To Wendy & Richard –
Thank ... again!
With ...
Penny ...

C000027419

A LAND OF PURE DELIGHT

Thomas Johnes of Hafod; by Thomas Stothard

(by permission of the National Library of Wales)

A Land of Pure Delight

Selections from the letters of Thomas Johnes of Hafod,
Cardiganshire
(1748-1816)

Edited and Introduced by:

RICHARD J. MOORE-COLYER

First Impression — 1992

ISBN 0 86383 751 4

© Richard J. Moore-Colyer

This book is published with the support of the Welsh Arts Council.

All rights reserved. No part of this book may be reproduced, stored in a retrieval system, or transmitted in any form or by any means, electronic, electrostatic, magnetic tape, mechanical, photocopying, recording or otherwise, without permission in writing from the Publishers, Gomer Press, Llandysul.

Printed in Wales by:
J. D. Lewis and Sons Ltd., Gomer Press, Llandysul, Dyfed

'There is a land of pure delight
Where saints immortal reign;
Infinite day excludes the night
And pleasures banish pain'
(Isaac Watts, 1674-1748)

Contents

Preface

Among the landed gentry of Wales flourishing in the late eighteenth and early nineteenth centuries relatively few contributed significantly to the cultural, political and literary climate of their times. Indeed, many of the printed sources suggest that as a race they had abandoned their native language and cultural traditions in favour of a lifestyle centred on the hunting field, the pleasures of the table and the cultivation of their local 'interest'. If the sweeping condemnations of the Welsh landowning class by earlier generations of historians bent on furthering the cause of nationalism no longer stand up to close examination, the fact still remains that the majority of landowners had but scant concern either for their own, or a broader culture. To this generalisation Thomas Johnes was a notable exception. During the course of half a lifetime in Cardiganshire he remodelled his estate and created a fine house and demesne, besides assembling a magnificent library and undertaking the prodigious task of translating the whole of Froissart's *Chronicles* along with other medieval French works.

Selecting items from his correspondence to illustrate the breadth and extent of these achievements is made the more difficult by the fact that Johnes burned most of his correspondents' letters once they had been answered, while any remaining material was destroyed by his wife after his death in 1816. Accordingly very few answers to his own letters remain extant. Equally, from what must have been an extremely wide correspondence, few extensive collections seem to have survived. These include letters to Sir Robert Liston and Dr Robert Anderson, located in the National Library of Scotland, and to George Cumberland, William Roscoe and Sir James Edward Smith, located respectively in the British Library, the Liverpool City Library and the library of the Linnean Society of London. Biographical details of these principal correspondents are given in the Introduction, while those of others are set out in the footnotes.

In selecting letters for publication I have been concerned to illustrate Johnes's life at Hafod and have thus included few of his numerous youthful epistles to his mentor Robert Liston, most of which deal with the trivia of family life. Some of these were written in French, Italian or Latin, apparently as exercises. Unfortunately and irritatingly, major gaps occur in the correspondence, often at crucial periods in Johnes's life. His letters to Liston, for example, appear to stop abruptly in 1779, only to begin again in 1783 and this, combined with a paucity of correspondence between 1784 and 1789, means that the early Hafod years are sparsely represented.

Readers of Horace Walpole's letters with their finely-honed phrases and polished elegance, who anticipate the like in the forthcoming pages of this volume will be sadly disappointed. Johnes, of course, did not write with a view to publication and his letters are hastily-produced affairs dashed off when he had a moment to spare. As a busy man who wrote principally to inform and to seek information, his letters are entirely without 'literary' pretension. They are, moreover, frequently repetitious, and in making the selection I have been at pains to eliminate those letters to Correspondent B which merely elaborate events detailed to Correspondent A. I have also avoided printing letters (including many to Robert Anderson) dealing with technical details regarding the translations of the French chronicles since, however interesting they may be to the specialist, they are hardly likely to excite the interest of the general reader.

Given the vagaries of Johnes's spelling, the eccentricities of his punctuation and his frequent disregard for the use of the higher case at the beginning of sentences, I have taken some liberties in editing the correspondence. Thus, while I have largely preserved Johnes's commas, I have from time to time silently inserted full points where appropriate, deleted repeated words and, very occasionally, interpolated a word or letter where this seemed necessary for the purposes of clarity. Such interpolations are indicated ( ) while the occasional indecipherable word appears thus (?). Johnes's contractions are preserved throughout the text except in the case of his valedictory 'Obt. hble Sert' and 'Compts', which have been expanded. I have allowed Johnes's spelling of personal and place names to remain as in the original, and have retained his renderings of 'honor', favor', 'Fryday', and other spellings commonly in use in the eighteenth century, without using [sic].

Thomas Johnes's correspondence embraces an extremely broad range of subject matter, extending from the technicalities of practical farming and forestry by way of local and national political matters to details of book collecting, literary criticism and publishing. This being the case I have provided an extended Introduction in order to minimise the proliferation of footnotes. In so doing I have enjoyed the benefit of the advice of numerous friends and colleagues including Professor and Mrs R.H. Macve, Dr. P. Bement, Mr E. Tudwal Jones, Mr G. Walters, Miss E. Rees and Professor P.D.G. Thomas, to all of whom I owe a debt of gratitude. I am also grateful to the Librarians and staff of the National Libraries of Wales and Scotland, the British Library, the Liverpool City Library and the Linnean Society Library, while to Mr N.D.H. Chapman I once again owe my thanks for converting my execrable manuscript into impeccable type.

Some of the material in the Introduction which relates to Thomas Johnes's literary activities has appeared in the *Welsh History Review*, and I am obliged to the Editor of that journal, Professor Kenneth O. Morgan, for permission to include it in the present volume.

R.J. Moore-Colyer

THE LINEAL DESCENT OF THOMAS JOHNES OF HAFOD
(1748-1816)

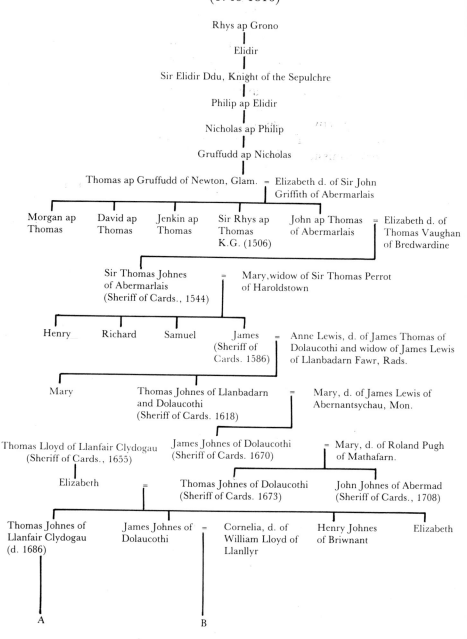

Rhys ap Grono

Elidir

Sir Elidir Ddu, Knight of the Sepulchre

Philip ap Elidir

Nicholas ap Philip

Gruffudd ap Nicholas

Thomas ap Gruffudd of Newton, Glam. = Elizabeth d. of Sir John Griffith of Abermarlais

Morgan ap Thomas | David ap Thomas | Jenkin ap Thomas | Sir Rhys ap Thomas K.G. (1506) | John ap Thomas of Abermarlais = Elizabeth d. of Thomas Vaughan of Bredwardine

Sir Thomas Johnes of Abermarlais (Sheriff of Cards., 1544) = Mary, widow of Sir Thomas Perrot of Haroldstown

Henry | Richard | Samuel | James (Sheriff of Cards. 1586) = Anne Lewis, d. of James Thomas of Dolaucothi and widow of James Lewis of Llanbadarn Fawr, Rads.

Mary | Thomas Johnes of Llanbadarn and Dolaucothi (Sheriff of Cards. 1618) = Mary, d. of James Lewis of Abernantsychau, Mon.

Thomas Lloyd of Llanfair Clydogau (Sheriff of Cards., 1655) | James Johnes of Dolaucothi (Sheriff of Cards. 1670) = Mary, d. of Roland Pugh of Mathafarn.

Elizabeth = | Thomas Johnes of Dolaucothi (Sheriff of Cards. 1673) | John Johnes of Abermad (Sheriff of Cards., 1708)

Thomas Johnes of Llanfair Clydogau (d. 1686) | James Johnes of Dolaucothi = Cornelia, d. of William Lloyd of Llanllyr | Henry Johnes of Briwnant | Elizabeth

A

B

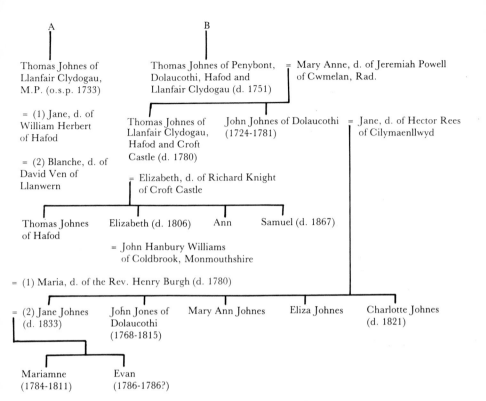

A

Thomas Johnes of
Llanfair Clydogau,
M.P. (o.s.p. 1733)

= (1) Jane, d. of
William Herbert
of Hafod

= (2) Blanche, d. of
David Ven of
Llanwern

Thomas Johnes
of Hafod

= (1) Maria, d. of the Rev. Henry Burgh (d. 1780)

= (2) Jane Johnes
(d. 1833)

Mariamne
(1784-1811)

Evan
(1786-1786?)

B

Thomas Johnes of Penybont,   = Mary Anne, d. of Jeremiah Powell
Dolaucothi, Hafod and   of Cwmelan, Rad.
Llanfair Clydogau (d. 1751)

Thomas Johnes of   John Johnes of Dolaucothi   = Jane, d. of Hector Rees
Llanfair Clydogau,   (1724-1781)   of Cilymaenllwyd
Hafod and Croft
Castle (d. 1780)

= Elizabeth, d. of Richard Knight
  of Croft Castle

Elizabeth (d. 1806)   Ann   Samuel (d. 1867)

= John Hanbury Williams
  of Coldbrook, Monmouthshire

John Jones of   Mary Ann Johnes   Eliza Johnes   Charlotte Johnes
Dolaucothi   (d. 1821)
(1768-1815)

Introduction

By the standards of any age Thomas Johnes the younger was a lucky man. His father had married the granddaughter of the immensely successful ironmaster Richard Knight of Downton (1659-1745) whose son, another Richard (1693-1765), had acquired Croft Castle in Herefordshire in 1746. Thus, in theory at least, young Johnes would enjoy the fruits both of the old family estates in West Wales and, by way of his mother's inheritance, of an enviable stretch of some of the finest country in Herefordshire. Having grafted a ready supply of new money onto a pedigree stretching somewhat obscurely and intriguingly into the misty reaches of medieval Welsh genealogy, the elder Johnes may have hoped that a few years of prudence and good husbandry would lay the foundations of the fame and fortune of his family for generations to come. His son, currently braving the rigours of Eton, would proceed via the University and the fashionable Grand Tour to a Parliamentary seat, an important position in county administration, and possibly even higher distinction in far-off Westminster. The newly-gothicised Croft Castle would echo to the portentous talk of men of affairs; politicians would decide the future of the country over its heavily-laden tables and as the port circulated, his son would discourse sagely on the great issues of the day. Or so he fondly thought...

Of the early years of the young Thomas Johnes we know very little. After a spell at a dame school in Ludlow and a few years at the free grammar school at Shrewsbury, he was packed off to Eton at the age of twelve and subsequently to the University of Edinburgh where he studied logic and moral philosophy. Here he came under the influence of Dr Drysdale, the friend of Adam Smith and David Hume, whose humanistic principles were to influence his thinking in the years ahead. Following what had by now become standard procedure for the sons of wealthy gentlemen, Johnes completed his studies in the enlightened (if insanitary) environs of Edinburgh and set off on an extended tour of Europe under the supervision of the brilliant Robert Liston, his lifelong friend and mentor. In the course of two years on the Continent he sowed a flourishing crop of wild oats, studied French and Italian and began to develop his fateful taste for collecting books and *objets d'art*—to the considerable discomfiture of his father who had to come to terms with his son's debts on the latter's return to England in the winter of 1769. For the next few years Johnes seems to have spent his days in Croft Castle and London, a regime occasionally punctuated by visits to the family properties in Wales and diplomatic calls on those dignitaries whose support he sought in his candidature for the Cardigan Boroughs parliamentary seat.

Social life in Herefordshire in the early 1770s seems to have held little appeal for Johnes after the heady delights of European travel. Ludlow and Hereford, pleasant though they may have been, provided little diversion beyond the usual provincial entertainments and his many letters to Liston, his '*Père confesseur indulgent*', suggest that he was both bored and uncertain as to the future course of his life. He complained in 1771 of the coarseness of the Bishop of Hereford, and of the tedium of the Balls, Concerts and Public Breakfasts as a result of which he believed, '*que dans neuf mois les registres de Baptisme seront un peu grossis*'. The dubious pleasures of Ludlow races and partridge shooting with his new gun—'*il faut le voir et en faire usage pour connaître sa beauté*'—provided a counterpoint to long and earnest sessions spent with Molière's works and the letters of Lord Chesterfield, and evenings of chilly formality with his family at Croft Castle. But this idle life was not enough. Johnes needed a purpose; he needed a stimulating project to carry him away from the stultifying confines of Croft Castle and the trivial and unprofitable company of county society in Herefordshire. A militia commission, a Parliamentary seat and ample cash to indulge his *dilettante* tastes merely spurred him on to hedonistic frivolities and the censure of his family. But Hafod was to change all that, and would provide Johnes with a lifelong source of pleasure and an outlet for his restless creative energies. The half-ruined family property in Cardiganshire, encircled by some 10,000 acres of upland populated by a hungry, ill-housed and despairing tenantry, had been leased for some years to a disreputable and rapacious mining engineer by the name of Paynter. This ruffian died five years before Thomas Johnes inherited the estate in fee simple on the death of his father in 1780. In the summer of that year, twelve months after his marriage to the ailing Maria Burgh, Johnes visited his Cardiganshire property for the first time, and as he travelled westwards through the open uplands his spirits slumped on drawing closer to his patrimony. Here was poverty beyond imagination residing in a country of glorious natural beauty suffering from generations of callous neglect. Starving tenants occupied fetid and airless cabins, semi-naked children begged for food, thatch rotted

on the roofs of barns and the treeless landscape presented a barren
and doom-laden aspect. Yet what a dramatic landscape it was! What
picturesque and romantic fancies could be created here in this heady
wilderness of moorland and stream! And Hafod itself, set in a deep
valley surrounded by hills— what a glorious setting for a fine house in
a carefully-moulded demesne! The die was cast. Johnes lost little time
in convincing himself that his future lay in Cardiganshire where he
would create a fantasy home in accordance with the picturesque ideal.
Prosperity would displace poverty, trees would flourish on the naked
hills and the land in this remote place would once again support a
vigorous and contented population. His family might condemn him
and his friends might declare him insane, yet Hafod would become
his home and its renovation his life's work. Croft Castle and his other
properties in Herefordshire and Monmouthshire were as nothing
compared to this; he was a Welshman and to Wales he would return.

As a collateral descendant of the celebrated Sir Rhys ap Thomas
who provided such sterling support for Henry Tudor on his march
towards Bosworth Field and the English crown, Thomas Johnes set
great store by his Welshness. But for all his impeccable Welsh
ancestry, he was nonetheless wholly ignorant of his native language,
a fact that he frequently confessed with some shame.[1] Many of the
Lhuyd manuscripts in the Hafod library, the delight of Welsh
scholars, would have been as obscure and inaccessible to Johnes as the
chatter of the labourers who wrestled with the task of realising the
Hafod dream. To a man with a scholar's inclinations — if not a
scholar's punctiliousness — his ignorance of Welsh may occasionally
have rankled. But it would have been no source of embarrassment
since it was a deficiency he shared with the majority of his peers who
had, by the late 18th century, despite their readiness to subscribe to
Welsh books and the publication of Welsh texts, come to regard the
native language and culture as a curiosity and an anachronism more
suited to the field and byre than to the drawing room and library.
Johnes himself probably took the view that since those of his fellow
countrymen with whom he might wish to converse could do so with
perfect facility in English, there was little purpose in his attempting to
master the baffling complexities of his native tongue. Equally, he may
have thought that if he was going to fulfil his plans for Hafod and
concurrently maintain the momentum of his literary activities, life
was too short to learn Welsh. Again, sympathetic though Johnes may
have been towards the ancient culture of Wales, its traditions

probably seemed homely, if not banal, to a man who had lived in
Madame du Deffand's Paris and had savoured the splendours of the
Roman campagna.

Despite his attachment to Hafod, Johnes's attitude towards the
native inhabitants of his domain was, to say the least, ambivalent. His
obituary in the *Gentleman's Magazine* spoke of his benevolence which,
'stooped to comfort the fireside of the lowliest cottager', while James
Edward Smith observed to a friend in 1799 that 'The family are the
guardian angels of the country and consequently not liked by the
neighbouring gentry who (as Mr. Johnes said to me today) want to
keep up all the old tyrannic notions and never think of other people's
starving, if they do but eat themselves'.[2] Johnes was certainly well
aware of his traditional duties as a landlord. His 'poor labourers'
enjoyed the benefits of a school and a dispensary and the services of
a surgeon and apothecary, while their daughters were given
instruction in sewing, knitting and spinning—from which emerged
the improbable myth that their benefactor invariably wore a shirt
knitted by these industrious maidens.[3] Work on the estate was always
available to those who took the trouble to ask for it although, as Johnes
himself hints, provision of employment was motivated as much by
fear of social disturbance, as by compassion.

But if he provided for some of the bodily needs of his labourers and
tenants, Thomas Johnes had little respect for their capabilities as
workmen and was wedded to the conventional view that they were
indolent, reactionary, untrustworthy, inclined to drink and quite
insusceptible to any suggestion by which their condition might be
improved. He saw his countrymen as being in all respects
diametrically opposed to the dour, thrifty and hardworking artisans
he had met during his Edinburgh days. With this in mind he set about
staffing his estate offices with Scotsmen (a practice also followed by
other landed gentlemen in south-west Wales) and went to great
lengths to attract capital-rich Scots tenants to the Hafod estate,
believing that by their example these worthies would encourage the
native tenantry to adopt more enlightened farming practices. We
know nothing of how the locals reacted to these implants with their
outlandish dress and impenetrable accents; they were probably
mortified.

Thomas Johnes's concern to create at Hafod a 'picturesque' estate
populated by a prosperous, contented and sober tenantry ran hand-
in-hand with his interest in attracting visitors to the remote reaches of

West Cardiganshire. The publication of William Gilpin's *Tours* of the River Wye and South Wales in 1783 and of the Lake District in 1786 set into motion the craze for 'picturesque' travel so mercilessly satirised in Rowlandson's drawings for the *Tour of Dr Syntax in Search of the Picturesque* (1812). Gilpin's suggestion that travellers should examine the face of a country 'by the rules of picturesque beauty' caused a tremendous stir. No longer was the viewer of the landscape expected to see the world around him merely according to the pictorial models of Claude or Salvator Rosa but, with careful mental editing, he was to look upon the landscape *as a picture*. By the judicious use of the 'Claude Glass' and other ingenious contrivances, the viewer was advised to adjust his position until he had obtained a view in accordance with the complex and fanciful dictates of picturesque theory. In essence, then, the picturesque was the art of 'cooking nature'.[4] Gilpin's theories emphasised the qualities of *roughness* and denigrated the cool rationality of Augustan architecture and the closely-shaven terrains of 'Capability' Brown. They were eagerly embraced by the movement's staunchest supporters, Richard Payne Knight and the latter's friend and neighbour Uvedale Price, both of whom published highly influential (if insufferably dull), tomes on picturesque theory.[5] Having grasped these new and slightly crazy theories, travellers began to flock to Wales in the later decades of the eighteenth century, carrying with them their attendant artists who were, of course, expected to produce works in accordance with the picturesque canon. To men like Robert Fulke Greville, who travelled to Wales in 1792 with the painters J. C. Ibbetson and John 'Warwick' Smith, the consciously picturesque elements in the Hafod landscape were a major attraction as indeed were the 'horrors' of the confluence of the Rivers Mynach and Rheidol at the celebrated Devil's Bridge. But however elevated a man's aesthetic senses, he still needs to be fed and watered, and to provide for the comfort of travellers Johnes built the Devil's Bridge Inn. This modest edifice, occupying the site of the present building, became a focal point for tourists. After braving the rigours of the turnpike from London they could wine and dine at Devil's Bridge and then proceed either to Aberystwyth which, as Johnes explained with some satisfaction in 1798, 'has been fuller this summer than ever known', or wend their way to Hafod, taking in Wyatt's little church of Eglwys Newydd *en route*. Johnes's creations at Hafod and his various efforts in attracting travellers with ample purses in the direction of West Cardiganshire were important elements in the increasing popularity of Aberystwyth as a resort in the pre-railway period.

Thomas Johnes derived enormous satisfaction and pride from his numerous ambitious projects at Hafod, and 'a very uncommon share of happiness' for which he frequently expressed gratitude. Yet he was unable to escape bouts of deep despair; 'of a most oppressive insight that sinks me'. When the bibliographer Thomas Dibdin wrote enthusiastically of the deceased Johnes in 1816, he noted that 'the same sensibility which was alive to his excellencies, could not but be painfully quickened on a contemplation of his schemes, plans and undertakings — not only too vast for his pecuniary means of carrying them into effect, but for any life to enjoy their completion.'[6] Undoubtedly Johnes's delight in fashioning a landscape miracle that 'fifty years hence will stand alone in grandeur' was tempered by the realisation that he would not survive to savour its full maturity. But this was of minor importance when compared to his anxiety over the health of his only child, the fruit of a deeply happy second marriage to a beautiful and understanding partner in the form of his cousin Jane. As his daughter's bouts of illness were relieved by recovery, Johnes's mood swung from the depths of gloom to light-headed happiness. Mariamne, 'dearer than the light', was his future and as the reality of her feeble health and the terrible inevitability of her permanent spinal curvature began to take root, he found it increasingly difficult to keep smiling. And yet, even after the girl's death in 1811 when he might easily have sold up, paid his debts and retired to comfortable obscurity in London or Bath, he continued to improve the Hafod estate until his own end five years later. On the face of it it seems remarkable that a man with no immediate heir and who held the rest of his family in contempt, should have any longer concerned himself with an estate which by now had become a financial millstone. But this is to ignore the depth of Thomas Johnes's antipathy towards his mother, brother and other members of his family who had both resisted his marriage and used every means in their power to cheat him of his patrimony and frustrate his plans for Hafod. Perhaps the continuation of his work on the estate and its eventual sale to a complete outsider was Johnes's ultimate revenge on his estranged family? Unfortunately, this is likely to remain an unresolved question since, in her wish to sever all remaining links with Hafod, Jane Johnes destroyed her husband's correspondence and estate papers after his death in Dawlish in 1816.

However much Thomas Johnes may have disapproved of his epicene contemporary William Beckford, whose lifestyle contrasted so starkly with his own, the two men's lives shared many common threads. Both enjoyed substantial incomes (although Beckford's might be more accurately described as princely) and managed, in the realisation of their dreams, to end their days far away from the extraordinary creations into which they had poured so much effort and cash. They both had mutual friends (including Lord Chancellor Thurlow), each had been tutored by a Scotsman, had assembled magnificent libraries and produced translations of major contemporary importance. Equally they held a common dislike of bloodsports (in Johnes's case developing later in life), a detestation of the cant of politicians and a lordly indifference to the notion of living within their means. Johnes would have found little difficulty in crying 'Amen' to Beckford's assertion that a Chancery suit brought more misery in its wake than invasion, inundation and earthquake![7] At this point, however, similarities give way to contrasts. To begin with, Johnes would have detested the egregious Beckford's snobbery, being himself a man whose friendships transcended social considerations. He was equally at ease with great magnates like the Dukes of Norfolk and Bedford as he was with the Liverpool banker William Roscoe, scholars of the standing of William Owen (Pughe) or the itinerant antiquary and stonemason Edward Williams (Iolo Morganwg). His acquaintance also reached across religious divides, and though a Churchman, he was closely associated with many Radical dissenters and included the Unitarian James Edward Smith among his closest friends. Like most of his contemporaries Johnes was deeply shocked by Beckford's perverted sexuality and would have recoiled with horror from the exotic goings-on allegedly taking place within the gloomy confines of Fonthill Abbey. To Johnes, the family man and supporter of the constitution, such moral turpitude and decadence was yet another manifestation of what he was fond of describing as 'this profligate and corrupt age'.

Oxford Dec 9. 1803

You must not think, my dear Sir, that I am insensible to the two excellent letters I received from you, by my delay in answering them. The truth is, at the moment they came here, my much employed about the defence of the country, I laid them aside so carefully I could not find them again. I am indeed very much obliged to you for the account you have of those respecting hard iron, being imported into this country. I adopt your idea, to say the truth I practised it, before I had come to it in your letter. I think, however subscription, would fail, and the moment I shall succeed to my whole fortune I will make the experiment on my own bottom. In the mean time I shall thank you to turn your thoughts on the best sorts of vessels for this importation, and lining them with copper would perhaps be as cheap, certainly lighter

Thomas Johnes's handwriting
(by permission of the National Library of Wales)

Political Life

After his election to the Cardigan Boroughs seat in 1774, Thomas Johnes was to occupy a place in the House of Commons for more than forty years. In the contest for the Cardigan Boroughs he stood against the powerful Peterwell interest whose candidate, Sir Robert Smyth, was an Essex man with neither landed nor commercial interest in the locality. Johnes seems to have had little time for his opponent, with whom he had become slightly acquainted on his European travels. As he wrote to Robert Liston in his less than perfect French shortly before the election, '*Vous (vous) souvenez que c'est lui qui a couché dans la même auberge à Narbonne et que son domestique disait qu'il ne se levait jamais qu'à midi.*'[8] Layabed he might have been, but Smyth was duly declared elected much to the annoyance of the Johnes party who promptly petitioned the House of Commons with the complaint that the returning officer, Thomas Colby, had accepted the votes of unqualified voters in order to favour Smyth's candidature. The petition was successful and after careful scrutiny of the pollbooks and examination of a variety of witnesses the House of Commons committee ruled that the return had been falsified and Johnes was authorised to take up his seat.[9] When his father died in 1780, he vacated the Boroughs in favour of John Campbell of Stackpole, and was subsequently elected to the Radnorshire constituency in a six day poll where he defeated the nabob Walter Wilkins of Maesllwch Castle.[10] Henceforth he was regularly returned for Radnorshire until 1796 when he was elected for the County of Cardigan, retaining this seat for the remainder of his life.

In a lengthy Parliamentary career Johnes seems never to have spoken in the House. Though a regular visitor to Westminster where he may have undertaken committee work, he only cast his vote when absolutely necessary and declined to become more than superficially involved with the political issues of the day.[11] He loyally supported Lord North's ministry and his approval of the war against the American insurrectionists probably earned him his secret service pension of £500 annually.[12] When this lapsed in May 1781 he managed, with the intercession of North, to obtain the sinecure of Auditor of the Land Revenues in Wales valued at the considerable sum of £1000 per year. This he was able to retain for life (despite Burke's bill for the abolition of sinecures) thanks largely to the support of Lord Chancellor Thurlow. By way of a *quid pro quo* Johnes worked actively to enable Thurlow to secure, in the teeth of Fox's opposition, the immensely lucrative office of Teller of the Exchequer. [13]

A supporter of the administrations of Pitt and Grenville and a vehement opponent of Addington, Johnes favoured both Catholic emancipation and political reform, and if inclined towards Whiggism he largely eschewed *active* political involvement. Accordingly it is extremely difficult to categorise his political stance, more especially as his support for, or opposition to, a particular cause was determined more by personal relationships and a sense of loyalty for favours received than adherence to party principle. Hence his support for Pitt in May 1804. The Prime Minister had given him the Lord Lieutenancy of Cardiganshire and in consequence, as he explained to George Cumberland, 'I should have been the most ingrateful [sic] fellow possible to have refused him when he asked'. Conveniently ignoring his own extremely valuable sinecures, Johnes often expressed his disapproval of the corruption, avarice and skulduggery of eighteenth-century political life and of the petty absurdities of party strife. 'Party', he declared, 'I have ever said, will ruin our country, and that ruin is coming on us with hasty strides without the proper preparations to arrest it.' As Roland Thorne has pointed out, Johnes was the despair of political calculators who were quite unable to guess how he would cast his parliamentary vote or, indeed, whether he would cast it at all. Among the papers of Sir John Sinclair, M.P., President of the first Board of Agriculture, is a note sketching the characters of those members of the House of Commons who might have been expected to support Pitt's first ministry in 1783. Johnes, Sinclair tersely remarks, 'Is much inclined to support administrations. Could not be got to support the new one immediately. But his absence might be procured.' [14]

Thomas Johnes rarely tired of protesting his abhorrence of public life, yet his letters clearly indicate that he was far from indifferent to the state of the nation's affairs. Recognising the genius of Napoleon, he nevertheless took the conventional view that the First Consul would best serve his people and the rest of the world by expiring at the earliest opportunity. Hence the need to prosecute the struggle against France with the utmost vigour. War, though, was a sickening business and 'The follies of Mankind would be laughable if they did not use such cursed instruments in the execution of them'. Humanitarian considerations apart, Johnes found the war with France extremely irksome from a personal point of view since it imposed serious restrictions on his work of translating the medieval French chronicles, at the same time precluding the importation of marbles from Italy for his house at Hafod. War, moreover, would have calamitous effects on the National Debt, and the inevitable post-war depression would bring in its wake scarcity, poverty, unemployment and the dreadful spectre of Jacobinism. Thus, he concluded, '. . . the further we advance in warfare the more we shall be bewildered'.

With that naive innocence characterising so many other areas of his life, Johnes believed in that ultimate of all impossibilities — the uniting of all parties for the common good. Such a measure he thought would resolve the dilemma of Catholic emancipation, prevent the outbreak of the absurd war of 1812 with America, and heal the growing and dangerous class rift in the country. Class alienation and its possible consequences really worried him and he was firmly of the view that unless politicians returned to the vague principles of 'morality, virtue and good faith', the people might be tempted to take power into their own hands. Yet, being finally convinced that the country's political masters would never awaken to the errors of their ways and would continue to be motivated merely by avarice and ambition, Johnes consoled himself with ostrich-like indifference to Westminster and all its works. He would remain at Hafod and maintain local peace and tranquillity by the application of the time-honoured paternalistic principles. 'For my part', he wrote to James Edward Smith as early as 1794, 'I am quite tired of a publick life and wish nothing so much as to fix my staff here, not to be removed until placed in the Black Box'.

Hafod: The House and Landscape

In his various writings on picturesque theory Thomas Johnes's cousin Richard Payne Knight developed the notion that the sophisticated artificiality of the formal landscapes of 'Capability' Brown and his followers was analogous to political despotism which inhibited human moral and intellectual growth. On the other hand, the ideal ('pictur-esque') landscape with its literary associations, its freedom from the strictures of reason and its appeal to the senses, carried with it a flavour of spiritual liberation in some ways akin to political revolution. In his dreary didactic poem, *The Landscape* (1794)—condemned by Horace Walpole as the 'insolent and self-conceited' work of a 'trumpery prosaic poetaster' whom he lampooned elsewhere as the 'Knight of the Brazen Milkpot'—Knight made his feelings about the Brownian landscape perfectly clear:

> 'See yon fantastic band,
> With charts, pedometers and rules in hand,
> Advance triumphant, and alike lay waste
> The forms of nature, and the works of taste!
> T'improve, adorn, and polish, they profess;
> But shave the goddess, whom they come to dress;
> Level each broken bank and shaggy mound,
> And fashion all to one unvaried round;
> One even round, that ever gently flows,
> Not forms abrupt, nor broken colours knows;
> But wrapt all oe'r in everlasting green,
> Makes one dull, vapid, smooth, and tranquil scene.[15]

Closely associated with the strong emotional appeal of the 'picturesque', with its emphasis on irregularity and 'roughness', was the Gothic style of architecture championed by Horace Walpole in his *Anecdotes of Painting* and realised in practice in his fanciful exercises at Strawberry Hill. Walpole had strongly argued that the Gothic style was suited not only to the sham ruins built with such enthusiasm throughout the 1740s and 1750s by Sanderson Miller, but to serious and scholarly architectural essays. Yet despite Walpole's efforts and the contorted attempts of Batty Langley to formulate rules for it, the Gothic remained for the most part a decorator's style, frivolous, lighthearted and — like those artificial ruins — improbable and escapist.[16]

In stark contrast to Walpole's rococo concoction at Strawberry Hill was Richard Payne Knight's remarkable achievement at Downton Castle in Herefordshire, wherein a Gothic outline was successfully united to the exigencies and practicalities of modern planning. In *An Analytical Inquiry into the Principles of Taste* (1805) Knight maintained that in the paintings of Claude 'we perpetually see a mixture of Grecian and Gothic architecture employed with the happiest effect in the same building', a view underpinning his approach to Downton which he began building to his own design in 1772. Emphasising the visual unity of the building with its physical setting, Knight combined a Gothic exterior with an interior in the style of Adam and in so doing created a house of major significance. Indeed, with its completion in 1778, Downton was to become one of the most frequently copied irregular castellated houses in England.

As a close friend of his cousin, Thomas Johnes was a regular visitor to Downton and could hardly have failed to be impressed by this singular building. Similarly he would have absorbed the Gothic elements at Croft Castle, substantially remodelled by his father in 1765 under the direction of the Shrewsbury architect T. F. Pritchard. Here, at one of the first houses in Herefordshire to be consciously gothicised, Pritchard threw up a curtain wall of mock towers, incorporated battlemented bay windows and created a rococo gothic interior of great warmth and charm.[17] Thomas Johnes's youthful home environment, allied to his expanding interest in medieval history, ensured that both gothic and picturesque notions would inevitably influence his ideas for Hafod.

Visitors to the Cardiganshire estate as it approached maturity bore witness to the consciously picturesque elements in the landscape and the degree to which the pensile gardens, chain bridges, rock-hewn caves and other artefacts had been conceived as a unity. 'Here all that is natural is grand and picturesque; all that is artificial, characteristic and appropriate', enthused the Rev. Richard Warner after a hearty breakfast and a walk round the grounds.[18] George Cumberland in his *Attempt to describe Hafod* talked of Hafod's 'sublime irregularities of nature' and Benjamin Heath Malkin, in a reference to Johnes's walks and viewpoints, observed that 'art has been no further consulted than to render nature accessible'. In similar vein the traveller Lipscomb noted approvingly that 'No *Brownian* attempts have been made to slope and swell it.'[19] Among the few detractors was J. T. Barber. Piqued by the obligation to tip the housekeeper and gardener for their courier service, he grudgingly conceded the Hafod domain to be, 'one of the most delightful rural retreats in the kingdom' but dismissed the house as '. . . a heterogenous jumble; wherein a bastard sort of Greek and Saxon architecture was blended with the prevailing Gothic'.[20]

The principal architect of this 'heterogenous jumble', of which the foundation stone had been laid in 1786, was Thomas Baldwin, at the time enjoying considerable success as Surveyor to the City of Bath. Baldwin's works in Bath, and his only building outside that city, the

Town Hall at Devizes, were exclusively in the classical style; cool, rather unimaginative and parochially pedestrian.[21] While he may have been influenced by other buildings in Bath, such as Lady Huntingdon's Chapel with its battlements and gothic windows, or John Palmer's St. James's Church, Baldwin seems to have had little interest in the gothic style. Accordingly the choice of this man, with his essentially classical training and outlook, as the architect of Hafod remains something of a mystery. After all, Johnes had probably conceived a full-blown gothic edifice as a complement to the romantic qualities of the setting and one which would provide an appropriate 'literary' atmosphere for his burrowings among the medieval French chronicles. What Baldwin eventually presented, apparently to his patron's satisfaction, was a basically symmetrical classical house embellished with a dressing of pointed windows and finials in the thirteenth-century style adopted by Batty Langley. In the absence of contemporary plans and drawings, (Johnes's copies having been destroyed by fire in 1807 and Baldwin's by his own hand following his discredit with the Bath Corporation in 1791-2), one is obliged to accept 'Warwick' Smith's 1792 painting to represent the completed building.

Several years after the completion of Baldwin's work in 1788, Johnes was already finding the house a little cramped for his purposes. His expanding library in particular was rapidly outgrowing the original provisions and he wrote to Bishop Percy in May 1794 that his books were lying topsy-turvy around the house pending the building of 'a new room' to accommodate them. This was to be the celebrated 'octagon library', alleged, in some sources, to have been designed by Johnes himself, but more probably the work of the young John Nash. That Nash worked at Hafod we have irrefutable proof in Johnes's letter to Robert Liston of November 1793 in which he writes with some irritation of the tardiness of the workmen engaged on the project. Nevertheless, '. . . Mr. Nash my Architect who has been here all the time promises to stay a fortnight longer if we will remain, and this will advance the building in a great degree. Uncomfortable as we are, this is such a flattering prospect of getting rid of such a set of rascals as I believe were never before collected together. . . ' Notwithstanding the obscurity of Nash's early life, we know that he was active in Wales after his bankruptcy in 1783. He re-roofed St. Peter's Church in Carmarthen in 1784-5 (in so doing destroying a number of antiquities), designed a bathroom at Golden

Grove in 1787 and completed Carmarthen Gaol the following year. In the same period he built a number of gentlemen's seats including, Ffynonau, Foley House and Sion House in Pembrokeshire, and Llysnewydd and Llanaeron in Cardiganshire. Moreover, he remodelled Dolaucothi in Carmarthenshire for Thomas Johnes's cousin John Johnes, gothicised Cardigan Priory and, in 1793, oversaw the building of Cardigan Gaol and the completion of his rather crude exercises on the west front of St. David's Cathedral. [22]

Like many aspects of the construction of the pre-1807 Hafod, there is some confusion as to whether the *first* octagon library was incorporated *within* the main body of the house, or built as a projecting wing. Johnes's concern over the discomfort occasioned by the workmen, combined with the lack of evidence for a projecting octagon in some published illustrations has prompted suggestions that initially at least, an existing internal octagonal space was converted into a library and that the projecting octagon was a later construction. However, the tendency for artists like 'Warwick' Smith to view the house from a westerly or south-westerly direction meant that both the octagon, conservatory and other offices would be obscured from view. This apart, the clear descriptions of both Warner and Malkin of an octagonal library leading out through plate glass doors to a conservatory, certainly seem to square with the notion of a projecting octagonal structure, and it is possible that after the 1807 fire Nash's *original* octagon was refurbished by Baldwin. In this case Johnes's reference in his letter to George Cumberland of Nash's building work having been entirely destroyed may relate to domestic offices to the north of the building. The various arguments have been rehearsed at some length elsewhere and will not be repeated here. [23] The only absolute certainty is that Nash was working at Hafod in 1793-4 where, in all likelihood, he designed an octagonal library besides undertaking various landscape works including perhaps the 'Adam and Eve' gateways to Jane Johnes's flower garden. [24]

In any event the library, described by Malkin as 'one of the finest rooms in the kingdom', was Johnes's pride and joy with its colonnade of marble pillars of the Doric order supporting a gallery lit by a domed ceiling. Below, Warner breathlessly observed, was 'a vast collection of valuable and rare publications, methodically arranged and carefully preserved.' [25] If the Gobelin tapestries in the drawing room and the collection of French, Dutch and Italian masters adorning the walls of other apartments excited the visitor, they formed a mere prelude to the pleasures of the library. Here, and in the adjoining conservatory, among the books, manuscripts and antique statuary were to be found several works by the modern sculptor Thomas Banks (1735-1805) of whom Johnes was a most appreciative and generous patron.

Having met with Johnes in Rome, Banks spent several successive summers at Hafod. According to his daughter, he 'revelled in undisturbed enjoyment of the sublime scenes with which that picturesque spot abounds' and warmed to the company of his patron, 'who was very partial to my father and loved the simplicity of his character'.[26] In a typically grandiose gesture Johnes had commissioned from Banks a colossal statue of Achilles lamenting the loss of Briseis which he had proposed erecting at some point on the Cardiganshire coast, and had duly acquired an enormous block of marble for the purpose. This ambitious project was eventually abandoned on the grounds of cost, and the bulk of the Carrara marble was used in Banks's celebrated *Thetis dipping the Infant Achilles into the Styx.*[27] Eventually removed to Clumber by the fourth Duke of Newcastle, the *Thetis* was among Banks's most original creations. Avoiding the temptation simply to treat the subject as a pastiche of the antique, he produced a dignified, unsentimental and sincere work and in so doing immortalised the serene beauty of Jane Johnes as the Thetis figure and the face of the child Mariamne as the infant Achilles.[28] Among other works executed by Banks for Johnes were busts of the daughter of the politician George Rose and those of Jane and Mariamne Johnes, the latter featuring as Lot 393 in the 1939 Sale Catalogue of the Hafod estate. Johnes's enthusiasm for Banks's talents also led to a commission for a library fireplace featuring the heads of Socrates, Plato, Alcibiades and Sappho, and when this was destroyed in the 1807 fire Johnes acquired a replacement at the Fonthill sale, paying 1400 guineas for a Banks chimney-piece incorporating figures representing Pan and Iris and Penelope and Ulysses.[29]

Indefatigable book collector as he was, Johnes was constantly plagued with the difficulty of shelving his collection, and in 1805 he found once again that his acquisitions were outgrowing the available library space. To resolve the problem he removed 'a bad circular stairs and all its dirty appendages' and created an anti-library [sic], described by Malkin as being, '. . . .in the form of a chapel in which is placed some very curious painted glass'. The origin of this painted glass, of which some found its way to the church of Eglwys Newydd and the gallery of the octagon library, is obscure. But the suggestion put about by the antiquary Meyrick that Johnes had removed it from the Priory Church at Cardigan has no basis in fact and in all probability the glass had been purchased in the Low Countries through the good offices of one of Johnes's numerous European correspondents.

As he wandered among his books and savoured that peculiar *frisson* enjoyed by a collector among his treasures, Johnes might happily have contemplated the agreeable prospect of spending his declining years in his exquisite home embraced by a landscape of ravishing beauty which was largely of his own creation. But such delectable musings were soon to be shattered when fire struck in March 1807, the horrendous extent of the tragedy being reported in the sober columns of the *Gentleman's Magazine* as printed below.[30]

Hafod 1795: John 'Warwick' Smith
(by permission of the National Library of Wales)

Fatal Accident at Hafod

In common with every admirer of Literature and the Polite Arts, we have most sincerely to lament the loss by Fire of the elegant and magnificent mansion of HAFOD in Cardiganshire, the hospitable residence of Thomas Johnes, Esq. the worthy Representative in Parliament for the County; and the theme of rapturous delight to every Traveller in that part of the Principality. The dreadful accident occurred early in the morning of Friday the 13th of March; and originated, it is supposed, in the apartments of the female servants. At a quarter after 3, Mrs Johnes was awakened by the Fire; and immediately, but with difficulty, alarmed the Family. So rapid was the progress of the flames, that some of the domesticks were with great difficulty rescued. The housekeeper was in the most imminent danger of perishing, before assistance could be rendered; and two or three other servants, who had made their way to the top of the house, were much scorched before they could be relieved by means of ropes, and conveyed to a place of safety. Scarcely covered, Mrs Johnes and her daughter, after saving some few articles from the wreck, took shelter at the Devil's Bridge, four miles distant, where the Family have since continued. Mr. Hanbury Williams, of Colebrook Dale, Shropshire, brother-in-law to Mr. Johnes, who was on a visit at Hafod, naked, and a few of the men-servants, by wonderful exertions, at the hazard of their lives, succeeded in saving most of the valuable plate, china, and a quantity of inferior furniture; the wine, the linen, Mrs. Johnes apparel, trinkets,&c. and the principal furniture, magnificent glasses, &c. were all lost. Mr. Williams also sustained a considerable loss, not being able to save his travelling equipage, bills, cash, and other valuables. Many of the splendid Books in the lower part of the Library were saved; but all the precious lore that was deposited in the Gallery and the Anti-library fell in the unrelenting flames, among which were the greatest curiosities—the Welch MSS, and the labours of Mr. Johnes for the last forty years; an irreparable loss to Society, and to the munificent Owner. We are afraid that the valuable Froissarts are to be included in the loss; but the copies of that work which, with so much credit to Mr. J. and his assistants in Typography, have issued from the Hafod press

(vol. LXXV.pp.141,633; LXXVI,137,433.) will immortalize
the Translator and the Printer. The Fire commenced at the hour
before stated; and at 6, only three hours time (excepting the
three turrets at the corners of the mansion and the
Conservatory), only the bare walls remained, a melancholy
momento of the former splendour of the place. The house,
library, &c. were valued at 140,000l.; and were insured (we
believe, at about half that sum) in the British and Imperial Fire
Offices; and those honourable Bodies, immediately on hearing
of the accident, dispatched their Surveyor to settle the claims
under the Policies. Fortunately no lives were lost, nor persons
injured. And it will be satisfactory to the extensive circle of the
friends of the amiable Family, to know that the calamity is borne
with fortitude becoming their exalted character. Mr. Johnes was
in town, attending his Parliamentary duties; and did not arrive,
to the solace of his family, till Wednesday evening, the 18th
instant.

Appalled by his loss, Johnes leased Castle Hill, Llanilar, a rather
gloomy mansion several miles from Aberystwyth where he spent
several months brooding over the future. His initial reaction,
catalysed by a tempting offer of a substantial sum of money for the
Hafod timber, was to buy a large house in London and to build a modest
cottage at Hafod to accommodate the family on occasional summer
visits. Concurrently he toyed with the idea of abandoning
Cardiganshire altogether in favour of either Prinknash Abbey, the
Gloucestershire home of the Bridgman family, or Houghton in
Norfolk, the palatial pile built by Colen Campbell for Sir Robert
Walpole, both of which were on the market. But as Miss Inglis-Jones
observes with her inevitable touch of romance, '....the mountains
had no intention of allowing their prisoner to escape. While he
wavered and built his airy castles, the spirits set to work, exerting
every wile of light and shadow, of breeze and tempest, to recapture his
allegiance.'[31] Whatever seductive web the airy spirits of
Cardiganshire may have woven, the blunt facts were that Nash's
work was virtually destroyed whereas the walls of Baldwin's house
remained sound; sufficiently so for Johnes to determine upon
rebuilding. Regardless of the remonstrations of his family, he would
realise the fable of the Phoenix, at least insofar as it was possible

within the constraints of the money released by the Imperial and British Insurance Offices.

According to Thomas Rees, Johnes's losses in the fire amounted to £70,000 although, as the *Gentleman's Magazine* hinted, this was probably a substantial underestimate, failing to take into account the value of the books, paintings and statuary consumed by the flames.[32] Johnes was grossly under-insured and the loss adjuster, a Mr. Abbott, '. . . . .who acted as agent for both offices with great ability, perspicuity and judgement', finally settled on a figure of £20,584.[33] Nevertheless Johnes decided to press ahead. He promptly re-employed Baldwin, ('. . . an able, and I believe, an honest man') who was probably glad to return to the peace and quiet of Hafod as his relations with the Bath Corporation grew increasingly strained. From the outset Johnes determined that the rebuilding of Hafod would be subject to the cash limits set by the insurance settlement and in August 1807 he and Baldwin agreed that the contractors would be tied down to specific contracts with heavy penalty clauses, rather than dangerously expensive generalised estimates. Shortly afterwards he busied himself with arrangements for the sale of his Cardigan Priory estate to Lord Lansdowne, hoping to use the proceeds for furnishing the new house. Although Lansdowne reneged upon the contract of sale and the Priory eventually realised less cash than he anticipated, Johnes set off for Wiltshire in September to visit Fonthill, where William Beckford was in the process of disposing of the contents of his father's classical house of Fonthill Splendens before moving into the ill-fated Fonthill Abbey. Here Johnes was in his element, spending freely on 'a grand heroic figure of Bacchus', a number of fireplaces and four superb French gilt mirrors which he claimed to be among the finest in Europe.

Meanwhile winter drew in and severe weather began to check the progress of the contractors at Hafod. By January 1809 the roof timbers were only partially installed and as he paced the damp and dreary corridors of Castle Hill, Johnes grew increasingly annoyed by what he considered to be the negligence and laziness of his builders. As winter gave way to spring he could take no more, and in the sanguine anticipation that the house would be completed in his absence he set off on a lengthy visit to Scotland with his wife and daughter. But the work dragged on long after the family's return in the summer, and to Johnes's considerable irritation he was unable to reoccupy Hafod before June 1810. Even then the place still echoed to the clatter of workmen and tranquillity was not restored until the end of August.

The new house, as Johnes wrote to William Roscoe, '. . . .is not larger than before, but I think better arranged'. The 1832 Sale Catalogue (which falsely proclaims Nash to have been the architect of the original mansion) probably represents Hafod in much the same form as Johnes left it. Besides bedchambers, dressing rooms and other offices, and an extensive range of stables and coachhouses, the Catalogue details a spacious entry hall paved with Anglesey marble [*sic*], giving access to a dining parlour (30'x19'), the long library (35'x 20'), the circular library (20' diameter), the octagon library (28'x 28'), the billiard room (28'x 18'), the vinery (68'x 22') and the conservatory (76'x 22'). Mentioned also is the 4 acre walled kitchen garden complete with a range of hot and forcing houses of no less than 240 feet in length. Johnes himself gave Robert Liston a full and detailed description of his intentions for the new building shortly before work commenced in the autumn of 1807. Underlining the cardinal importance of securing the place against fire he explained that the libraries and servants' rooms would be equipped with iron or copper doors, and the bulk of the house heated with enclosed stoves with any open fireplaces guarded by wire fenders. The family bedrooms, moreover, would be located on the ground floor to facilitate escape should the unthinkable occur again. These rooms, together with his and his wife's respective dressing rooms and bath, would occupy the south face of the building and the pavilions flanking either end of it, connected by the vinery (or colonnade) which would be open in the summer and glazed in the winter months. The hall and dining room would be much the same as in the original house, with a double door opening from the latter into the long library, itself being divided by columns from a circular library with a domed roof. From here a further double door would give access to the octagon library whose dome would be supported by sixteen double columns of green marble. On the opposite side of the circular library would be a marble staircase to the first floor and beneath this staircase the billiard and music rooms, the latter accommodating Johnes's collection of paintings. Thomas Rees's account shows that the octagon library was completed without the marble columns of Johnes's original proposal, presumably on the grounds of cost or unavailability of marble of sufficient quality. It is clear, however, from Dibdin's comments in 1817 that the conservatory, separated from the octagon library by folding plate-glass doors, had been completely restored, if substantially curtailed in length.

Two years previously Dibdin had spent much of the summer at Hafod and had passed many happy hours in the octagon library in his friend's company. Surrounded by books and statuary and enjoying the exotic perfumes drifting through the open conservatory doors, the two men sipped their hock and white burgundy in a delectable atmosphere of quiet contentment. At such times Hafod must have seemed paradise indeed.[34]

The notion of creating a sylvan paradise to complement his home had been uppermost in Thomas Johnes's mind since his first fateful visit to Hafod in the early 1780s when he had travelled through a landscape virtually denuded of timber by the depredations of shipbuilders and charcoal burners. From an aesthetic standpoint it would be essential to nurture the surviving ancient woodlands and to dress out the banks and glades of the demesne so as to provide an appropriately picturesque setting for the new house. Visual considerations apart, Johnes was only too aware that his financial position was not as sound as he might have wished, and he reasoned that investment in saleable timber —particularly on those parts of his estate of limited agricultural potential —would provide a bulwark against future economic illwinds. Thus he optimistically declared in the summer of 1799 he would plant, 'as my sinking fund', up to a million larch trees per year as long as space remained to do so. In fact, Johnes had already begun to plant extensively as early as 1782 and as the years passed so did the rate of planting accelerate to the extent that he was able to inform George Cumberland that in the 1797-98 season he had set upwards of 600,000 trees. Henceforth planting continued at a frenetic pace, and in 1800 and on four subsequent occasions Johnes received gold medals from the Royal Society of Arts in recognition of his monumental afforestation activities. The antiquary Walter Davies (Gwallter Mechain), maintained that almost four million trees were planted at Hafod between 1796 and 1813, although given the total timbered area of between 1000 and 1200 acres, Davies may well have underestimated by as much as one million.[35] It should also be noted that planting on the estate continued at the rate of some 200,000 trees annually for some years after the death of Johnes's only child in 1811. 'I shall continue to plant and improve', he told William Shepherd in 1812, 'just the same as if we were not the miserable branchless trunks we are'.

Occasionally broken up with blocks of Norway Spruce, the Hafod plantations principally comprised stands of larch, a species thriving well on the shaly soils of the Cardiganshire uplands. The lower slopes of the hills and the valley bottoms were planted predominantly with beech and oak with, for example, 58,600 oaks and 96,000 beech being set in 1804, several years after a 55 acre block of upland had been sown with acorns.[36] By 1803, Malkin tells us, the hills around Hafod had 'risen into opulence of timber', while the alder, ash, wych elm, black poplar and mountain ash interspersed with the plantations of oak and beech on the lower-lying areas were beginning to make some headway.[37] So too were the various exotics planted by Johnes around the demesne, including material from India *via* his niece Charlotte, and from Tsarskoe Selo in Russia— probably obtained by way of one of Robert Liston's many friends in the diplomatic service.

The communications of James Todd, Johnes's Scots gardener, with the Royal Society of Arts reveal various details of the sylvicultural methods employed on the Hafod estate. Stocks of the less common species were apparently bought in from nurserymen in Liverpool and Scotland, with the estate nurseries producing the bulk of the larch and oak seedlings. The latter, of which 922,000 trees were raised between 1798 and 1805, were sown as acorns at twelve inch spacings in the nursery and after periodic thinning planted out at permanent sites as seedlings of two or three years old.[38] Nursery-raised larches were transplanted after two years when they had attained a height of twelve inches, and though some one and three year old transplants were produced, the former were preferred on the grounds that they would suffer relatively little from wind damage as their roots became established.[39]

In view of the incompatibility of sheep farming and the establishment of timber stands, Johnes realised that an essential prerequisite to success was the secure enclosure of the land to be planted. To this end potential plantations were either walled to a height of five feet or, where appropriate, surrounded by turf banks of similar height topped with willow cuttings. In either case the enclosures were maintained by a man, '. . . .who has a yearly allowance for the purpose', while another individual regularly patrolled the plantations with a dog in order to deter both four- and two-legged trespassers.[40]

Setting out larch transplants was a highly organised operation with great care being taken to see that the planting material was in good order before being placed in the soil. To avoid root desiccation transplants from the nursery were drenched in a solution of water and leaf mould and then drawn through dry soil so that, '. . . the fibres of the roots are prevented from hardening and drying as they would otherwise do'. By this simple means trees could be persuaded to establish in rainless conditions and it was with some satisfaction that Todd reported to the Royal Society of Arts that during the drought of April, May and June 1786, he had planted 80,000 larches on a dry hillside and lost a mere two hundred.[41] Armed with spades and accompanied by small boys, each struggling under the burden of a bundle of transplants, the planting teams set to work on a task both arduous and tedious. Each man simply made a cross-cut notch in the bare unploughed turf, whereupon the boy introduced the transplant and his senior partner pressed it firmly into the ground with his foot. The minds of both individuals were concentrated on their task by the ever-present field supervisor whose duty it was to make sure that each tree was securely in place. On the assumption that this was so, each man/boy team was expected to plant up to 1000 larch trees per day, with four teams completing an acre in that time. The same teams were involved with acorn planting. In this case the turf was pared off with a spade and the soil loosened before the boy threw in several acorns which were immediately trodden in.[42]

By all accounts Johnes's larch plantations were a great success. At the end of the 1810 growing season the Hafod bailiff, John Greenshields, reported larch growth rates of between seven and nine rings per inch, and fifty years later some 700 acres of larch timber (notably free of larch canker) yielded specimens of one hundred feet in height containing up to one hundred and twenty cubic feet of timber. As William Linnard has noted, the Hafod sylvicultural techniques were well in advance of their time and indeed, '. . . .some of the techniques have scarcely been improved upon in the period since Thomas Johnes started his planting. . . . .' Thus it was with ample justification that Linnard awarded Johnes the accolade of 'pioneer of upland afforestation in Wales'.[43]

Farming at Hafod

Rural Cardiganshire in the late eighteenth century carried about it a flavour of mild decay and dilapidation. Of those landlords who may have wished to put into practice on their home farms the new methods and techniques pioneered elsewhere, most had not the money to do so, while others took little interest in their estates beyond receiving their rents and exercising their seigneurial rights. In general, incomes relative to the size of land holdings were low, leaving little net rental for reinvestment on the part of those gentlemen who chose to live on and work their home estates. Others, as total or partial absentees, left their land to the tender mercies of agents, more often than not trained as lawyers and attorneys, who concerned themselves more with maximising rents than developing rational systems of management and organising estates along the lines of a true partnership between landlord and tenant.[44] Tenant farmers, distrustful of innovation and shrouded in a miasma of inertia, were unwilling to invest their limited capital in their farming operations, and in many cases pursued husbandry practices which had changed little since medieval times. For generations the system of life leases at absurdly low rents had been a positive disincentive to the improvement both of farm management and capital structure, and since this system obliged tenants to maintain their own farm buildings, the latter were for the most part in a sad state of dereliction.[45]

Thus was Thomas Johnes confronted by a community of inept and largely indifferent landlords holding sway over a stubborn and suspicious tenantry whose outlook on life was tempered by a fierce pride in their ancient lineage and a deeply-rooted sense of attachment to their home soil. He would have noted too, that in the days before large scale emigration to the valleys of South Wales or the shores of America, Cardiganshire supported a teeming mass of rural workers, their economic and physical condition varying according to the vagaries of the seasons. Labourers on the land, in the lead mines and at the coastal lime kilns; hat and clog makers, wool workers, stocking knitters, drovers, wheelwrights, carpenters and the whole complex of craftsmen necessary to sustain what was in essence a self-supporting community, thronged the countryside. Both skilled and unskilled labour was cheap and plentiful and in the uplands of Cwmystwyth and Pontrhydygroes there were many who probably looked forward with eager anticipation to the rewards they might reap from participating in Johnes's grand schemes for Hafod.

Johnes was aghast at what he saw. How could estates be anything but mismanaged, he asked George Cumberland, when they are turned over to attorneys and agents? Only by landlords remaining at home and providing guidance, advice and encouragement would the attitudes of tenants be changed and their lot improved. True enough; but how could he, Thomas Johnes, with all his energy, zeal and determination, create a thriving and profitable estate and rouse other landlords from their lethargy by his example? To begin with, he would secure the co-operation and collaboration of his tenants and after developing his home farm to perfection would persuade, cajole and coerce them into effecting similar improvements to their own holdings. After all, apart from any other considerations it was *aesthetically* necessary that farms on the Hafod estate be upgraded from their present squalid condition.

To put such a plan into effect tenants would need to be made aware of new agricultural methods, and to come to terms with the necessity for drainage, rotational husbandry and other essential prerequisites of efficient farming. On neighbouring estates, he hoped, they would be galvanised into action by their landlords who would themselves be stimulated by the activities of the Cardiganshire Agricultural Society with which he was closely involved following its foundation in 1784.

As an honorary member of the First Board of Agriculture, Thomas Johnes put a great deal of effort into the Cardiganshire Agricultural Society. With the able assistance of the Rev. David Turnor of Wervilbrook he managed to accumulate numerous subscribers and even when membership began to drop off in 1799 his enthusiasm was unabated, and he wrote to Arthur Young that '. . . .no exertions of mine shall be wanting for its support'. But in common with many other county agricultural societies of the time, Cardiganshire's achievements probably amounted to very little. In the final analysis attempts to encourage a traditionally-inclined tenantry to adopt 'fancy' and expensive farming methods that rarely produced profits at the end of the day were doomed to failure, and the possibility of winning one of the Society's cheap medals was hardly likely to turn farmers away from well-tried and proven systems, however inefficient these were alleged to be. Nor were tenants likely to be over-impressed by landlords who used their rental incomes to put into practice on their home farms techniques of questionable local relevance. Yet, if proposals for the creation of model farms and the offers of premia for husbandry activities of dubious value were regarded as rather whimsical notions by most tenants, meetings of the County Agricultural Society at least provided a forum for landlords to discuss agricultural conditions and the potential for change. Such gatherings probably resulted in a chink of light penetrating the heavy veil of ignorance and indifference which had descended on so many Cardiganshire estates.[46]

Among the many factors limiting the potential development of farming in Wales was the virtual absence of printed information in the Welsh language, a matter of some significance considering the high proportion of monoglot Welsh speakers in the Principality. By the turn of the eighteenth century such technical literature as was available was almost exclusively in English and although Welsh-language newspapers were eventually to publish agricultural material, the most informative and influential publications were quite beyond the comprehension of most farmers in the western counties of Wales, if not the rest of the country. Indeed, apart from the translation of 'some tracts of plain instruction', by such luminaries as the Rev. John Owen of Tynllwyn (1808-1876) and, much later, the publication of bilingual versions of the Board of Agriculture's advisory material, works in Welsh entirely devoted to agriculture were few and far between.[47] Thomas Johnes, therefore, was breaking new ground when he arranged for the translation into Welsh of his *A Cardiganshire Landlord's Advice to his Tenants* (1800), a slender affair comprising a compendium 'of extracts from the best authors and facts from my own observation.' The Welsh version, *Cynghorion priodor o Garedigion i ddeiliaid ei dyddynod,* translated by William Owen (Pughe), appeared in the same year as the English original and was printed in an edition of 400 for free distribution to the Hafod tenants and other deserving local farmers. Unfortunately however, Pughe's eccentricities of spelling and his forlorn attempts to give the translation a dialect cast might in themselves have rendered the work incomprehensible to the majority of farmers.

The introductory and concluding paragraphs of *Landlord's Advice* underline Johnes's fundamentally paternalist philosophy:

'The long attachment which has subsisted between most of your families and mine,—the natural connexion which ought always to subsist between landlord and tenant,—added to a long and anxious desire for improving your condition, have induced me to make the following extracts from the most approved writers on Agriculture. I have been led to this undertaking from the fullest persuasion that it was necessary only to point out to you a better mode of farming, to induce you to follow it.'

And in conclusion:

'Wishing, most sincerely, that any of the facts and observations which I have collected for your service, may prove of that utility that I think an attention to them will show, I shall now conclude with assuring you, that you will always find in me a landlord eager and willing to recompense good farmers, and an assured friend'.

The volume was precisely as Johnes described it; a well-intentioned pot-pourri of advice, some of it sound and practical; some of it fanciful and irrelevant. Tenants were encouraged to adopt a more rational approach to cropping systems and the use of manures besides receiving instruction in the most appropriate equipment for their farms, of which threshing machines, seed drills, ploughs, waggons and harrows were fashioned by the Hafod estate workshop according to approved models. These were available for purchase, 'at modest price'. The prevailing mood of encouragement was occasionally tempered by unequivocal warnings to those farmers who persisted in their slovenly ways. All holdings would be inspected regularly and where poor farming was apparent Johnes would hold 'a very bad opinion' of the perpetrator, 'and consider him as undeserving of any assistance or support.'

Johnes was determined to bring to an end the deleterious practice of continuous cropping with cereals which rapidly exhausted the already hungry Hafod soils. This he achieved by inserting restrictive clauses in tenancy agreements, and where soil conditions were suitable, promoting the cultivation of 'break' crops of turnips. 'Estimating the value of a turnip crop as highly as I do, I shall lay it down as a rule that no tenant shall be entitled to any premiums from me who has not first acquired a premium for a turnip crop'. However valuable these turnip crops in terms of improving soil conditions and providing livestock feed, they were both very expensive to grow and technically difficult to establish on the acidic soils of Cardiganshire, and it is questionable whether this particular advice was acted upon to any extent. Indeed one is inclined to wonder whether in fact Johnes's well-meaning work had any significant influence beyond emphasising its author's admirable intentions.

Until midway through the first decade of the nineteenth century Thomas Johnes was himself an enthusiastic farmer. Guided by his friend and mentor, the Scots agriculturist James Anderson, through whose efforts 'my farm will be most respectable and all my estates put on the best footing both for tenants and landlord', he strove to create a profitable model farm on the Hafod demesne. Disregarding the scepticism of his friends and the blank incomprehension of many locals, he forged ahead and proved, at least to his own satisfaction, that respectable yields of harvestable crops could be obtained in this unpromising environment of high rainfall and thin acidic soils. 'Although the neighbouring farmers laughed at the idea and insisted upon it that it would not answer', wrote Thomas Martyn after his visit to Hafod, healthy crops of wheat and flax flourished at considerable altitudes.[48] By 1797 Johnes was confidently declaring that the pundits would soon sit up and take notice, for even now, he told his cousin John, 'People get off their horses as they pass to see if their eyes have not deceived them in respect to the Crops'. But to grow these crops, heavy applications of manure were essential. Traditionally local farmers had manured both their arable and pasture lands with a compost of dung and ditch scrapings intermixed, perhaps, with seaweed and lime. All too often, however, the effort put into the creation of the compost midden was wasted when it was stacked out of doors and subject to the combined effects of leaching and desiccation. Realising that this would lead to serious losses of plant nutrients, Johnes counselled his tenants to cover their middens, and included in *Landlord's Advice* a wood engraving of an 'improved dunghill' wherein the midden was protected from the elements.

Fundamentally important to farming in Cardiganshire were ample supplies of lime to counteract the natural acidity of the soil. Burnt lime was obtained from the numerous limekilns located at various points on the coastline to which limestone and the culm required for burning it were delivered by sea from the quarries of south Pembrokeshire.[49] Unfortunately many farmers found difficulty in financing both the purchase of lime and the burdensome turnpike charges payable as they returned home, and more often than not as Warner observed, liming was 'scantily and slovenly done'.[50] As a major user of lime, sometimes applying up to 200 bushels per acre on his hill lands, Thomas Johnes was anxious to secure ready supplies of the material as cheaply as possible and throughout 1802 and 1803 he even contemplated the potential for importing shiploads of ready-burnt lime directly from Glamorgan to Aberystwyth, thereby saving on local kiln charges. Nothing seems to have come of this potentially dangerous undertaking, nor indeed of his later attempts to persuade magnates and businessmen to subscribe towards the construction of a railway from South Wales into Cardiganshire along which lime, coal and culm could be hauled in horse-drawn rolling stock and thereby imported more cheaply than by sea. If these projects were fruitless, they once again emphasise Thomas Johnes's concern with resolving the agrarian problems of his locality, and the very fact that he thought at all about such matters stands him in stark contrast to most of his fellow landowners.

Although successful as an arable farmer, Johnes was fully aware of the comparative advantage of pastoral farming in the moist climate of west Wales. In the context of the picturesque ideal, moreover, he probably took the view that pastoralism was more appropriate than the business of growing crops. If the claims made by some contemporary observers were grossly exaggerated, Johnes nevertheless seems to have achieved spectacular results with his grassland improvement exercises, particularly on the peat soils of the hillier parts of his property. Directed by James Anderson and supervised by the estate's Scots bailiffs and their henchmen, the process of pasture improvement in these areas was relatively simple. Once the area to be improved had been drained with open catchment ditches, the existing turf surface was removed, dried, and burnt in heaps, the resulting ash being spread over the soil surface. [51] Into this rich medium rape (*Brassica napus*) was sown and subsequently grazed off during the winter by folded sheep before being sown to grass under a 'nurse' crop of oats the following spring.

We know little of the seeds mixtures and grass species used by Johnes in the earlier phases of his hill improvement schemes. [52] Supplies both of rye grasses and clovers were available at the time although both were frequently contaminated with weed seeds, notably of the vigorous couch grass (*Agropyron repens*) so that whatever species were planted, the sward in its early stages would have played host to a flourishing weed population. [53] In one of his numerous publications on grassland James Anderson had recommended the planting of herbs, in particular Yarrow (*Achillea millefolium*), to yield pastures which have, ' . . . a closer pile than they would have done had they been left entirely to themselves'. [54] Quick to accept the advice of his agrarian *guru*, Johnes set about obtaining supplies of this excellent herb with its deep, widely-ranging roots capable of absorbing minerals from the soil to greater effect than the monocotyledonous grasses, and we can assume that yarrow was extensively sown on the hills around Hafod.

In 1812-13, regardless of his growing financial difficulties, Johnes was, '. . . still planting and farming as if we were in the most happy state'. Influenced by the writings of the Irish agriculturist William Richardson (1740-1820), he had by this time become interested in the potential of Fiorin Grass (*Agrostis stolonifera*) as a pasture species for his upland moors.[55] The main virtue of Fiorin, for which Richardson had made extravagant claims, lay in the ability of its stolons rapidly to colonise wetter soils and to produce an ample bulk of herbage in the latter part of the season when most other grass species had ceased to grow. Undeterred by the laborious task of planting stolons as opposed to broadcasting seed, Johnes successfully established several hundred acres of *Agrostis* dominated pasture, observing to James Edward Smith that he was, 'more and more convinced that it will prove the most beneficial discovery that has been made and all travellers now stop and look at what plantations I have made of it on the roadside'.

These extensive pasture-land improvements increased the availability of summer grazing and winter hay supplies, so creating a more suitable environment for livestock production, to which Johnes turned with his usual enthusiasm. Although many of the small, hardy, black cattle of the Cardiganshire uplands had been improved by crossbreeding in the late eighteenth century, there was still a great deal of prejudice among Cardiganshire farmers against any but the local cattle types. To some extent this was justified, in that the native cattle could survive, and indeed flourish, under the poor nutritional régime of the hills,where other 'improved' cattle types often failed. Johnes, however, appreciated that where grasslands had been improved, larger and more productive cattle could be supported. He had experimented on his exposed hills with crosses by Shorthorn, Hereford, Devon and Scots bulls out of the local cows and had achieved some success in breeding animals suited to producing meat under those environmental conditions. 'My farm is answering amazingly', he wrote proudly in 1799, 'A few years ago I had my meat from Kington and Newtown. This year I shall fat for sale 50 head of cattle. I am now building the most complete feeding house that ever was. . .' This 'complete feeding house' accommodating 12 cattle was particularly remarkable in that it foreshadowed developments in livestock feeding normally associated with the mid-nineteenth rather than the late eighteenth century. Moreover, the building incorporated many features included in contemporary intensive livestock housing systems. Thomas Martyn described the 'beast-house' as follows:

'The house for fattening Beast is admirably constructed. This was a new scene to me and therefore it engaged my intention. Each beast has a stall for itself either a rack or trough for his hay and a smaller one for turnips below it, a constant stream of water clear and transparent runs beneath. The animals stand on a false floor the boards of which were about 2 inches asunder for the soil to pass through, which is carried off through a hole behind each stall into a spacious receptacle covered by a penthouse. In front of the cattle is a passage for the feeder to pass and a convenient opening at the head of each to put in the different food without going into the stall. At the front of the door is a weighing machine by which you have the exact weight of the beast immediately that he steps over the threshold.'

The success achieved with this remarkable building was not paralleled by Johnes's dairy enterprise. Dairy farming was practised on a small scale on many Cardiganshire farms in the early-nineteenth century, although the production of store cattle for export to the border counties or to England was the predominant feature of cattle husbandry. Indeed, contemporary evidence indicates that where a constructive breeding policy was followed, animals tended to be selected for meat rather than milking potential. Johnes was not satisfied with the milking performance of local cattle breeds nor, for that matter, with his Hereford, Longhorn and Devon crosses.[56] Hence his decision to import 40 heifers from Holland to form the basis of a 'winter dairy'. According to Thomas Martyn these animals were milked in a spacious building, '. . . in the form of an amphitheatre, the cows being housed every night during the winter'. Following contemporary practice, Johnes concentrated on producing butter and cheese, in which procedures he laid heavy emphasis on cleanliness, considering easily-cleaned stoneware pans, leaden troughs and a continual flow of fresh water to be essential to success.[57] Typically, he eschewed the manufacture of the rather bitter locally popular cheese and concentrated instead upon making exotic Stiltons, Gloucesters, Cheshires and Parmesans—the latter to a recipe drawn up by a relation of Signor Trossarelli, Mariamne Johnes's drawing master. Oblivious to the difficulty of marketing such products in a locality where traditional tastes prevailed, Johnes found himself with 5 tons of unsold cheese in the autumn of 1803 which he disposed of cheaply to his labourers. Learning an expensive lesson, he abandoned exotic cheese production thereafter in favour of the more readily marketable butter and skim-milk cheeses. But even this seems to have been an equally unsuccessful venture and the dairy and its fittings were sold as a job lot in the winter of 1806.

Although he ultimately lost interest in sheep production, principally on the grounds of 'the wretched management of sheep in this country' by which his neighbours' flocks joined forces with his own in a frontal attack on his young plantations of trees, Johnes in his earlier years raised sheep on a very large scale. Ignoring the local type, described as 'very small, long-legged and narrow in the chine', he experimented with various breeds and by the turn of the eighteenth century had established a hardy and productive Cheviot-Ryeland cross as the basis to his flock.[58] Notwithstanding the relative tolerance of this cross to harsh conditions, the flock was decimated by the severe winter of 1799 when almost a thousand ewes and lambs were lost. The remainder were saved by being driven off the mountains to be hand fed in the lowland meadows—an almost unprecedented move according to Arthur Young for, 'In this country it is not the mode to think even of giving sheep anything in the winter'.[59]

In 1788 King George III had been presented with a small flock of Merino sheep by the Supreme Junta of Spain.[60] As numbers increased the King charged his equerry Robert Fulke Greville with the task of presenting rams from the flock at Kew to improving landowners, thereby '. . . to extend throughout the country a general benefit'. Greville decided that among Welsh landowners Phillip Yorke of Erddig, Lord Cawdor of Stackpole, Mr. Morris of Swansea and, '. . . my Friend Mr. Johnes of Havod in Cardiganshire' were most deserving of the King's munificence and rams were accordingly despatched to these far-flung outposts of the kingdom.[61] Had they known the climatic conditions of their destination the wretched animals would probably have left Kew with some reluctance. Their evolutionary background and superb fine wool hardly suited them to the damp and chills of upland Cardiganshire and those rams managing to survive for any length of time soon succumbed to the foot-rot disease prevalent on the soft, wet soils of the hills. Johnes, as usual, was stoical and heedless of the astronomical prices commanded by the King's rams, we find him writing to Greville in 1804 to ascertain the availability of Merinos at Kew since he wished, once again, to attempt a cross with his own stock. But this was probably no more than a token gesture for by this time the seeds of disillusionment with sheep farming, if not model farming as a whole, were beginning to germinate in his mind.

By 1807 Thomas Johnes had come to realise, like so many innovators before and since, that exciting and satisfying though it may be, the experimental approach to agriculture had an unerring tendency to absorb enormous resources without yielding a great deal in the form of tangible returns. Besides, he now inclined more to forestry than farming, believing it to be more profitable on '. . . large extensive tracts of little or no value in their present state'. From now on his own farming would be of limited scale on land immediately adjacent to the house, its sole object being to yield provisions for his own consumption. To this end the home farm was wound up in the Spring of 1807 and the land leased to a tenant after the buildings had been pulled down to provide stone and timber for refurbishing other holdings on the estate. Subsequently Johnes would continue with his extensive programme of pasture renovation and other improvements designed to advance rentals and attract 'substantial tenants' to the estate. But his principal effort would now be directed towards his first love, the afforestation of Hafod.

The Hafod Library

In the middle years of the eighteenth century the ancient Universities of Oxford and Cambridge had descended into a state of moral and intellectual torpor. The dons occupied themselves with those deep and dull potations so derided by Gibbon, while gentleman students looked upon a spell at either institution more as an opportunity for uninhibited whoring and drinking than a chance to attain learning and wisdom. The frivolities of Oxbridge contrasted sharply with the austere intellectual climate of the University of Edinburgh where Thomas Johnes and Paul Panton junior, two of the more scholarly scions of the Welsh gentry, were sent to complete their education. In the process each developed a life-long interest in book and manuscript collecting and the esoteric, and often eccentric, world of the bibliophile.

There was, of course, nothing new in the idea of a Welsh gentleman disposing of his patrimony in the civilised pursuit of bibliomania. In the previous century men like Robert Vaughan of Hengwrt and William Maurice of Cefn-y-Braich had amassed remarkable manuscript collections, while the herculean efforts of the great antiquary Edward Lhuyd to collect Welsh manuscripts had profoundly influenced Welsh antiquarianism and served as a major stimulus to the endeavours of the Morris brothers, Thomas Pennant and Iolo Morganwg among many others.[62] The difference, possibly, between Thomas Johnes and the earlier collectors, with their laudable concern for conserving Welsh material, lay in Johnes's broader cultural horizons and more extensive social milieu. He was, after all, the cousin and close friend of Richard Payne Knight, the most distinguished dilettante and connoisseur of his time, and as a Fellow of both the Royal and Linnean Societies was acquainted with many of the foremost scientific and literary figures of the day. A particularly close associate was the London-based bookseller and bibliographer James Edwards (1787-1816), a man whose enthusiasm for his calling was so intense that he instructed his executors to arrange for his coffin to be fashioned from library shelves! Edwards was Dibdin's 'Rinaldo' who '. . .did such wonderful things towards the acquisition of rare, beautiful and truly classical productions. . . .he was probably a born bibliographical bookseller and had always a nice feeling and accurate perception of what was tasteful and classical'.[63] Johnes often stayed with Edwards at his Pall Mall home and attended the celebrated dinners given by the latter for his literary and political friends. He may even have been present on the occasion when Sheridan, noted for his legendary capacity, became so drunk that he entirely lost the power of speech![64]

Thomas Johnes had begun to collect books as a young man and had probably assembled the nucleus of a library by the time he arrived at Hafod in the early 1780s. Thereafter he became an assiduous scrutineer of sale catalogues, keenly seeking the advice of his friends as to those items which might be worthy of shelf space in the libraries of his new home. In 1793 he completed his first major purchase, an important group of Froissart manuscripts from the collection of Paris de Meyzieux, allegedly costing him upwards of £2,000.[65] This enormous expenditure, along with other financial strictures, seems to have clipped his wings for a time and it was with some disappointment that he told James Edward Smith in 1794 that he was prevented 'by circumstance' from purchasing extensively at Lord Bute's sale. Two years later, by a remarkable stroke of luck, he was presented with a major collection of the Welsh manuscripts of Edward Lhuyd by the Whig politician Sir John Sebright of Beechwood in Hertfordshire. Described by Maria Edgeworth as '. . . very clever—very vain—very odd—full of fancies and paradoxes', Sebright was an expert on animal husbandry and field sports besides being a scholar of some eccentricity, who took great pleasure in lecturing visitors to Beechwood on the mysteries of dog training, pigeon fancying and rabbits.[66] Having little interest in the collection, Sebright probably thought that since both Jesus College and the Bodleian Library had turned them down at Lhuyd's death, the manuscripts, originally purchased by his ancestor Sir Thomas Sebright, might as well be returned to Wales. Johnes was delighted. The Sebright collection would lend lustre to Hafod and act as a magnet to Welsh scholars who would flock to Cardiganshire to peruse and transcribe the manuscripts. Not for him the selfish attitude of Sir Watkin Williams Wynn to whose great library at Wynnstay even accredited readers were denied access; on the contrary, the Hafod library would provide a public service. And he was not to be disappointed, for once the manuscripts were safely deposited at Hafod numerous Welsh scholars, including William Owen (Pughe) and Iolo Morganwg followed in their wake and busied themselves with the exacting task of transcription. Iolo's transcriptions in particular, if suspect like much of his work, provide virtually the only clues as to the contents of the Sebright collection and the other Welsh manuscripts destroyed in the fire of 1807.[67]

With the assistance of Robert Liston, Johnes had attempted in 1804 to acquire the library of Johann Meerman, the widely-travelled Dutch scholar and statesman whose collection embraced both medieval volumes and numerous legal, historical and linguistic works, some of his own compilation.[68] When this fell through he cast about for other complete collections and in 1805 succeeded in purchasing the remarkable Pesaro Library, a superb assemblage primarily reflecting the interests of the Pesaro family of Venice. This mouthwatering collection, claimed by Johnes to have been acquired, '. . . .from the profits of my pen', exemplified the finest productions of the European presses. Apart from some 550 Aldine editions, 300 Latin volumes and 800 Italian titles, the Pesaro library included French works (with 50 volumes of Voltaire) besides more than 150

Spanish titles concerned, *inter alia*, with history, geography and travel. As the library laboriously made its way by sea from Venice to London, where it arrived in October 1806, Johnes commissioned craftsmen in Carmarthen to prepare bookcases and then waited in eager anticipation for the delivery of his treasures. As he did so, he reflected upon the library catalogue and noted that for all its glories the Pesaro collection was lacking in examples of early printing from Germany and England. To rectify the deficiency he purchased (from Thomas Payne, the Prince Regent's bookseller) the small, but important collection of Stanesby Alchorne, previously Master of the Mint between 1789 and 1800. This admirably filled the gap since it contained works from a variety of northern European presses among which were 9 Caxtons, 23 de Wordes, various early Mainz imprints and 16 Pynsons, including Lord Berners's Froissart translation of 1523-25.[69] Most of the manuscripts and many of the books in the gallery and anti-library [sic], were destroyed in the 1807 fire, but thanks in large measure to the valiant rescue efforts of Jane and Mariamne Johnes, the Alchornes escaped the flames. Nevertheless the collection was not to remain long at Hafod. Seven years after the original purchase a near-bankrupt Johnes was forced to part with his Alchornes and the 120 items — by now in less than perfect condition—were sold to Lord Spencer of Althorp for £3500. On discovering that the collection embodied numerous duplicates, Spencer sold these on in May 1813 to the bookseller R.H. Evans of Pall Mall.[70]

As far as his books were concerned, Johnes viewed the calamitous Hafod fire with commendable *sang froid*. Once the initial shock at the loss of his manuscript collection had evaporated, he began rearranging the remnants of his library which lay 'in grand confusion' around him, and in so doing quietly counted his blessings. By happy accident the Pesaro library had been detained in London, thereby escaping the conflagration, while the Alchornes were virtually complete and many other miscellaneous volumes had escaped all but minor damage. Moreover, several months after the fire he had bought the library of the numismatist Rogers Ruding, a choice collection of items of heraldic, genealogical and topographical interest including works by Ashmole, Camden, Dugdale, Leland and Pennant. Thus as the new Hafod took shape he was able to advise his various correspondents that he was richer in printed books than ever before. These, he fondly imagined, would be a source of comfort and solace to his declining years.

The Hafod Press and its Productions

If the assembling of a fine private library was a costly venture, so too was the establishment, maintenance and operation of a private press. Following the precept of Horace Walpole, whose Strawberry Hill press had been set up in 1757 under the direction of Thomas Kirkgate, several English gentlemen established private presses with the primary object of printing their own works of antiquarianism or connoisseurship. In Wales, William Turton of Swansea (1762-1835) printed various medical and zoological treatises on his own press. In the north Paul Panton Jnr. of Plas Gwyn, Anglesey launched his press in 1784, although, in contrast to the Hafod press, Wales's only other private publishing enterprise, no example of Panton's works remains extant. [71]

It seems in many ways extraordinary that Thomas Johnes should ever have contemplated a printing press at the remote location of Hafod unless he were consciously attempting to emulate Panton or the more ambitious pretensions of Walpole. Whatever the benefits, as Dibdin wrote, of '....gentlemen of classical education, good fortunes, or fine patrimonies (devoting) some portion of the leisure of retirement in enquiries connected with the ancient history of their country....', private printing ventures were rarely commercially successful and, in catering more or less exclusively for the tastes of their owners, bore little relationship to the mainstream book trade. [72] Apart from the capital cost of purchasing equipment, and the frustrations of employing printers and compositors, who, as Johnes found to his discomforture could be an irritating and temperamental species, the law demanded that presses be licensed; a procedure not without its anxieties and pitfalls. Besides, ink and print had to be bought from outside Wales while paper; the most expensive item in the operation, required to be purchased either from London or from papermills at Haverfordwest and Wrexham. 'Remember', wrote Johnes to George Cumberland in response to the latter's urging the establishment of a press at Hafod, 'in this insulated spot I must have every material and apparatus sent at a vast cost'. But if Johnes were to proceed with his translations of the French Chroniclers, argued Cumberland, it was essential that the printing be carried out *locally* to facilitate effective supervision by the translator. A sensible suggestion, perhaps, but Aberystwyth had no commercial printer before 1809, while Titus Evans of Machynlleth, some 30 miles distant, produced somewhat shoddy work offensive to Johnes's taste.[73] Evans apart, the nearest printing operations capable of competently tackling work on the scale envisaged by Johnes were located at Wrexham or Carmarthen. He could, of course, have had his translations printed in London or Bristol, but then he would have been faced with considerable logistical problems when it came to correcting and re-correcting proofs, organising bindings and undertaking the other technical tasks associated with ushering a work into print. It occurred to Johnes, that without spending long periods away from home (which he detested) it would have been virtually impossible to oversee satisfactorily the printing of his works by one of the metropolitan houses. The fact that his first literary venture, *A Cardiganshire Landlord's Advice to his Tenants*, was printed in 1800 by Biggs and Cottell of Bristol, suggests that he had no initial intention of printing his own translations and that he was forced *faute de mieux* along this road. His seemingly reluctant decision to go ahead with the Hafod press may also in part have been encouraged by members of the literary coterie associated with his friend James Edwards, or he may even have entertained hopes that in the longer term the press might yield bankable returns.[74]

In the event, the Hafod press, set up at Pwllpeiran some distance from the house, commenced operations early in 1802. With the assistance of the publisher John White of Fleet Street, Johnes had obtained both a pair of presses and the services of a printer who, for £1-14-0 per week and a tied cottage on the estate, began the exacting task of printing his patron's first translations from the French. But for some reason relations between translator and printer soon became strained. Whether this was due to the former's impatience or the latter's idleness is not clear, but when his printer requested an increase in wages early in 1803 Johnes decided that the time had come for a parting of the ways, and he wrote to Robert Anderson in Edinburgh about the prospect of securing a Scots compositor and printer who might achieve a more satisfactory output at a lower level of disgruntlement than the present man. Ever ready to oblige, Anderson scoured Edinburgh and finally found a printer prepared to forego the sophistication of the northern capital for the less salubrious environs of west Cardiganshire. Thus came James Henderson to Hafod to join the growing throng of Johnes's Scots entourage. A tall, scholarly man whose considerable linguistic abilities enabled him to master Welsh relatively quickly, Henderson was to remain at Hafod until the press was finally wound up around 1810. If from time to time his association with his employer was less than convivial, the volumes bearing his name on the title page lend testament to the overall quality of his workmanship.

Throughout eight busy years Henderson and his assistants at the Hafod press were principally concerned with the printing of Thomas Johnes's translations of the histories of the medieval French chroniclers Froissart, Joinville and Monstrelet. Like the poet Thomas Gray and that extraordinarily industrious copyist and annotator La Curne de Sainte-Palaye, Johnes loved the lively style of the chronicles of Froissart, which for all their numerous errors and inaccuracies, remained, and still remain, important sources for students of the Hundred Years War. [75] With the exception of an undated three-volume edition published by Antoine Vérard in Paris, the first printed edition of Froissart's chronicles had been produced in the same city by Michel le Noir in 1505, almost a century after the chronicler's death. Others followed, culminating in Denis Sauvage's Paris production of 1574. Realising their historical importance, eighteenth-century French scholars combed the libraries of Europe for copies of the Froissart manuscripts, hoping that by careful collation a definitive edition might finally be produced. Thomas Johnes himself was an enthusiastic collector and in the 1810 edition of his *Memoirs* of Froissart he refutes Sainte-Palaye's claim that England could boast only three sets of Froissart manuscripts, pointing out that besides copies in the British Museum and various Oxford and Cambridge college libraries, '. . .I have in my library not less than six; but not one in a complete history'. [76] In fact Johnes owned four volumes of the manuscript chronicles (originally from the library of the Prince de Soubise) having bought them at the sale of Paris de Meyzieux in the early 1790s. Spurred on by encouragement from his wife and his friends James Edwards and Lord Chancellor Thurlow, Johnes decided to produce a definitive modern English edition, based to some extent, on the manuscripts in his possession. An earlier translation, produced at the command of Henry VIII by John Bourchier, Lord Berners (1467-1533) had appeared between 1523 and 1525. Printed by Richard Pynson, Berners's translation was of considerable contemporary importance both as a fine example of Tudor prose and for the stimulus it gave to general historical reading in the sixteenth century. Johnes, however, had little time for Berners's performance and he determined upon bringing Froissart into the contemporary light by giving the world a translation which was at once accurate and lively and without its predecessor's obsolete language.

Johnes's basic strategy was to collate with the printed copies the Froissart manuscripts in the Hafod library, the British Museum, the Bibliothèque Nationale and the Elizabethan Library in Breslau, thereby to produce an accurate translation without, as he observed in the *Advertisement* to the folio edition, becoming 'servilely literal'. As it happened he was unable to obtain transcriptions of the Breslau material until the summer of 1806 and these were eventually incorporated in the 1810 edition of the *Memoirs of the Life of Froissart*. In fact the *Memoirs* were the first fruits of Johnes's work. A translation of Sainte-Palaye's *Vie de Froissart* (which had first appeared in the *Mémoires de l'Académie des Inscriptions et des Belles Lettres*) the volume was printed by Nichols of Fleet Street and published by John White in 1801 a year before the Hafod press began operations. As Johnes often pointed out, the *Memoirs* were completed in no more than a week and had been produced merely to test the extent of public interest in Froissart, and thereby to assess the potential market for his translations of the Chronicles. The critics were less than charitable, and one is left with the distinct impression that Johnes regretted releasing this inaccurate and rather shoddy work whose many imperfections were rectified in the 1810 Hafod edition. If the *Memoirs* did little to enhance Johnes's reputation as a scholar, their production alerted him to the avarice and rapacity of John White, if not the general run of contemporary publishers. As he complained to James Edward Smith, '. . . he seems to charge us poor authors most exorbitantly. I pay all the expenses of printing (and) when the book is sold for 5/- he quickly accounts to me for only 3/-. This is an easy way to get rich and yet they can combine so much together that you cannot help yourself.'[77]

Johnes had begun the enormous task of translating the Froissart chronicles as early as 1794. Disregarding the advice of his friend Thomas Percy, Bishop of Dromore, he made no attempt merely to update Berners's work which he only consulted 'when in great doubt', preferring instead to work from page to page of the collated manuscript and printed material to produce an entirely new translation. As the work progressed he encountered increasing difficulty in identifying personal and place names, many of which were indecipherable in the manuscripts, and in wrestling with these problems frequently sought the assistance of Robert Liston and Robert Anderson. He finally concluded (in common with the compiler of the most recent translation) that complete accuracy in this respect was a virtual impossibility and in the *Advertisement* preceding the text of the first edition craved the public's indulgence for, '. . . when it is considered that this work was printed in a very remote part of the Island, great allowances should be made. . . '

In the early stages the translation made unsteady progress as Johnes busied himself with farming and planting and struggled to come to grips with the prodigious complexities of his finances. In January 1800, however, he took up his pen 'with the ardour of renewed love', explaining to George Cumberland that the project would benefit from having been temporarily shelved, '. . . for I take now much more pains. . . ' Time and again Johnes's letters reveal the pleasure and solace which Froissart afforded him. Rising at 5 a.m. and translating for several hours before breakfast he could luxuriate in Froissart's action-packed tales and ignore the realities of his money problems, the iniquities of lawyers and the machinations of his estranged family. The translation, he maintained, was undertaken primarily for his own self-gratification and as copies rolled off the press, some of them marred by over-heavy impression and smudging, he was generally stoical about the numerous printing errors which he attributed to inadequate and insufficient proof-reading. Yet, after the completion of the first folio volume, 'I trust that the general amusement it must give will serve as a passport for its errors'.

The fourth and final volume of Froissart was ready for sale in November 1805, some 2 years after the young Duchess of Bedford had pulled the first sheet of Volume II from the press at Hafod. Previous volumes were already on the market, Johnes having sold the whole impression of 25 folio and 300 quarto volumes to John White for £2800. The former were embellished with sumptuous hand-coloured engravings traced from illustrations identified by James Edwards in the Bibliothèque Nationale, the quarto edition having the same plates in black and white only.

On the appearance of the first Froissart volume in 1803 the critique in the *Gentleman's Magazine* was limited to minor strictures about language, the reviewer concluding that the Hafod Press 'may be considered as the Strawberry Hill of Wales, and Mr. James Henderson a fit representative of Mr. Robert Kirkgate.'[78] The *British Critic* was similarly gracious in its praises. Johnes, 'being universally known as an elegant and accomplished scholar', had produced an admirably-illustrated work of translation and if the absence of notes or an index was unfortunate, '...There is...but little occasion or opportunity for complaint'.[79] Walter Scott's contribution to the *Edinburgh Review* placed Johnes's work in a somewhat different light. Comparing the new translation with that of Lord Berners rather than the original French, Scott castigated Johnes for his style, 'timidity' of language and inaccuracy in heraldic matters. Although he grudgingly commended the translator for correcting many of Berners's errors respecting Froissart's *dramatis personae*, he concluded that a new edition of Berners, reduced to 'a systematic orthography', would better have served scholarship than Johnes's performance. Nevertheless, '...we are more disposed to be grateful for what may be considered as a free gift made to the public, than strictly to examine how far it might have been made more acceptable. If the Hafod press performs what is incumbent on that of Clarendon, the founder is surely entitled to choose betwixt the character of a translator and editor: and while, as a private individual, he discharges at his own expense a public duty, we willingly say, God speed his labours'.[80]

Johnes was piqued but not unduly disturbed by Scott's patronising remarks. As far as he was concerned the enthusiastic reaction of the book-buying public vindicated his efforts; the quarto edition was sold out by 1806 and the octavo edition printed by Longman eagerly sought after. Impressed by public demand he set about preparing a supplementary volume incorporating the various readings and additions from overseas libraries until these (with the exception of the Breslau transcripts) were destroyed in the 1807 fire.

Shortly after he had begun work on Froissart Johnes had told Robert Anderson that, 'Froissart's great beauties are his naiveté and simplicity. I was afraid I couldn't attain the last, but find I have and shall be careful of polishing. Our later historians are I think much too florid, more especially Gibbon'. Gibbon, of course, was one of the great writers of English prose; Thomas Johnes was manifestly not so. His writing is rather tame (and in Walter Scott's words, 'over-genteel'), while his attempts at the pseudo-archaic seem sadly flat by both medieval and modern standards. Yet he remains the only man to have undertaken the formidable task of translating Froissart's chronicles in their entirety and the appearance of further editions of his translations in 1842, 1882, 1884 and 1906 testifies to their worth. Readers will gain some of the flavour of Johnes's prose from the paragraph printed below in juxtaposition with appropriate passages from Lord Berners's translation of 1523-25 and that of Geoffrey Brereton in the *Penguin Classics* edition of 1967.

Berners

'In this season a frerre minor full of great clergye was in the cytie of Avigno, called frere Johan of Rochetayllad, the whiche frere Pope Innocent the vi helde in prison in the castell of Baignoux for shewinge of many mervailes after to come, principally he shewed many thinges to fall on the prelates of the church for the greate superfuitye and pride that was as then used among them. And also he spake many thinges to fall of the realme of Fraunce and of the greate lordes of Christendome for the oppressions that they dyd to the pore comon people. This frere sayde he wolde prove al his sayynges by the auctorie of the Apocalippys, and by other bokes of holy sayntes, and prophettes the whiche were opened to hym by the grace of the holy ghofte he shewed many thinges harde to beleve, & many thinges fell after as he sayde. He sayd them not as a prophette, but he shewed them by auctorite of auncient sciptures, and by the grace of the holy ghoste, who gave him understanding to declare the auncient prophicies and to shew to all christen people the yeres and tyme whan suche thinges shulde fall.'

Johnes

'About this period, a Franciscan friar, full of knowledge and understanding, was at Avignon: his name was John de Rochetaillade: and Pope Innocent VI kept him a prisoner in the castle of Baignoux, not only on account of the great prophecies he made of the times to come, chiefly and principally relating to the heads and prelates of the holy church, by reason of their pride, and the expensive life they led, but also concerning the kingdom of France, and the great Lords of Christendom for their heavy oppressions on the common people. The above-mentioned John was willing to prove all he said from the Apocalypse, and by the ancient books of the holy prophets, which were opened to him by the grace of the Holy Ghost, by which he uttered things that were difficult to be credited. Some of the predictions he had made were seen to come to pass within the time; which he never could have foretold as a prophet, but by means of the Holy Scriptures, and the Holy Spirit that had given him the power of understanding these ancient prophecies, and of announcing to all Christians the year and time when they were to be fulfilled'.

Brereton

'In those days there was a Franciscan friar at Avignon, a very learned and intelligent man, called Brother Jean de la Roche-taillade. He was kept imprisoned by Pope Innocent VI in the castle of Bagnols because of the extraordinary misfortunes which he predicted, firstly for the prelates and princes of the Church, on account of the excessive luxury and pomp in which they lived; and also for the Kingdom of France and the great lords of Christendom, because of the way in which they oppressed the common people. This Friar John claimed to prove his utterances by the Apocalypse and the ancient books of the holy prophets, whose sense was made clear to him, he said, by the grace of the Holy Spirit. Many of his predictions were hard to believe, yet some came true within the period in which he placed them. He did not speak as a prophet, but knew about them through the old Scriptures and by the grace of the Holy Spirit — as one says—who had granted him understanding to make clear all those ancient prophesies and writings, so as to announce to all Christians the year and the date when the troubles were to come'.

With the completion of the translation of Froissart the Hafod press was moved to Pendre, a small farm above the mansion whence, in 1807, issued two further works. The most substantial of these was the Joinville *Memoirs,* a translation of Joinville's *Vie de Saint Louis* of 1305-6 along with the various commentaries and notes of du Cange, de la Bastie, de la Ravalière and Falconet.[81] Johnes's translation was based on the edition forming part of the *Mémoires relatifs à l'Histoire de France* while the second work, the fifteenth century *Travels of Bertrandon de la Brocquière,* derived from le Grand d'Aussi's edition originally published in the fifth volume of the *Mémoires de l'Institut*. The *Joinville*, dedicated to Johnes's friend and financial advisor Hugh Smith of Bloomsbury, was issued in two quarto volumes with maps and plates published by Longman, Hurst, Rees and Orme. To the translator's great annoyance his work was savagely mauled by an anonymous critic in the *Edinburgh Review* who, pulling no punches, maintained 'that the merest drudge, who knew a little of French, was as competent to have produced this publication as the proprietor of the Hafod Press'. Having criticised Johnes for failing to provide any introduction or commentary, the reviewer took him to task over a number of inaccuracies, arguing that these arose from his rejection of the 1761 Louvre edition in favour of the interpolated edition from which the translation was derived. Allowing that the work 'is not unsuccessful in point of expression, which is generally free and idiomatic without too much affectation of antiquity', he went on to condemn the 'ignorant or parasitical eulogy' bestowed upon Johnes's other translations and finally wound up a review so astringent as to verge on the insulting with the conclusion that '...Mr. Johnes has done nothing, as yet, upon which a reputation of authorship can fairly be erected'.[82]

Whatever the motives behind this extraordinary and largely unjustified assault, it cut little ice with the public, and the first edition of Joinville soon sold out as indeed did the de la Broquière *Travels*. The latter, published in octavo (except for twelve small quarto copies) was dedicated to the memory of Johnes's sister Elizabeth Hanbury Williams who had died in March 1806 and whose 'virtues will live, to his latest breath, in the remembrance of the translator of the following work...' The rather heavy impression and other indications of poor finish, suggest that the *Travels* were produced somewhat hastily. This, however, does not seem to have worried the critics who were uniform in their praises. The *British Critic* saw the description of de la Broquière's adventures in Palestine, Western Asia and Eastern Europe as 'a valuable accession to all collections of voyages and travels' while the *Gentleman's Magazine*, sympathising with Johnes over the dual calamities of the Hafod fire and the death of his sister, commended the efforts of a man, '...superior to the weakness of sinking under the inflictions of misfortune.'[83] Even the *Edinburgh Review* was disposed to be charitable and in thanking Johnes for the 'amusement' afforded by the *Travels*, hoped that, '...he will

THE

CHRONICLES

OF

ENGUERRAND DE MONSTRELET,

A gentleman formerly resident at Cambray in Cambresis;

CONTAINING

AN ACCOUNT OF THE

CRUEL CIVIL WARS BETWEEN

THE HOUSES OF ORLEANS AND BURGUNDY;

OF THE POSSESSION OF PARIS AND NORMANDY BY THE

ENGLISH,—THEIR EXPULSION THENCE,—AND OF OTHER MEMORABLE

EVENTS THAT HAPPENED IN THE KINGDOM OF FRANCE AS WELL AS IN OTHER COUNTRIES.

A HISTORY OF FAIR EXAMPLE AND OF GREAT PROFIT TO THE FRENCH,

BEGINNING AT THE YEAR MCCCC. WHERE THAT OF SIR

JOHN FROISSART FINISHES, AND ENDING AT THE

YEAR MCCCCLXVII. AND CONTINUED

BY OTHERS TO THE YEAR

MDXVI.

Translated

BY THOMAS JOHNES, ESQ.

VOL. I.

At the hafod press,

BY JAMES HENDERSON.

MDCCCIX.

Title page of Johnes's *Monstrelet* translation

(from copy in possession of the Editor)

persevere in his gentlemanlike, honourable and useful occupations'.[84]

Perseverance ranked highly among Johnes's many qualities and though mortified by the tragic events of March 13th 1807, he continued to work on his monumental translation of the *Chronicles* of Monstrelet which he had begun towards the end of 1806. Monstrelet's compilation picks up the saga of Anglo-French relations at the point where Froissart finishes in 1400, and carries the story forward to May 1444, when it is taken up by various other continuators. Derived from a printed edition of 1512 and incorporating marginal corrections set out by du Cange, Johnes's translation occupied four enormous quarto volumes of text averaging almost six hundred pages apiece. Anxious to complete the translation so as 'to enjoy my idleness at Hafod', he worked at a frenetic pace and by the spring of 1809 two volumes were already printed. Towards the end of August the second two volumes of text appeared, these being followed several months later by a fifth volume comprising outline plates and a full index. So great was public anticipation that the 300 quarto edition was sold (at 20 guineas per set) prior to publication in the summer of 1810, as indeed was the special edition of 25 folios with their magnificent hand-coloured engraved plates. Johnes's apparent rush to bring Monstrelet to his readers probably explains why he employed the Blackfriars printer Henry Bryer to print Volume IV and the 'notes and emendations' to volume III. Volumes I and II were entirely the work of James Henderson. In his Preface, following a fulsome dedication to John, Duke of Bedford, the translator observed that he had originally intended his work to provide, '. . . some claims upon the gratitude of the student of history, by the extensive notes and memoranda which I have collected. . . .' Though these had been lost in the Hafod fire the indomitable Johnes had refused to give in to despair. 'On the contrary I have been happy to beguile my sense of that, and of still more serious losses, by prosecuting my task with increasing ardour'. The Monstrelet translation, lavishly praised by the ever-faithful Dibdin, passed through a number of editions, beginning with an octavo set of twelve volumes in 1810. Subsequently a further octavo edition appeared in 1840 followed by two volume editions by William Smith of Fleet Street and Henry Bohn of Covent Garden respectively in 1845 and 1853.

Excepting the 1810 edition of the Froissart *Memoirs* (which included an Index to the Chronicles), the Monstrelet translation was the last major product of the Hafod press. For Johnes it had been a rewarding and fulfilling venture and besides giving him enormous personal pleasure, had enhanced the prestige of his beloved Hafod. He would have readily admitted that his literary talents were less than first rate, yet he could have claimed with justifiable pride that whatever his limitations and however careless and inaccurate some of his trans-lating work, he would leave behind him 'an honourable testimony of well directed study and commendable devotion of time'.[85]

The Published Works of Thomas Johnes

A Cardiganshire Landlord's Advice to his Tenants, Bristol, printed by Biggs and Cottell, 1800.

Cynghorion priodor o Garedigion i ddeiliaid ei dyddynod, London, printed by S. Rousseau, 1800. [Translated by William Owen (Pughe)].

Memoirs of the Life of Froissart, with an Essay on his works and a Criticism of his History. Translated from the French of M. de la Curne de Ste. Palaye, London, printed by Nichols and Son, Red Lion Passage, Fleet Street, 1801.

Sir John Froissart's Chronicle of England, France and the adjoining countries, from the latter part of the reign of Edward II to the coronation of Henry IV. Newly translated from the best French editions with variations and additions from many celebrated manuscripts, Hafod, printed by J. Henderson, 1803-5 [4 vols. 4to].

Memoirs of John, Lord de Joinville, Grand Seneschal of Champagne, written by himself, containing a History of part of the Life of Louis IX, King of France, surnamed Saint Louis, including an account of that King's expedition to Egypt in the year 1248. To which are added the Notes and Dissertations of M. du Cange on the above; together with the Dissertations of M. le Baron de la Bastie on the Life of Saint Louis, M. L'Evesque de la Ravalière and M. Falconet on the Assassins of Syria, from the *Mémoires de L'Académie de Belles Lettres et Inscriptions de France.* The whole translated by Thomas Johnes Esq., Hafod, printed by J. Henderson, 1807.

The Travels of Bertrandon de la Brocquière, Counsellor and first Esquire-Carver to Philippe Le Bon, Duke of Burgundy, to Palestine and his return from Jerusalem overland to France during the years 1432-1433. Extracted and put into modern French from a MS. in the National Library at Paris, and published by M. le Grand D'Aussy, in the fifth volume of the Mémoires de L'Institut. Translated by Thomas Johnes Esq., Hafod, printed by James Henderson, 1807.

Memoirs of the Life of Sir John Froissart, to which is added some account of the Manuscript of his Chronicle in the Elizabethan Library at Breslau, and a complete Index, Hafod, printed by James Henderson, 1810. [The text includes a revision of the 1801 *Memoirs*.]

The Chronicles of Enguerrand de Monstrelet, a Gentleman formerly residing at Cambray in Cambrensis. Containing an account of the cruel civil wars between the houses of Orleans and Burgundy; of the possession of Paris and Normandy by the English: their expulsion thence, and of other memorable events that happened in the Kingdom of France as well as in other countries. A history of fair example and of great profit to the French, beginning at the year 1400, where that of Sir John Froissart finishes, and ending at the year 1467, and continued by others to the year 1516. Translated by Thomas Johnes Esq., Hafod, printed by James Henderson, 1809 [published 1810] [5 vols 4to of which the fifth contains outline engravings].

Minor publications from the Hafod Press
1803—1807; *Reports* of the Cardiganshire Agricultural Society for 1803, 1804 and 1807.

1806; *A Catalogue of the late Pesaro Library at Venice, now forming part of the Hafod Library.* Since this volume gives no indication of its compiler, printer or place of publication, it can only be assumed that it emanated from the Hafod Press. In advising George Cumberland on November 17th, 1806 that 'the Catalogue is now in London', Johnes presumably refers to the original Venetian catalogue since the collection had yet to arrive at Hafod.

Thomas Johnes's Financial Affairs

Like any sensible man, Thomas Johnes of Hafod enjoyed spending money. A typical landed gentleman of his time, he could see little purpose in having an ample patrimony if this were not to be employed towards the improvement of his property, the enhancement of his social position or the exhilarating pleasures of self-indulgence. To Johnes and his fellows, any suggestion of retrenchment or careful husbandry of financial resources would have been greeted with derision and written off as a business more suited to a middle-class merchant than a territorial magnate. Avarice was mean-spirited and contemptible, and quite beyond the contemplation of a gentleman of ancient lineage. Money was to be spent, and spent freely.

Thomas Johnes's ancestors in the early years of the eighteenth century had acquired land by the time-honoured manner of marriage supplemented by prudent purchases. Thomas Johnes M.P. of Llanfair Clydogau had secured the Hafod estate by way of marriage to the daughter of William Herbert of Hafod. This union proved fruitless and when Johnes died in 1733 he left Hafod and his other properties to his cousin Thomas Johnes of Penybont (d. 1751), who in turn willed it to his eldest son Thomas, the father of Thomas Johnes of Hafod. [86]

Meanwhile Thomas Johnes of Penybont had been steadily purchasing lands in south Cardiganshire and Carmarthenshire all of which were settled at the time of his son's marriage to Elizabeth Knight of Croft Castle for the dual purpose of securing her portion of £1,000 per year and of providing fortunes for any younger children of the union. [87] Since his father had gained the extensive property of Croft Castle along with a capital sum of £70,000 by way of his marriage, the eldest son Thomas was ensured a more than adequate patrimony.

With these happy circumstances in mind the young Johnes saw little reason not to indulge himself and during his European tour and subsequent adventures in London and elsewhere, he accumulated debts of such magnitude that his father was obliged to mortgage his manors of Cellan and Arglwyddiaeth Sir Rees in 1778. [88] The following August Thomas the younger married the ailing Maria Burgh thereby increasing his income by £2000 per year besides gaining a life interest in his new wife's Monmouthshire property. His brief, and apparently happy, first marriage seems not to have steadied his extravagance and by the time his father died in 1780 the Cardigan-shire mortgage debt had increased to £15,000, from which it had climbed to £30,000 in 1792.[89] By now, of course, Johnes was pouring money into his various projects at Hafod and in order to supplement borrowings for this purpose was anxious, in the face of the vehement objections of his family, to sell Croft Castle. But this was to prove less than straightforward. His mother enjoyed a life interest in the property and in 1797, as if to spite her estranged son, she announced her intention of felling large areas of timber on the estate. After lengthy negotiations wherein Lord Thurlow and Richard Payne Knight acted as intermediaries, Johnes had no alternative but to file a bill in the Court of Chancery so as to obtain an injunction against his mother's depredations. Naturally, this did little to thaw the chilly relations between Johnes and the rest of the family and some time elapsed before he was finally enabled to offer the estate for sale. By any standards it was a desirable property with a demesne of some 1400 acres containing mature timber valued at upwards of £20,000. Even so, the effects of the law's delay and kindred frustrations held up matters and when the estate was sold in 1799 it realised some £10,000 less than the vendor had anticipated. Accordingly Johnes was brought abruptly to heel by the contemplation of the need to make large financial sacrifices. Purchasing his mother's life interest had cost him dear and if the pace of the Hafod development was to be maintained, other property would have to go. In rapid succession Johnes sold Stanage Park in Radnorshire, the home of his deceased Knight grandmother (thereby losing the estate income of £1400 per annum), together with various outlying properties in Cardiganshire and Carmarthenshire. With a rental income of barely £3,000 from Hafod itself, sales of real estate were essential if he were to execute his plans without sinking hopelessly into debt. By 1800 loans from the family were out of the question and other sources of cash were becoming rapidly depleted, and in what was probably a rather desperate frame of mind he fomented the idea of selling the reversion of the Dolaucothi Estate near Pumsaint in Carmarthenshire to his cousin and brother-in-law John Johnes, thereby embroiling himself in a legal wrangle of awesome complexity.

The basic point at issue was that Thomas Johnes had no legal rights to Dolaucothi until the expiry of his mother's life interest, the estate having been settled on her by her husband with *reversion* to her son. Thus the unfortunate and impecunious John Johnes found himself in

the unenviable position of occupying a property over which he had no
inalienable rights, besides being assailed with demands for rent from
the dowager Mrs. Johnes's agents who regarded him as a mere
tenant. The situation dragged on until the summer of 1807 when the
dowager promptly announced that she proposed to sell the Dolaucothi timber and insisted upon right of entry. There now followed an
increasingly vituperative exchange of letters between her London
solicitors and John Johnes's representatives in which it became clear
that Thomas Johnes had acted illegally in selling the reversion and
that John would be attacked with the full rigour of the law if he
continued to refuse her agents access to the timber. At the instigation
of the Carmarthen attorney Herbert Lloyd and with the support of
Thomas Johnes's friend Hugh Smith of Bloomsbury, John stood firm
and declared that since he had never paid a penny of rent to Mrs.
Johnes he could not be a tenant, and indeed, regarded himself as the
absolute owner of Dolaucothi. Under no circumstances would he
allow a single tree to be felled unless the dowager could establish her
title by decree in Chancery.[90] His subsequent bill of injunction
against his adversary was not, however, effected in time and John was
unable to prevent the felling and sale of the timber.[91] The angry
dowager reacted against John Johnes's bill by filing her *own* Chancery
suit claiming compensation for trees which John himself had felled
and sold. When judgement was pronounced against him and he was
faced with costs amounting to £3500, John abandoned the struggle to
obtain title to Dolaucothi and in 1810 reluctantly signed a lease from
the dowager, '...knowing the consequences of refusing.'[92]
However, explained Mrs. Johnes's lawyer in advising John to take
action against his cousin Thomas, '....you are not without your
remedies for any imposition that may have been practised upon you
on the occasion of your purchase. You cannot blame Mrs. Johnes in
not suffering herself to be the Dupe of any such practices.'[93] As John
turned to his cousin for redress, Thomas indicated that all
material relative to the case should be referred to Hugh Smith,
claiming rather lamely that, '...It has not been any fault of mine; for
you must know how cruelly I have been treated by the old Lady's
advisers'.[94] Smith assured John that his client would reimburse both
the former's legal costs *and* the arrears of rent claimed by the dowager
provided any threat of legal action were withdrawn. 'I can only account
for such conduct in one way', he wrote to John in May 1811, 'and that
is a course to put Col. Johnes to all the expense possible to erect a long

bill of costs—which motive I am sorry to say motivates too many of our profession to the ruin of many an honest man.'[95] But as John came under increasing pressure to settle his arrears, his cousin showed little inclination to pay up, and prompted by the rapacious Herbert Lloyd, he proceeded against Thomas Johnes in the Court of Chancery. The long and acrimonious case was eventually decided in John Johnes's favour in December 1814, a year after the dowager's death. Thomas Johnes had no alternative but to settle, and a sum exceeding £5300 was paid to the late Mrs. Johnes's estates, the money finding its way to the pocket of his younger brother, the Rev. Samuel Johnes, principal beneficiary of his mother's will.

John Johnes resolve in the matter of the Chancery suit had been steeled by the attorney Herbert Lloyd of Carmarthen, an ambitious and acquisitive character who gained greatly from the financial discomfiture of many of the gentry families of south-west Wales. Described in his obituary as 'a gentlemen of great professional talent and private worth', Lloyd was viewed in a less than favourable light by his many enemies who saw in him 'a reckless streak [which] had blurred the distinction between the pursuit of reputation and notoriety'.[96] Prior to 1803 he had acted on behalf of both the Hafod and Dolaucothi parties in legal and political matters, but during the course of that year he seems to have turned completely against Thomas Johnes so as to employ his energies in serving the interests of the latter's creditors. Possibly sensing rich pickings for himself, he launched a frontal attack on the financially-embattled owner of Hafod. This culminated in an attempt to distrain upon the mansion for the recovery of certain petty debts, an action only averted by the loyalty of the estate tenants by whose 'handsome conduct' Lloyd's bailiffs were turned away.[97] The absent Johnes was infuriated, appalled and not a little worried. But however much he might remonstrate against Lloyd, the fellow had to be paid and with unusual despatch he arranged a loan of £1000 for the purpose from his neighbour Thomas Parry of Llidiadau.[98] In the following year, 1804, he was again being pressurised by Lloyd for the settlement of a debt of £7600 due to his cousin John Johnes of Dolaucothi, while the Equitable Assurance Company to whom his property was mortgaged for £34,425 were demanding additional security for their money.[99] Something had to be done. Into the breach clambered (and, one suspects, rather wearily) Hugh Smith of Bloomsbury who managed to reduce the Hafod mortgage to £20,000, but not without first assigning to the Assurance Company Johnes's life interest in his first wife's estate of Park Lettice in Monmouthshire.[100] Smith, 'who has absolutely saved me from destruction', managed somehow to extricate his friend from his immediate difficulties. By reassigning mortgages, juggling with loans and selling off remaining outlying properties, he was able to realise a substantial capital sum which, in the event, could be used as a marriage portion for Johnes's daughter. For all Smith's wizardry, Johnes still continued to feel the pinch and between 1807 and 1810 his mortgage commitment to the ever-bountiful Equitable Assurance Company continued to mount at an alarming rate.

Two years after his daughter died in 1811, Thomas Johnes of Hafod concluded that strict measures were necessary if he were to avoid saddling his wife with an intolerable financial burden following his own death. Sixty-five years old with no next of kin worthy of his consideration, he decided to clear the slate of debts in a single dramatic move by selling the reversion of the Hafod estate and remaining as a life tenant. By so doing he would leave his wife free to retire in comfort to their recently-purchased home of Langstone Cliff Cottage near Dawlish in Devon. He was advised from various quarters that the estate, lock, stock and barrel, would fetch in the order of £90,000, so that by the time his residual debts of £30,000 had been cleared he would be left with a more than ample sum to service a quiet retirement by the banks of the Exe. The locals could hardly believe it and suspected that the so-called 'sale' of Hafod was being put about as a rumour to distract Johnes's growing flock of creditors. John Johnes of Dolaucothi, for example, still trying to coerce his cousin into settling the award in the Chancery case, was mortified to learn from his attorney in November 1814 that, '. . . the sale of Hafod is all a Juggle to cheat the Creditors', and a subterfuge designed to make life as difficult as possible for sheriff's officers wishing to distrain upon the property. But Thomas Johnes was in earnest, and when in the same year William Roscoe's colleague, the Warrington solicitor John Fitchett, entered into negotiations on behalf of an unnamed client, he was delighted. Fitchett's client proved to be the Lancashire salt-manufacturer and dealer Thomas Claughton of Haydock Lodge to whom a proportion of the estate would be immediately conveyed on the receipt of £35,000, the remainder to come into his hands at Johnes's death when the balance of the £90,000 purchase money would be paid to the latter's estate. Claughton, who had anticipated selling on the estate at a substantial profit, was prevented from doing so by the post-Waterloo depression in land prices and shortly after Johnes died in April 1816, his lawyers sought means of renouncing the contract of sale—albeit forgoing the £35,000 already paid. Hugh Smith immediately went to Chancery, but his efforts to enforce the contract were frustrated by Claughton's bankruptcy in 1824 and the estate once again returned to the market.[101]

In raising objections to the title of the Hafod estate Thomas Claughton's legal representatives had claimed that out of a total of 13,000 acres, some 8,000 were in fact Crown Lands illegally encroached upon by Thomas Johnes during his ownership. This allegation was reinforced by the Crown's Commissioners of Woods and Forests even though they were prepared to admit the extreme difficulty in upland areas of ascertaining a clear boundary between private and Crown Lands.[102] Realising that the vexed question of title to the disputed lands would have to be resolved if the estate were to command a reasonable price, Hugh Smith and Johnes's other executors conceded that their deceased client had originally encroached upon Crown property, but argued that he had established title to these encroachments by enclosing them many years before his death. Yet, they would be prepared, provided the Commissioners could firmly establish that the encroachments *were* on Crown wastes, to negotiate for the purchase of the title to the enclosures. There now followed an extensive correspondence between the executors' lawyers and those of the Crown. The Crown Commissioners fully recognised that the executors needed the estate in fee-simple to facilitate its sale, which would prove difficult if the Crown's claims to the encroachments were still pending. They realised also that if they exercised their rights as Lord of the Manor and ordered the fences around the plantations on the encroachments to be opened, the estate would be substantially reduced in value. It was therefore agreed in principle in 1830 to sell the Crown's interests (less the mineral rights) to the executors, and after various details had been resolved the Commissioners of Woods and Forests recommended that the Treasury accept the executors' offer of £800 rather than risk the expense of arbitration.[103] The way was now clear for the sale of Hafod which took place under an order of the Court of Chancery in September 1832. The property, averred the Sale Catalogue, had been in Chancery for thirteen years and now at last the mansion, lands, timber, books, statuary, pictures and effects were on offer to the public.

Sitting in his heavily-fortified home at Clumber, Henry Pelham, 4th Duke of Newcastle, pored over the Catalogue. An arch-conservative, opposed to Parliamentary reform and religious emancipation, this ageing widower had succeeded throughout the course of his life in exciting the animosity of virtually everyone he met. Deeply unpopular with his Nottinghamshire tenants, the arrogant and autocratic Newcastle needed a bolt-hole —somewhere far removed from his turbulent past where a tame and pliant tenantry would leave him in peace. Hafod must have seemed ideal, and he lost little time in instructing his agents to attend the auction with a view to purchase. A year after the sale the Duke rode into the Hafod demesne having paid £62,038-16-8 for a property which was to prove a haven of tranquillity for him and his family for more than a decade.[104]

Meanwhile Jane Johnes had died in Exeter in 1833 after seventeen years of widowhood. If the long years at Langstone Cliff Cottage had occasionally been lonely and punctuated with worries about Hafod, there were at least the compensations of her books and plants and the financial wherewithal to live and entertain in fine style. As the principal beneficiary of her husband's will, she was left with a capital sum of £40,000-£50,000 for her own use.[105] Well may she have written to George Cumberland after the death of Thomas Johnes, 'Few indeed were blessed with such a heart as his; all his thoughts, all his wishes were for the good of his fellow creatures.....'[106] Her lines, heartfelt as always, serve as a final reminder that for all his follies, for all his costly and oft-misplaced enthusiasms, the master of Hafod was in the end a deeply human man.

Thomas Johnes's Principal Correspondents

SIR ROBERT LISTON (1742-1836)

Robert Liston was born on October 8th, 1742, the second son of Patrick Liston of Torbanehill, West Lothian. After graduating from the University of Edinburgh (which awarded him an honorary LL.D. in 1785), he was appointed tutor to the sons of Sir Gilbert Elliot of Stobs. He subsequently accompanied the boys Gilbert and Hugh,

Sir Robert Liston; by Wilkie

(by permission of the National Galleries of Scotland)

respectively 12 and 10 years old, for several years study in Paris under the general direction of the historian and philosopher David Hume. Hugh was later to take up a diplomatic career and on missions to Munich, Ratisbon and Berlin his old tutor accompanied him as his private secretary. Liston himself gained his first diplomatic assignment in March 1783 when he was appointed Embassy secretary to Lord Mountstewart whom he succeeded as Minister Plenipotentiary at Madrid later the same year. This post he held until the summer of 1788 when he was moved to Stockholm and thence to Constantinople late in 1793. He remained as Ambassador Extraordinary at Constantinople until February 1796 when he returned to Glasgow to marry Henrietta Marchant, daughter of a Jamaican 'nabob'. Around this time he was accredited Ambassador Extraordinary and Minister Plenipotentiary at Washington whence he travelled later in the year and where he was to remain until the Peace of Amiens. Subsequent appointments took him to the Hague and Copenhagen before he retired on pension in May 1804. After seven years of inactivity he once again became Ambassador at Constantinople in 1811, remaining in post until his final retirement in 1821 after more than 30 years of diplomatic service.

When he died at Millburn Tower in Edinburgh at the age of 93, this master of no less than ten languages was described as 'the father of the diplomatic body throughout Europe'. [107]

ROBERT ANDERSON, M.D. (1750-1830)

The son of a small farmer of Carnwath in Lanarkshire, Anderson's early education at Lanark Grammar School was followed by spells at Edinburgh and St. Andrew's universities, graduating M.D. from the latter in 1778. After a few years practice as a surgeon at Bamborough Castle in Northumberland, he inherited a modest independence and moved in 1784 with his ailing wife and three infant daughters to Edinburgh where he devoted his time to literary pursuits and the cultivation of the local literati. As editor of the *Edinburgh Review* for a number of years, Anderson was in a good position to encourage and assist the many promising and talented young men that he regularly met in the salons of the bustling city. Among the more celebrated of Anderson's protegés was Thomas Campbell (1777-1844) who visited Edinburgh for the first time in 1797, and was launched into local

Dr Robert Anderson; artist unknown
(by permission of the National Galleries of Scotland)

literary circles by the older man. Anderson also found a publisher for Campbell's *Pleasures of Hope*, being rewarded with the dedication of the volume wherein the poem first appeared.

Around 1790 Anderson began work upon what was to become a 14 volume compendium of biographical and critical sketches of British poets, appearing between 1795 and 1807. The *British Poets*, of which several parts were subsequently to be expanded and published separately, gained wide approval. Southey in particular praised the man who for the first time made the Elizabethan poets readily access-ible to the reading public, while Wordsworth held its editor in high regard. James Hogg recalled that when he and Wordsworth were journeying south from Edinburgh, 'Old Dr Robert Anderson travelled along with us as far as the source of the Yarrow, and it was delightful to see the deference which Wordsworth paid to that venerable man.'

Between 1786 and 1820 Anderson was constantly working at his evolving biography of Smollett. A tireless and prolific researcher, his several biographies, though heavy-handed and often inaccurate, cleared up some of the factual obscurities of the writer's life. Although he was not above making vague and undocumented assertions, Anderson's work was largely instrumental in establishing Smollett's popularity in the opening decades of the nineteenth century. [108]

By all accounts Robert Anderson was an amiable, kind and hospit-able man whose house in Edinburgh continued to be one of the foremost literary venues in the city until his death from dropsy on February 20th, 1830. His biographer in *Chambers Eminent Scotsmen* (1875) noted; 'As a literary critic Dr Anderson was distinguished by a warm sensibility to the beauties of poetry, and by extreme candour. His character as a man was marked by perfect probity in all his dealings, and unshaken constancy in friendship. His manner was lively and bustling; and from his long-continued acquaintance with the literary world, he possessed an unrivalled fund of that species of gossip and anecdote which gives so much pleasure to Boswell's *Life of Johnson*'. [109]

GEORGE CUMBERLAND (1754-1848)

By way of a series of prudent marriages, the Cumberland family, descended from a seventeenth-century London scrivener, steadily rose from obscurity, spawning several distinguished churchmen and, in due course, the dramatist Richard Cumberland. An elder son of the scrivener had had the satisfaction of seeing his grandson George marry Elizabeth Balchen of the well-known naval family. This couple, living in the Mile End Road, had two sons, Richard Denison (b. 1752) and George (b. 1754). With the death of their father in 1771 the Cumberlands found themselves rather hard up and George was obliged to abandon his studies at the Royal Academy to seek a living as a clerk at the Royal Exchange Assurance offices in 1772. His brother, meanwhile, left Cambridge to become vicar of Driffield in Gloucestershire.

George Cumberland as a young man; artist unknown
(by permission of the National Portrait Gallery, London)

A restless character of wide literary and artistic interests, George was hardly suited to the humdrum clerking life which he abandoned in 1785 after inheriting enough money to allow him some independence and to enable him to travel to Paris. Against the wishes of his family he married in 1788 and left with his wife for Rome where he continued to develop his interest in Italian art and to begin to assemble an impressive collection of prints and coins. Returning to England in 1790, he lived for a while at Lyndhurst in Hampshire before purchasing a house at Bishopsgate near Egham in Windsor Great Park from whence he regularly visited his friend William Blake at Lambeth.

Cumberland had already published *A Poem on the Landscapes of Great Britain* (1780) and over the coming years was to produce a range of works of varying quality. *Lewina, the Maid of Snowdon* appeared in 1793 as did *The Life of Julio Bonasoni* (the Bolognese artist) to which Cumberland prefixed *A Plea for the Improvement of the Arts in England*. This work was partially influential in stimulating the move to found the National Gallery. Cumberland's best known book, *Thoughts on Outline*, followed in 1796. Here he was much influenced by Blake who contributed the engraved folding map of the Hafod estate in *An Attempt to describe Hafod*, published the same year.

In 1801 Cumberland left Bishopsgate, and having for some years toyed with the idea of farming, leased land at Axbridge in Somerset, and later near Weston-Super-Mare. The bucolic life, however, does not seem to have appealed to him and by 1808 he was living in Culver Street, Bristol. Meanwhile he continued to correspond with Blake, whom he had befriended as a young man, their letters being concerned primarily with the contemporary artistic scene and the technicalities of printing and engraving. Their correspondence and friendship continued over 40 years and when Blake died in 1827 Cumberland did all in his power to help Mrs Blake and to perpetuate his friend's genius. Cumberland was deeply appreciative of Blake's qualities as an artist, but in common with many contemporaries (including Thomas Johnes) he was puzzled by Blake's eccentricities and thought him not a little mad.

Cumberland's *Original Tales* and *Birthday Ode to Horne Tooke* were published in 1810, followed, the next year, by a description of his friend Charles Long's seat at Bromley Hill. He seems to have written little else until the appearance of *Religae Conservatae,* a description and classification of the fossil corallines in 1826, *An Essay on Italian*

Engravers (1827) and *Outlines from the Ancients* (1829) whereupon he laid aside his pen only to pick it up again to contribute a somewhat incredulous appendix to Dix's *Life of Thomas Chatterton* (1837). He died eleven years later at the age of 94.[110]

WILLIAM ROSCOE (1753-1831)

Born at Liverpool in the early spring months of 1753, William Roscoe was the son of a substantial market gardener and publican. Leaving school at the age of twelve, he worked for some time with his father, concurrently devouring books and committing vast chunks of Shakespeare and other poets to memory. In his late teens he began to prepare for a legal career and in 1774 set up business as an attorney, continuing in practise until 1786. As his legal work expanded so did his reading of the Latin and Italian classics, so that by the time of his marriage in 1781 he had become an accomplished Latin scholar and had perfected his knowledge of the Italian language and its literature.

His wife Jane, daughter of a local tradesman, described by Maria Edgeworth as 'an honest-faced, fat, *hearty*, good-natured hospitable body, without the least pretensions to polish', was eventually to bear her husband seven sons and three daughters. Meanwhile Roscoe began to publish what was to become a substantial corpus of widely influential writings. As a passionate liberal he produced numerous pamphlets condemning the slave trade, concurrently labouring away at his *Life of Lorenzo de'Medici* which appeared in 1796 to wide critical acclaim both at home and abroad. Despite Southey's strictures, *Lorenzo* was soon translated into a number of European languages, and Horace Walpole wrote of the 'Grecian simplicity of the style' and its 'judicious candour'. Having given up his legal practice in 1786, Roscoe involved himself (somewhat injudiciously as matters turned out) in a banking concern, played a leading role in the reclamation of Chat Moss near Manchester, and became immersed in local political and commercial activities. He purchased Allerton Hall, some six miles from Liverpool, and over the the next 12 years partially rebuilt the house to accommodate his expanding collection of books and paintings. Against the background of all these ventures he continued with his Italian studies and published his *Life and Pontificate of Leo the Tenth* in 1805, of which Southey was able to speak, '. . . in terms of decided praise'. Elected to Parliament as member for Liverpool,

William Roscoe; stipple vignette by T. Woolnoth
(by permission of the Liverpool Record Office)

Roscoe argued in favour of the Bill to abolish the slave trade. His speech, though widely praised by his supporters, did not go down at all well in Liverpool, much of that city's wealth having been founded on the returns from slavery, and Roscoe did not seek re-election after the dissolution of Parliament the following year.

In 1816 Roscoe's bank experienced a serious run and for all his efforts to weather the storm by selling off his private collection of books and paintings, he was declared bankrupt in 1820. At the intercession of his many friends, who had purchased the bulk of his library and placed it in the Liverpool Athenaeum, Roscoe was ultimately granted an honourable discharge from his bankruptcy and was enabled to continue with his literary pursuits, publishing, among other works, *Observations on Penal Jurisprudence* (1819), *Memoirs of Richard Jones of Aberdaron* (1822), an edition of Pope's works (1824) and a folio monograph on the *Monandrian Plants* (1828), before succumbing to influenza on June 30th, 1831.

Some years previously he had been invited to visit Holkham by the wealthy and urbane Thomas Coke, but for various reasons, including diffidence and pressure of work, he had turned down what were to be repeated invitations. In 1814, he was persuaded by Sir James Edward Smith to travel to Norfolk and he soon became close friends with the master of Holkham to whom he presented a bound copy of *Leo the Tenth*. The superb if rather disorganised library at Holkham, choc-à-bloc with volumes and manuscripts purchased by Coke on the Continent, was a source of endless fascination for Roscoe who suggested that he might assist with the binding and arrangement of the collection. Coke was delighted and over the next two years Roscoe regularly journeyed into Norfolk to work towards producing a catalogue of the enormous collection of Holkham manuscripts.

Described by De Quincey as, 'simple and manly in his demeanour', Roscoe was a sensitive and conscientious man, honest and courageous in his views and with an acute sense of duty. Maria Edgeworth, invited to Allerton in 1813, left a worthy tribute to Roscoe in her letters. 'Mr. Roscoe is a benevolent-looking chearful [sic] gentlemanlike old man —neither thin nor fat—with a peaked forehead—thick grey hair, *tufty* about the face—rather longer than North the hairdressser would allow it to be—looks as if it was blown by the wind in a picturesque style'. His manner, she maintained, was without pretension and his memory quick and retentive. He, '. . . speaks excellent language but with a strong provincial accent which at once destroys all idea of elegance. This at first disappoints, but in a short time his chearful [sic] kindness entirely effaces the recollection of this and even the perception of it.' While they were at Allerton Maria and her friends were shown the Liverpool Botanic Gardens, which Roscoe had opened in 1802, and in whose planning he and his friend Sir James Edward Smith had played a significant part. Later they walked the length and breadth of the house and viewed its owner's splendid collection of paintings. Here Roscoe was in his element, talking with enthusiasm of his collection in a manner 'free from all the cant of a connoisseur.' At dinner they listened to Roscoe and William Shepherd discussing poetry and exchanged coy glances with the Roscoe sons, 'tall blackeyed, bashful young men', who sat in silence. Roscoe's talk, wrote Maria, was never *too* literary, being a happy mixture of anecdote and fact and delivered in an atmosphere of warm family affection. She clearly enjoyed her visit.[111]

SIR JAMES EDWARD SMITH, F.R.S., (1759-1828)

James Edward Smith was born in Norwich where his father was a wealthy Unitarian wool merchant. Being of delicate health he was initially educated at home before being sent to the University of Edinburgh in 1781 ostensibly to study medicine, but mainly to continue the pursuit of the botanical studies which had excited his interest as a child. In the autumn of 1783 he moved to London to work under the direction of John Hunter and William Pitcairn in whose company he was introduced to the celebrated scientific patron Sir Joseph Banks. Shortly before, at the death of Linnaeus's son, Banks had been approached with a view to purchasing the Swedish botanist's library, manuscripts and herbarium, but had not been disposed to part with the 1000 guinea asking price. Smith, however, jumped at the chance of possessing this superb collection and by the winter of 1784 he was busy organising the Linnean material at his Chelsea apartments. From this point onwards he virtually abandoned his medical studies in favour of natural history and botany. On a lengthy continental tour taking up most of 1786 and 1787 he met many of the great contemporary figures of the scientific and philosophical world, gained an M.D. at Leyden for his thesis *De Generatione*, and described his adventures in the three volume *Sketch of a Tour on the Continent* (1793). It was this work which, as he wrote in his

Sir James Edward Smith; by John Rising
(by permission of the Linnean Society of London)

dedicatory letter to Thomas Johnes in *A Tour to Hafod* (1810), 'first procured me the pleasure of your acquaintance'.

On returning to England in the autumn of 1787 Smith took a house in Great Marlborough Street where he held the first meeting of the Linnean Society, delivering his presidential lecture, 'Introductory Discourse on the Rise and Progress of Natural History'. The Great Marlborough Street house now became a regular meeting place for scientists and aristocratic amateurs keen to listen to Smith's courses of lectures on Botany and Zoology and to view the treasures of the Linnean collection. Concurrently Smith was at work on the celebrated 36 volume masterpiece in which he described the botany of all the known British plants. *Sowerby's English Botany,* the series being named after its illustrator, appeared between 1780 and 1814.

Shortly after he married Pleasance, daughter of Robert Reeve of Lowestoft, Smith retired to Norwich, visiting London for several months each year to lecture to the Royal Institution and to supervise the Linnean Society whose President he remained until his death. His *Flora Britannica* appeared between 1800-1804, being followed by *Prodromus Flora Graeca* (1806-1813) and what was to become the highly successful *Introduction to Physiological and Systematic Botany*, which went through six editions in his lifetime. These apart, he contributed over 3000 entries to Rees's *Cyclopaedia*, 52 articles to the Transactions of the Linnean Society together with a variety of other publications concerned with religious affairs, the sexes of plants, the botany of Europe and the butterflies of Georgia (dedicated to Mariamne Johnes). A number of Smith's hymns were regularly sung at the Octagon Unitarian Chapel in Norwich where he was for many years a deacon. The last seven years of a busy and fruitful life were taken up with the compilation of his finest work, the *English Flora*, whose first two volumes were published in 1824 with subsequent volumes appearing in 1825 and March, 1828, a few days before the author's death.

As the owner of the Linnean collection, Sir James Edward Smith was able to exert enormous influence in scientific circles both at home and abroad and yet, despite the academic honours bestowed upon him throughout Europe, he remained essentially a kind, sensitive, and humble individual who enjoyed with his circle 'that true union of hearts and minds which is the essence of friendship'.

Two months after Smith's death, his obituarist in the *Philosophical Magazine* summarised his life and achievements:

'He found the science of botany, when he approached it, locked up in a dead language; he set it free by transfusing it into his own. He found it a severe study, fitted only for the recluse; he left it of easy acquisition to all. In the hands of his predecessors, with the exception of his immortal master, it was dry, technical and scholastic; in his, it was adorned with grace and elegance and might attract the poet as well as the philosopher.'[112]

NOTES

[1] For example, to Walter Davies [National Library of Wales (N.L.W.) MS 1805E, f.517; 1810]. The Hafod demesne is located to the east of Pontrhydygroes; OS 1:50,000 Sheet 135; 760734.

[2] *Gentleman's Magazine, 86(1), 1816*, pp.563-4; Linn. Soc. (Smith) 18, f.206.

[3] D. J. Morgan, Johnes of Hafod Uchtryd, Cardiganshire, as an Agriculturist, *Jour. U.C.W. Agri.Dept. IX, 1920*, p.36.

[4] P. Bicknell, *Beauty, Horror and Immensity, Picturesque Landscape in Britain, 1750-1850,* Fitzwilliam Museum, Cambridge, 1981; K. Clark, *The Gothic Revival: an Essay in the History of Taste*, 4th Edn., London, 1975.

[5] R. Payne Knight, *The Landscape; A Didactic Poem in Three Books, addressed to Uvedale Price Esq.,* London, 1794; Uvedale Price, *An Essay on the Picturesque: as compared with the Sublime and the Beautiful and on the use of studying pictures for the purpose of improving real landscape,* London, 1794.

[6] T. F. Dibdin, *Bibliographical Decameron*, III, London, 1817, p.357.

[7] B. Alexander, *England's Wealthiest Son*, London, 1962; B. Fothergill, *Beckford of Fonthill*, London, 1979.

[8] Liston MS. 5514, f.14.

[9] H. Lloyd-Johnes, The Cardigan Boroughs Election, 1774, *Nat. Lib. of Wales Journal, 7(1), 1972*; J. Hughes, *A History of the Parliamentary Representation of the County of Cardigan*, Aberystwyth, 1849.

[10] J. Williams, *A General History of the County of Radnor,*, Brecknock, 1805.

[11] Speeches attributed to Johnes in some sources were almost certainly by Thomas Jones (1768-1811) the member for Shropshire. (R. G. Thorne, *History of Parliament, The Commons, 1790-1820, IV*, London, 1986, pp.310-11).

[12] L. Namier and J. Brooke, *The House of Commons, 1784-1780*, London, 1964, p.683.

[13] W. R. Williams, Colonel Johnes of Hafod, *The Red Dragon, x, 1886*, p.135.

[14] R. Mitchison, *Agricultural Sir John, The Life of Sir John Sinclair of Ulbster, 1734-1835,* London, 1962, pp.234-7.

[15] Payne Knight, *The Landscape*, 1794.

[16] T. Davis, *The Gothick Taste*, David and Charles, 1974.

[17] For Croft Castle, see, *Country Life,* April 28th and May 5th, 1950.

[18] R. Warner, *A Second Walk through Wales,* 2nd edn., London, 1800, p.148.

[19] B. H. Malkin, *The Scenery, Antiquities and Biography of South Wales,* London, 1807, p.360; R. Lipscomb, *Journey into South Wales,* London, 1802, p.127.

[20] J. T. Barber, *A Tour through South Wales and Monmouthshire,* London, 1803, p.121.

[21] W. Ison, *The Georgian Buildings of Bath,* London, 1948, *passim.*

[22] T. Davies, *John Nash, The Prince Regent's Architect,* Newton Abbot, 1973; J. Summerson, *John Nash, Architect to King George IV,* London, 1935; J. Piper, Decrepit Glory: A Tour of Hafod, *Architectural Review, 87, 1940,* p. 207.

[23] J. Thomas, The Architectural Development of Hafod, *Ceredigion, VII(2), 1973,* pp. 153-170.

[24] Piper, *op.cit.,* p.208.

[25] Warner, *op.cit.,* p.148.

[26] *The Builder, XXI, 1863, p.4.*

[27] *Gentleman's Magazine, LXXXI, 1811,, p.168.*

[28] As *The Morning Post,* of Nov. 26th, 1789 noted, Jane Johnes was ' . . . a lady whose worth and accomplishments entitle her even to the celebration of such an artist as Banks'.

[29] *Hafod Estate Sale Catalogue, 1832*; C. F. Bell (ed.), *Annals of Sir Thomas Banks,* Cambridge, 1938, *passim.*

[30] *Gentleman's Magazine, cxxvii, 1807,,* p.269.

[31] E. Inglis-Jones, *Peacocks in Paradise,,* Golden Grove Editions, Carmarthen, 1988, p.207.

[32] T. Rees, *The Beauties of England and Wales,* 1815 edn., p.420.

[33] G. Nicholson, *The Cambrian Traveller's Guide,* Stourport, 1808, p.218.

[34] Dibdin, *op.cit.,* p.358.

[35] W. Linnard, Thomas Johnes of Hafod, Pioneer of Upland Afforestation in Wales, *Ceredigion, VI, 1970,* p.311.

[36] *Transactions of the Royal Society of Arts, 23, 1805,* p.28.

[37] *Ibid., 20, 1802,* pp.185-6.

[38] *Ibid., 23, 1806,* pp.26-8.

[39] *Ibid., 18, 1800,* pp.81-2.

[40] *Ibid., 20, 1802,,* pp.185-9.

[41] *Ibid, p.189.*

[42] *Ibid., 18, 1801,* pp.78-80.

[43] Linnard, *op.cit.,* p.318.

[44] See *inter alia,* D. W. Howell, *Land and People in Nineteenth Century Wales,* London, 1977; *Ibid., Patriarchs and Parasites,* Cardiff, 1986; R. J. Moore-Colyer, The Land Agent in Nineteenth Century Wales, *Welsh History Review, 8(4), 1977.*

[45] R. J. Moore-Colyer, Crop Husbandry in Wales before the onset of mechanisation, *Folk Life, 21, 1983; Ibid.,* Aspects of the Pastoral Economy in pre-industrial Wales, *Jour. Royal Agricultural Society of England, 144, 1983.*

[46] R. J. Moore-Colyer, Early Agricultural Societies in South Wales, *Welsh History Review, 12(4), 1985.*

[47] A. O. Evans, Some Welsh Agricultural Writers, *Welsh Journal of Agriculture, VIII, 1932,* pp.74-84. I am informed by Miss Eluned Rees that the 4th edition of a Welsh work on the culture of turnips, *Hwsmonnaeth mewn pethynas i faip,* was printed in Dolgellau in 1802.

[48] N.L.W. MS. 1340C.

[49] For details see, R. J. Moore-Colyer, Of Lime and Men: Aspects of the Coastal Trade in Lime in the eighteenth and nineteenth centuries, *Welsh History Review, 14(1), 1988.*

[50] Warner, *op.cit.,* p.151.

[51] Johnes was well aware that this process of 'paring and burning' could only be justified on peaty soils with an excess of undecomposed organic matter. Elsewhere it could be highly injurious; hence his warnings to tenants in *Landlord's Advice.*

[52] Which, incidentally, forestalled the work of the Ministry of Agriculture, Fisheries and Food at their Pwllpeiran Experimental Husbandry Farm by some two centuries. Pwllpeiran is located on the old Hafod estate.

[53] See n. (45)

[54] James Anderson, *Essays relating to Agriculture, II,* London, 1800, pp.355-6.

[55] Richardson's publications on the subject included; *The Utility of Fiorin Grass: a Prize Essay,* London, 1811; *Letter to the Marquis of Hertford on Fiorin Grass,* London, 1810; *A Letter to the Bath and West of England Agricultural Society,* Bath, 1812.

[56] T. Lloyd and L. Turnor, *General View of the Agriculture of Cardiganshire,* London, 1794, p.22.

[57] *Landlord's Advice,* pp.83-113.

[58] Lloyd and Turnor, *op.cit.* p.24.

[59] A. Young, *Annals of Agriculture, XXXIII, 1799,* p.200.

[60] For which see, A.M.W. Stirling, *Coke of Norfolk and his Friends,* London, 1907; A. Aspinall, (ed.), *The Later Correspondence of George III,* London 1966-1970; H. B. Carter, *His Majesty's Sheep Flock,* London, 1964.

[61] F. Bladon, (ed.), *Diaries of Col. R. F. Greville,* London, 1930.

[62] E. Rees, An Introductory Survey of Eighteenth Century Welsh Libraries, *Journal of the Welsh Bibliographical Society, X(4), 1971,* pp.199-200.

[63] Dibdin, *op. cit.,* pp.14-16.

[64] A. Dyce (ed.), *Recollections of the Table Talk of Samuel Rogers,* London, 1886.

[65] Rees, *op.cit.,* p.212.

[66] C. Colvin, (ed.) *Maria Edgeworth; Letters from England 1813-1844,* Oxford, 1971, pp.325-6.

[67] Rees, *op.cit.,* p.219. Some Lhuyd items, presumably from the Sebright collection were sold off following the fire of 1807 and apparently came into the possession of William Lawrence Banks of Brecon (*Archeologia Cambrensis, Ser. ii(v), 1854,* p.111). See also, E. Rees and G. Walters, The Dispersion of the MSS of Edward Lhuyd, *Welsh History Review, 7(2), 1974,* p.p. 148-178.

[68] For Meerman see *Gentleman's Magazine, LXXXVI, 1816,* p.638.

[69] J. A. Dearden, Thomas Johnes and the Hafod Press, *The Book Collector, 22, 1973,* p.331.

[70] Dibdin, *op.cit.,* p.83; S. de Ricci, *English Collectors of Books and Manuscripts, 1530-1930,* Cambridge, 1930.

[71] E. Rees, *The Welsh Book Trade before 1820,* Aberystwyth, 1988, p.LX; E. Rees and G. Walters, Thomas Pennant and Paul Panton Jr: Their Printing Contacts with George Allen and Luke Hansard, *Journal of the Printing History Society, 7, 1971,* p.62.

[72] Dibdin, *Bibliomania,* p.361.

[73] Dearden, *op.cit.,* pp.323-4.

[74] Meyrick, apparently, had considered having his magisterial *The History and Antiquities of the County of Cardigan* printed on the Hafod press but being obliged to wait so long for the press to become available he turned to London. (Rees, 1988, *op.cit.*, p.LIX)

[75] L. Gossman, *Medievalism and the Ideologies of the Enlightenment; the World and Work of La Curne de Saint-Palaye,* John Hopkins, 1968, p.246.

[76] Froissart, *Memoirs*, 1810, p.61

[77] Benjamin White (1725-1784) had two bookselling businesses in Fleet Street. His sons Benjamin and John had succeeded in 1793 and by 1798 John was working alone at the premises at Horace's Head, remaining in business until his retirement in 1812.

[78] *Gentleman's Magazine, LXXV, 1805*, pp.141-3, 633-38.

[79] *British Critic, XXV, 1805*, p.2; *XXXI, 1808,* p.342.

[80] *Edinburgh Review, V, 1804-5*, pp.347-362.

[81] A. Foulet, Joinville's *Vie de Saint Louis, Romanic Review, 1941*, p.243.

[82] *Edinburgh Review, XIII, 1809*, pp.468-477.

[83] *British Critic, XXXII, 1808,* pp.146-150; *Gentleman's Magazine, LXXVIII, 1808,* pp.1001-1007.

[84] *Edinburgh Review, X, 1807*, pp.329-33.

[85] Dibdin, *op.cit.*, p.361.

[86] N.L.W. Crosswood Deeds and Documents, II, 172.

[87] *Ibid.*, 211.

[88] *Ibid.*, 438.

[89] *Ibid.*, 475, 507, 521.

[90] N.L.W. Dolaucothi Correspondence, L.290.

[91] *Ibid.*, L.291.

[92] *Ibid.*, L.335.

[93] *Ibid.*, L.25.

[94] *Ibid.*, L.113.

[95] *Ibid.*, L.293.

[96] R. G. Thorne, Herbert Lloyd of Carmarthen, *Transactions of the Cymmrodorion Society, 1977.*

[97] National Library of Scotland MSS, 140, 75, f.72.

[98] N.L.W. Llidiadau MSS (unnumbered).

[99] N.L.W. Dolaucothi Correspondence, L.329, 330, 196, 197.

[100] N.L.W. Crosswood Deeds and Documents II, 626, 627.

[101] Nottingham University Library, NeD, 4479.

[102] For details see, *Return to an Order of the House of Commons, 6th March, 1845, concerning the sale of the Hafod Estate* (N.L.W. Dep. 583B); *The Cambrian*, 21st February, 1835.

[103] In fact, the eventual sum paid was reduced to £7328 when it was established that the extent of Johnes's encroachments was 7,438 acres rather than the original estimate of 8061 acres. Ultimately the £7328 was paid by the Duke of Newcastle when he purchased the estate out of the Court of Chancery.

[104] Nottingham University Library, NeD, 8411. The purchase money was used to wind up Thomas Johnes's remaining debts which were finally discharged 3 years later (N.L.W. Crosswood Deeds and Documents, II, 1061).

[105] T. Knight to J. E. Smith, June 12th, 1816, Linn. Soc. (Smith), 16, f.201.

[106] Add.MS. 36506, f.342

[107] *Dictionary of National Biography; Gentleman's Magazine, ii, 1836.*

[108] *The Life of Tobias Smollet, M.D., with Critical Observations on his Works,* London, 1786, 2nd Edn. 1800; 3rd Edn. 1802; 4th Edn. 1803; 5th Edn. 1806; 6th Edn. 1820.

[109] *Dictionary of National Biography; Chambers Eminent Scotsmen,* 1875; L. M. Knapp, *Tobias Smollet,* Princeton, 1949; G. S. Rousseau and P. G. Bouce, *Tobias Smollet, Bicentennial Essays presented to Lewis M. Knapp,* New York, 1971; D. S. Black (Ed.), *James Hogg, Memoirs of the Author's Life and familiar anecdotes of Sir Walter Scott,* Edinburgh, 1872.

[110] C. F. Bell (Ed.), *Annals of Sir Thomas Banks,* Cambridge, 1938; C. Black, *The Cumberland Letters, 1771-1784,* London, 1912; G. Keynes, Some Uncollected Authors, XLIV, George Cumberland, 1754-1848, *The Book Collector, 18, 1970,* pp. 31-65.

[111] *Dictionary of National Biography; Encyclopedia Britannica* (11th edn.); K. Curry (Ed.) *New Letters of Robert Southey,* I, Columbia, 1965; C. Calvin (Ed.), Maria Edgworth, *Letters from England, 1813-1844,* Oxford, 1971; A. M. W. Stirling, *Coke of Norfolk and his Friends,* London, 1908.

[112] M. Walker, *Sir James Edward Smith,* London, 1988; Lady P. Smith, *Memoir and Correspondence of Sir James Edward Smith,* London, 1832; J. E. Smith, *A Tour of Hafod, Cardiganshire,* London, 1810.

Selections from the Letters of Thomas Johnes of Hafod

To Robert Liston, in Edinburgh Liston MS. 5514, f.178

April 27th, 1773
No. 8, Cockspur Street.

My dear Bob,

I have been this long time in expectation of having the Pleasure of receiving an Answer to my last from Coldbrook.[1] I have not thought the less about you, & I hope the following *Expectancy* will be agreeable to you. Lord Clive's Son is soon to go abroad; Smith of Glasgow was intended to go with him, but that is now off.[2] I proposed you; and I have been warmly seconded by Elliot, so much so, that I think you stand a very fair Chance. As to the Terms, as I have not as yet spoke to his father on the subject, I can not as yet tell you but make no doubt but they will be agreeable to you.[3] Write to me immediately, but remember at present this is all *entre nous*. I shall hope soon to be able to write to you *par ordre*.

Adieu,

Believe me ever yours, etc.

Thos. Johnes Jnr.

[1] Coldbroook House, Abergavenny, seat of John Hanbury Williams who had married Johnes's sister Elizabeth several years previously.
[2] Edward Clive (1754-1839), son of Robert Clive of India. After some years as Governor of Madras he became Earl of Powis in 1804.
[3] Hugh Elliot (1752-1830), diplomat; son of Sir Gilbert Elliot, Lord Minto. Like Johnes, Elliot had been under Liston's supervision in Europe and was subsequently to do much to advance the latter's career. Elliot himself held a number of important diplomatic appointments leading to the governorship firstly of the Leeward Islands and then of Madras, before he retired from the service in 1820.

To Robert Liston, in Edinburgh   Liston MS. 5514, f.188

London, June 22nd, 1773

My dear Bob,

I am very sorry to have delayed writing to you for such a length of time, & I am afraid you will already have blamed me (to say no more) for it. However, dont condemn me unheard. My reason for delaying myself that Pleasure was in the hope of being able to send you the agreeable news of my having fixed something clever for you. But in this, as in many other of my projects I have been most terribly disappointed; at least I am afraid I shall be so. But I will give you a succinct account of ye facts, and the Ground I have now left to go upon. As I told you in my former Letter, I had proposed you to Mr. Clive, as the properest person he or any other young man could possibly have as a Companion to travel with. I had every hope of success as I believe I was warmly seconded by the Elliot family & Wederburne.[1] Lord Marchmont very unluckily step'd in during these negociations, & said so much in Frazer's favor that what with his fine speeches, & the *critical situation* of Affairs there that Mr Frazer to my great sorrow has succeeded.[2] Lord Clive nor Lady C ever spoke to me on the subject, but ye young man *seem'd* very much for it. Indeed he is a very agreeable Character, & too much cannot be said in his Praise.

While this was in agitation Lady Hertford gave a most magnificent Ball. I was there, as was also Lady Powis. As I was looking over her Ladyship whilst she was at Cards, I said I was very sorry that Ld Clive had Resolved on hiring Frazer to go with his son. She immediately asked if you were disengaged. I said yes, & at the same time wished you had some employment properer for you than living so retired in the Country. She desired me to say no more upon that subject then, but that she & I must have some further conversation on that subject. I was immediately for fixing a day, & she named any

[1] Alexander Wedderburn, 1st Earl of Rosslyn (1733-1805). As Baron Loughborough he succeeded Thurlow as Lord Chancellor in 1792, remaining in that office until 1801.

[2] Hugh Hume, 3rd Earl of Marchmont (1708-1794), Lord Keeper of the Great Seal of Scotland and friend of Bolingbroke and Pope.

morning. I called there as soon as I could without appearing to be too pressing but she was never at home. I dined there some time afterwards, & then desired her to name a time for our Conference. She fixed a day & hour; I was as punctual as ye Clock, she was gone out. I returned again with no better success. I have made many excursions into the Country to the D. of Dorsets etc. but always at my return, endeavoured with no better luck to catch her at home. This Morning however I wrote her a note a little angrily to know if she meant anything or not; when lo my note was returned as she was gone to ye country for a Month.

Here then we rest at present, but as soon as ever I have an Opportunity I'll see if she means anything, or if she only intends to hammer me with hopes 'till the General Election. My Paper obliges me to conclude, and I am very sorry I could not make this a more interesting letter. You are perfectly right with regard to Mrs H. I am much obliged to you for it.

Believe me, ever yours etc,

Thomas Johnes

Pray write soon & direct to me at Colebrooke [sic].

To Robert Liston, in Edinburgh   Liston MS. 5515, f.5

Croft Castle, January 9th, 1774

My dear Bob,

I am ashamed to have left your last letter so long unanswered, and the more so as this will (I am afraid) be a very short letter. But the truth is, notwithstanding what you said, I cannot put it out of my head but that I am to have ye pleasure of seeing you every day. I cannot help expecting you, and own I am disappointed at night when you are not come. However the time is now almost elapsed when *you yourself* have fixed the time for your arrival. My only reason for writing so short a letter, is, my expecting to see you so soon y' I reserve everything for *word of mouth*. I have had three days very good Skaiting, but it has since thaw'd & now it snows & rains alternately—*quel temps*!

I cannot write any more. You know I am impatient, but now I am more than ordinarily so to see you. I foolishly think you are on the road & that I shall see you before you receive this Letter. Pray write immediately (if you are not set out) & fix when I shall see you.

Believe me, ever yours most sincerely,

Thos. Johnes Jnr.

My grandmother begs you will bring with you for her Six pound of *Scots Snuff*.

Venez vite.

To Robert Liston, in Edinburgh   Liston MS. 5515, f.25

Croft Castle, March 25, 1774

Ever since I had the Pleasure of receiving your last letter (which was about a fortnight ago on my return from Wales) I have deferred writing 'till I could give you some certain account of what my intended operations were to be. But they are now as uncertain as ever. I write however to thank you for your very obliging letter. One part of it, vanity has made me read over very often, & you may be assured I am not a little proud of it. I should shew it to everybody, but the same vanity & a *little* modesty prevents me. You know me better than anybody, but even *you* cannot know what I feel on reading y commendations. I will try however to observe them. I was in hopes you would have followed y' letter immediately; & then I should have had ye pleasure of y' company here for sometime.

I am obliged to attend my Father *now* whenever he goes to Wales. He always goes in May to receive his rents, but *now* he will add to it the *attendance* of ye *Court Leets*. I have been just asking him, what time he would chuse I should go to London; whether for the month of April, since we have heard nothing from you; or any other time? He tells me it is impossible for him to fix, as it is so uncertain how soon he may be called into Wales. For God's sake let me hear from you immediately, that if you are more fixed than I am, we may meet somewhere; I had rather see you here than anywhere upon many accounts, and I should then have you all to myself, which would be no small pleasure considering how long it may be before I see you again.

If I go to London before summer it will be with Mr Knight the first week in April, but as I am situated it is quite uncertain whether I shall go at all.[1] My doubts concerning myself are nothing to the purpose, for I must & will see you before you quit England. With respect to Dodwell & his wife when last I saw them they seemed to agree perfectly well. She was to pay a visit to Madame de Fitzjames & some other of her friends that were educated with her at the Convent & I have since heard that Dr Hunter had recommended to her husband that she should live from him as long as possible on account of her breeding too fast for her Constitution; which he seems to think a good deal improved already.[2]

You will see by this being wrote in English, besides many other things, the hurry which I write it. The Truth is, I have waited till I am almost too late, for ye arrival of my Father in order to fix some plan for me. But in vain. I am now as uncertain where I shall be next week as ever (more indeed) I was in my life. But I am never in doubt that I shall always remain,

Yours most unalterably,

T. Johnes

There's a finishing worthy a Modern novel, with this difference only; that (it) is truth. Pray write immediately.

---

[1] Richard Payne Knight (1750-1824) of Downton, Herefordshire, dilletante, art historian and connoisseur. Besides being an expert on ancient art, an insatiable reader and an indefatigable foxhunter, Knight was considered an excellent landlord, a characteristic probably commending him to his friend and cousin Thomas Johnes, who hung his portrait by Lawrence in the Music Room at Hafod.

[2] William Hunter (1718-1783), Scots anatomist and brother of John Hunter (1728-1793). William had taken a special interest in obstetric matters and became Physician Extraordinary to Queen Charlotte in 1764.

To Robert Liston, in London   Liston MS. 5521, f.9

Feb. 6th, 1778

My dear Liston,

Had I not promised to write by this post, I should not have done it, not having a great deal to say. The morning after I saw you I sent my letter with a few alterations. The force was the same. Ld Bateman knows of it, which I am very sorry for. [1] He wants to see me, but I have avoided it, and as for my father I dont believe he wishes to see me. I am now at the House where I should not have been had not Harley desired it, Mr Rigby having asked where I was these 2 last days. [2] [3]

My Father will pay everything but insists on my settling the Estate so that I cannot sell it. I will send you a more particular account when I know it, probably next post. With regard to Miss H., for Pardoe told him everything, he says he is only averse to it because there is not a Competency. [4] I am determined to abide by my original resolution, for he seems to expect I shall go on amending with ye same allowance. [5]

I am very unhappy, but will write more fully when I am more composed.

Yours ever & ever,

T.J.

[1] John, 2nd Viscount Bateman of Shobden; Herefordshire landowner and friend of Thomas Johnes, senior.

[2] Thomas Harley (1730-1804), 3rd son of Edward Harley, Earl of Oxford. A wealthy merchant and banker, he represented the City of London in Parliament from 1761-1774 and became Lord Mayor in 1767. In later years Harley's wine business supplied the cellars at Hafod until Johnes's tardiness at paying his bills led to legal action and the end of this arrangement.

[3] Richard Rigby (1722-1788), placeman and political trimmer *par excellence* who rose to become Paymaster of the Forces from 1768 to 1782.

[4] 'Competency' here is used in the sense of financial sufficiency—i.e. having adequate means to live comfortably ['Superfluity comes sooner by white hairs, but competency lives longer', *Merchant of Venice I, ii, 9*].

[5] This letter clearly refers to Johnes's growing burden of debts which had steadily accumulated since his return from Europe in 1769. The unidentified 'Miss H' appears to have been a lady at Court whose financial means, whatever her other virtues, were insufficient to commend her to the elder Johnes.

London, Feb. 23rd, (Monday) [1778]

My dear Liston,

I have been so long silent, because I had nothing relating to myself to acquaint you with. I never saw my father before yesterday, just 3 weeks since His arrival in town. He agrees to pay everything, & I am to settle the Estate; first to myself in fee, then to my Children supposing I have any, then to my Brother, his Children, my Sisters etc.[1] He has reserved a power of jointly revoking all this settlement. Rigby & Harley are so kind as to advance him the Money. We were to have met yesterday at the Pay office, but the Master of the House was so much engaged with the Attorney General, that it is put off till tomorrow. I met my Father in the Park; I shall leave to a future opportunity an account of our meeting. It was *too Cold* for me. It has made me however much easier by it and I hope now to recover some flesh again, for since you left I have thinned very much. I met him today in the House (from where I write this & where probably we shall be till 12 at night) and we speak as if nothing had happened. With regard to . . . . he (by what I can learn) does not object to it, but asks only how we are to live. He only wishes a Competency for us. I have not seen her since you left me, but I could not refrain from going to Court on Thursday last to have that pleasure. I intend going to take leave before I set out for Wales. Mr Rigby has told my father he would get me a place; & my Father has desired me to endeavour to gain every friend in Wales in order to secure my Seat to be re-elected. Campbell has behaved in the most kind manner imaginable. Indeed I shall never be able to make him the least adequate return for his kindnesses.[2]

Poor Dodwell has had a very severe loss, his Eldest Boy is dead. He & his wife are in town, they have been here this week.

Lord Bateman affects to look shy. I admire him! I have avoided seeing him before tonight—he was coldly civil.

---

[1] Thomas Johnes senior agreed to pay his son's debts on condition that the family properties were legally settled in order to prevent the latter from selling real estate and squandering his patrimony.

[2] Probably John Campbell of Stackpole Court, Pembrokeshire who succeeded Johnes as M.P. for the Cardigan Boroughs in 1780. He was created Lord Cawdor of Castlemartin in 1796.

I have ten thousand little circumstances which I should be happy to relate to you but which would be as tiresome to write as to read. Adieu for the present, I will finish this tomorrow.

Tuesday

We met today at Rigby's. Everything passed off, signing, sealing etc., better than I expected. But I have made a cursed blunder, in the account I gave into my father's lawyers hands. I forgot J. Boissin's debt of 600£ although I had put it into the list I gave Mr Harley. This has vexed me most exceedingly—it has the appearance of Deceit. Luckily Mr Harley I hope has kept the list I gave him of my debts, that will acquit me of that at least. Mr Harley is not in the House tonight. I intend going there tomorrow early to acquaint him with it.

Lord Carlisle is to be one of the Commissioners to restore Peace to us. We did not break up before one o'clock this morning. It is said we shall have a very late night tonight.

I have mentioned my blunder to my Father, and he made me no Answer.

Believe me ever yours most sincerely & affectionately,

Thos. Johnes

Burn this when read. Mrs Dodwell has miscarried today and is very ill.

To Robert Liston, in Barcelona   Liston MS. 5521, f.122

Monmouth, Sept. 12, 1779

My dear Liston,

I have deferred myself the pleasure of writing to you sooner, because I waited to inform you of my marriage. I am now a Benedict of a fortnight old, and am so happy that (although I have every day intended writing to you) I could not find time before. I shall say nothing of my Wife, not to forestall your pleasure; yet this much I must say that I think myself most lucky in point of Beauty, Sense & Virtue, & what you will think of more value (knowing me), Prudence. You are so thoroughly acquainted with my character that I shall say nothing of my past follies. You I know thought I was too humble; yet allowing everything that can be said against me, surely I have made

Posterity ample atonement by uniting 2000£ per ann: with only a debt of 12,000£ to my Estate. I say nothing of Manors & other feathers [sic], nor of Life Leases which must rise the present income considerably.[1] My Father has given up to me the Stanage Estate of 870£ but when I am to receive anything God knows, for you will scarce believe even me that he has refused to give us a guinea on our setting out, and this year I have only received 56£.[2] He has indeed written to us kind letters, but my Mother, Brother nor Sister have not even thought this necessary. This will appear the more extraordinary when I can shew you Letters under his hand where he says he cannot contain himself for joy on my informing him of my having gained Miss Burgh's affection. If I had not married a most extraordinary Woman, and we had not the best tempers this behaviour would render us both miserable. But we are determined to be happy & contented.[3]

My Father has gotten the Lord Lieutenancy of Carmarthenshire upon Rice's death; he has given me the command of the Regt. of Militia. I do not expect to be anything, but as the Irishman expresses it, a Gainer of a Loss.[4] The Regt. is at Bristol, where I expect to go this week, but I doubt whether our poverty will permit my taking my Wife with me. You may guess from this it is very bad indeed. At present we have not the smallest idea of seeing Town next winter. You may form your opinion from this what sort of people we are; & you will the more esteem us. I cannot write more. Mrs Johnes unites with me (though not *personally* known to you) in every good wish.

I remain,

My dear Liston,

Yours ever & ever most affectionately,

Thos. Johnes Jnr.

[1] On August 26th 1779, Johnes married Maria Burgh, the only surviving child of the Rev. Henry Burgh whose father had served as agent to the Duke of Beaufort and had purchased the estate of Park Lettice in Monmouthshire. Maria, who had never enjoyed good health, died on April 1st 1782.

[2] Stanage Park, Radnorshire, part of the Knight family properties.

[3] Johnes's father, who died in May of the following year, had expected his eldest son to select a bride of rather more distinguished family than the unfortunate Maria.

[4] Henceforth styled 'Colonel', Johnes attended assiduously to his duties with the Militia, spending lengthy periods away from Hafod with his men and actively participating in training and manoeuvres. By exercising 'a happy mixture of strictness and liberality' he is said to have earned the affection of those who came under his charge.

To Robert Liston, in Madrid   Liston MS. 5538, f.105

Hafod, Oct. 31, 1783

My dear Liston,

Your letter of the 2nd of this month which I found here last night on my return from the Audits, has made me very uneasy. I received your letter from Lyons, & one from Barcelona, which I much enjoyed as it consisted of that species of buildings I am happy in; I mean Castles in the Air, & I shall be ever ready to join you in them.[1] I also received yours of 29 Augt. from St. Ildefonso. These are all I have yet had, & your last but one (that of ye 29th) was so short I waited for another to thank you for both—it was not one side of Gilt paper. Now I wrote to you a very long letter from Paris the day before I left it and, I guess it was cursedly stupid, for I never left any place with more regret. I wrote to you from London, & as I think inclosed in it the Cover which brought you the one you mention. I cannot think what is become of it. It was not signed by my name, and as yet I have not heard one word about it. I am very sorry you did not receive it as I spoke very frankly on many subjects which I should be extremely sorry any one else saw but yourself.[2] I there mentioned the narrow escape I had in crossing from Calais. We were obliged to run for ye Downs; I never was out such a night; the Pacquet Boat left Calais about 4 p.m. and could not get into Dover before 6 o'clock the evening after. I came here as soon as I could, & found everything going wrong, at least not one third done, which I expected. I hope however things are more orderly. I shall endeavor not to leave this place before Christmas, but if I am summoned my Poverty will make me comply.

[1] Following the death of his wife, Johnes spent much of the year 1782 travelling in Europe. On his return he was invited by Liston, who had recently been appointed British Minister in Madrid in succession to Lord Mountstewart, to join him as Embassy Secretary. Johnes set out in June 1783 with great enthusiasm, but as the weeks went by his keenness lost its edge and he relinquished his post before reaching Madrid. Retracing his tracks he visited Paris where he remained until the Autumn.

[2] Probably setting out the reasons why he had failed to take up his post, doubtless to Liston's embarrassment. Whether a sense of inadequacy, a dread of shouldering responsibility, homesickness or sheer perversity caused Johnes to act in this manner is a matter for surmise. In any event, however angry Liston may have been at the time, Johnes's behaviour does not seem to have soured the two mens's mutual affection and readiness to be of help and encouragement to each other throughout various trials and tribulations.

This place appears more beautiful than ever. I long most exceedingly to shew it to you. I am but just returned from the Audits & I can assure you I have not seen anything which is to be compared with it. My friends I understand are scolding me confoundedly for living here & quitting Croft. They have houses of their own and do not consider what importance that monosyllable *own* gives to a place. I cannot be idle; employ me, & I never wish to leave the Country. Now was I to go to Croft I am to buy everything, gardens, trees & all, & was I to cut down any trees which I certainly should do, to make walks etc., this would soon be misrepresented, and I a poor tenant at will should be served with an ejectment.[1] This place is my own, and I trust when finished will realize my idea of ressembling a fairy scene.[2]

Adieu my dear friend. Believe that no-one can love you more sincerely than

Your,

T. Johnes

To Robert Liston, in Madrid   Liston MS. 5540, f.50

London, Feb. 17, 1784

My dear Liston,

I have not written to you for some time because everything has been, I mean public affairs, in so extraordinary a situation that I could not send you any thing decisive. Nor indeed can I at present, but as I know your anxiety I merely write to let you know only my guesses upon the Subject. I believe I have received all your letters, and I had sent your Franks before the receipt of your last (the 8th January).

---

[1] Although Croft Castle had been settled on Johnes at the time of his marriage to Maria Burgh, his mother retained a life interest which inevitably would have placed constraints upon his freedom of action to 'improve' the house and grounds.

[2] Johnes had inherited Hafod and several other Cardiganshire properties in fee simple, free of encumbrances.

Mr Pitt etc still remain in power, and I hope long will remain so. All the cry of the Country is in his favor; this is so well known, that a dissolution which must take place is dreaded as decisive against the present opposition. It perhaps had been better to have dissolved us at once, but there were many reasons against it.[1] I was last Saturday at the meeting in Westminster Hall, with Lingreet. I never saw such a defeat as Fox met with. Lingreet's expression was marked, for we were everywhere in the crowd. *Jamais de ma vie j'ai vu une defaite plus complette, car M. Fox a quitté le champ de Bataille.* He hired some Blackguards to drag his Chariot from Palace Yard, but you may guess how it was with him, when upon his coach box sate Captain O'Byrne the gambler, Major Stanhope, & Will Hanger; behind as footmen were Geo. North & Willy Adam, not one of which I believe have a vote for Westminster.[2] They have been driving for some time at an Union, & some country gentlemen as the(y) call themselves have assembled at ye St Alban's Tavern for the purpose of easing the King of his Prerogation in naming his Ministers.[3] There was a kind of a meeting on Sunday between some of the Ministers & the Duke of Portland, but it ended in nothing, as they insisted as a preliminary article that Mr Pitt should resign. It thereupon ended. I think if Pitt joins, he ruins himself for ever, for what has the famous coalition done but hurt both.[4] The Prince of Wales has taken a determined part with Fox. He does not see that his interest must be interwoven with his father's. Tomorrow I understand they mean *to postpone*, (as being a softer term than stop) the Supplies.[5]

I have spoken as much as possible about you, but that damned fool the Earl of Chesterfield has thought proper to fix upon a relation of his

[1] In the turbulent Westminster election of 1784, where the poll extended from April 1st until mid-May, Fox eventually defeated the government candidate Sir Cecil Wray.

[2] At a pre-election meeting on February 14th Fox, overcome by a stinkbomb of asafoetida, was jostled out of Westminster Hall. After haranguing the crowds from the King's Arms Tavern, he was drawn in his chariot by a mob of his supporters to Devonshire House. [C. Hobhouse, *Fox, London, 1934;* L. Reed, *Charles James Fox, A Man for the People, London, 1969;* J.W. Derry, *Charles James Fox, Batsford, 1972.*]

[3] Following the dispute over the India Bill, a number of country M.P.s met at St. Alban's Tavern to discuss the union of all parties, and appointed a committee to sound out Portland, Fox and Pitt on this issue.

[4] i.e. The Fox-North coalition of 1783.

[5] In an attempt to embarrass Pitt and to enforce his resignation, Fox and his followers were contemplating bringing before the House a motion to postpone the supply of funds to the Navy.

own.[1] You have however an excellent friend in Rose, who has assured me how very sorry he is, but that you *must be provided for*. This has made me easy, for he does not make such declarations as mere words of course.[2]

Adieu my dear Liston, believe me ever yours most sincerely. I wish you would think about some wines for me, & some handsome matts, 30 by 20 feet & smaller proportions.

Once more adieu.

[letter ends]

To Robert Liston, in Stockholm   Liston MS. 5567, f.15

Hafod, March 25, 1789

My dear Liston,

I cannot express my disappointment in not having the pleasure of seeing You here, but your reasons are too just for me to find fault with you. I have three things that I am very anxious to shew you, as I am not a little proud of them all, and for two of them I have not been a little found fault with; but I am convinced in my own mind they are two of the wisest acts of my life & I have not many to boast of. What I wish to shew you is my Wife my Child & this place, almost all of them my own creation.[3] I had really set my heart on seeing you; but this King of Sweden who seems in my opinion not a little rash, unless he is assured of strong support, has totally routed me as well as his

[1] Philip Stanhope, 5th Earl of Chesterfield (1755-1815), a man of unaffectedly bucolic tastes and manners had been appointed Minister Plenipotentiary to Madrid on January 1st 1784. In fact he never visited Spain and resigned the nominal post in 1787. Throughout this period Liston himself served as the active British Minister in Madrid and Johnes is presumably referring to an official appointment which Chesterfield had arranged against Liston's wishes.

[2] George Rose (1744-1818), Tory politician and friend of George III.

[3] Johnes had married, in secret, his cousin Jane Johnes of Dolaucothi, Carmarthenshire, sometime in 1783-4. Their daughter Maria Anne (Mariamne) was born on June 30th, 1784. His mother and immediate family were not informed of his new domestic situation until April 1785.

Jane Johnes: plaster bust by Thomas Banks

Nobles.[1] I trust you will return in the Winter, for my health has been long unsettled, so that unless you keep your promise we may never meet here again. Do not think I am low spirited. I have for sometime made up my mind to it, and shall be exceedingly sorry to quit the very very happy state I enjoy here, but I really do not expect it will last long. Well, no more of this.

We have shockingly cold weather & the roads are execrable, so you would not have seen my place or this country to advantage.

Pray write as often as you can; I will be very punctual indeed. Mrs Johnes wishes you would in your way thro' Holland order her 100 roots of the finest Hyacinths, 100 Narcissus's of sorts, 100 Jonquils. She is very anxious for a collection of Green house plants, but that you must take your time as you will be too much hurried at present.

Adieu, my dear Liston, believe me ever (to) remain your very affectionate & sincere friend.

T. Johnes

To the Marquis of Buckingham[2]   N.L.W. Dolaucothi MS. Vol. 3, f.39

Hafod, May 17, 1789

My Lord,

I have no other apology to make your Lordship for troubling you with this letter & request, than of having the honor of your Lordship's acquaintance & being attached to the same political sentiments.

The Bearer of this is my Brother in Law, Lieutenant Johnes of the 64th Regt. now on duty in Dublin.[3] As he is the Son of a younger

---

[1] Liston served as Envoy Extraordinary at Stockholm between 1788 and 1793, his former pupil Hugh Elliot being at the same time Ambassador in Copenhagen. [For Gustavus III's difficulties with the Swedish nobility, see C. Hallendorf and A. Schuck, *History of Sweden*, London, 1929]

[2] George Nugent-Temple Grenville, (1753-1813), Marquis of Buckingham and Lord Lieutenant of Ireland (1787-1789).

[3] John Johnes (1768-1815), Thomas Johnes's cousin and brother-in-law. Having run away from Charterhouse, this weak and vacillating individual had been purchased a commission by his father. This he sold on reaching his majority, thereafter retiring to his estate at Dolaucothi in Carmarthenshire, the bottle and the chase and eventually expiring from gout in the head.

Brother, his fortune is not great; his ambition is the army & hitherto he has purchased every Step. His Character & conduct are irreproachable, as his Corps will eagerly testify, & if your Lordship would shew him any kindness through me, towards advancing him to a Company, I should ever esteem it a most particular & personal mark of your friendship & always happy to shew my gratitude for it. I am convinced he will not do any discredit to your Lordship's patronage. Not to trespass any longer on your Lordship's time,

I remain, my Lord,

Your Lordship's most obedient humble servant,

Thos. Johnes.

To John Johnes, Dolaucothi, Carmarthenshire   N.L.W. Dolaucothi MS.
Vol. 16, f.42

(n.d.) [1792]

Dear John,

The Bearer of this is Mr Raspe a very learned German Minarologist [sic] but who speaks and understands English perfectly well.[1] I wish you would shew him Cogové & give him every information about it as it may turn our to our mutual benefit.[2]

I am,

Yours ever,

T. Johnes

Your sister (though in great tribulation for the death of the White Peacock) writes with me in kind love to you all.	Shew Llandre water as he says Lime *must* be there.

[1] Rudolf Eric Raspe (1737-1794), natural scientist, antiquary and rogue. After various picaresque adventures leading to his arrest for theft in Germany, he fled to England around 1775 where he spent most of his remaining years as a translator and *soi-disant* mineralogical expert, finding time also to piece together the immensely

To Robert Liston, in London   Liston MS. 5568, f.109

Hafod, Nov. 10, 1792

My dear Liston,
    We were very happy to hear of your safe arrival in London, & hope that your expedition to the north will be equally so. Min thanks you herself for your letter & present & is so proud of it that it is never off. [3] She is more ridiculous than ever, but yesterday she indeed surprised us all. A Mr Raspe, a German Mineralogist & Chymist (who has been examining the Western Islands & found some of the most beautiful marbles in Icolmkill I ever saw) came here to examine my Mines, as I wished for better information than can be had here. After dinner he was spouting to M. Trossarelli some verses from Tasso in compliment to her, when she cried out that they were very like one of her songs 'La piu Vezzosa' from Milico. I said, 'Sing it Min'. She said she could not without the accompaniment, upon which Trossarelli ran to the Harpsichord & played it and I cannot express our astonishment at the little figure at the Bottom of the Table singing without note or book with a precision & Taste that must be heard to express. [4]
    I have had a long letter from a particular friend of mine, who you may guess, when I mention some *recommendatory* Letters to you at Stockholm, expressing great alarms at the present Crisis, and very great fears. I answer it this post, and as in a Case of mortification, shall prescribe losing one limb to save the Vital parts. This will not please, but it is the only means left, or we shall be in as bad a situation as our Neighbours. Something essential must be done, & that soon, for though I really believe the Storm is forming, yet God knows how

successful *Baron Munchausen's Narrative of his marvellous Travels and Campaigns in Russia*, with which his name was not associated until after his death. Visiting the north of Scotland in 1791 he falsely claimed to have discovered enormous mineral wealth and after persuading Sir John Sinclair to supply money for exploration, he disappeared to Donegal, and still masquerading as a mining expert succumbed to scarlet fever in 1794.
    [2] Cogové = Ogofâu, Pumsaint, Carmarthenshire, location of the celebrated Roman gold mines.
    [3] Mariamne Johnes is also termed 'Min' or 'Mary' in her father's letters.
    [4] According to Elizabeth Inglis-Jones, Trossarelli was engaged to teach Italian to Mariamne Johnes. A reference to 'Trusserella', Italian painter, appears in the Book of Visitors to Strawberry Hill for 1794 and probably refers to Gaspare Trossarelli (1763-1825) [W.S. Lewis (ed.), *Horace Walpole Correspondence, 12*, Oxford, 1944].

soon it may burst. I wish I was to make the King's Speech at the opening of Parliament. I think it should be a safe conductor.[1]

Our united kind wishes attend you & believe me always yours most affectionately,

T. Johnes

Whenever you are inclined to write no-one will thank you more.

To Matthew Boulton in Birmingham[2]   N.L.W. Fac. Vol. 77, 16.

Swansea, May 8th, 1793

Dear Sir,

I take the liberty of enclosing to you two of the Buttons of the Carmarthenshire Militia; and as I am not a little proud of so very Fine a Body of Men I wish to set them off by every means and shall beg of you to exert yourself in making us a handsome Button, and as

[1] The growing strength of radicalism in England, fuelled by events taking place in France, provoked a nervous reaction from the Establishment. In May Pitt's government reacted with a proclamation against seditious practices and the indictment (*in absentia*) of Tom Paine whose *The Rights of Man* appeared in 1791-2. Burke had predicted the anarchy and military dictatorship which would follow the French Revolution. The outbreak of war between France and Austria, the September massacres and the overthrow, trial and execution of Louis XVI seemed to have vindicated his predictions and many felt that it was only a matter of time before the contagion spread across the Channel. In a sense a 'safe conductor' was provided by France's declaration of war against Britain in February 1793 when many radicals who had previously exchanged fraternal greetings with their French brethren disclaimed any seditious intent and protested their loyalty to Crown and Constitution. [For this and other general historical footnotes I have relied heavily upon I.R. Christie, *Wars and Revolutions in Britain, 1760-1815*, London, 1982; J.B. Owen, *The Eighteenth Century, 1714-1815*, London, 1974.]

[2] Matthew Boulton, F.R.S. (1728-1809), engineer and close acquaintance of Priestley, Wedgewood, Franklin and other liberal luminaries. Besides coins, buttons and buckles contributed significantly to the output of Boulton's Soho works in Birmingham, with prices varying according to design and degree of ornamentation from 3d to 140 guineas per gross. [H.W. Dickinson, *Matthew Boulton*, Cambridge, 1937]

reasonable as you can—for it is not to save my own pocket that I wish it, but from the King's allowance to lay more out on the men. I wish that the Shanks may be made particularly strong. I wish you would send some patterns & the prices to me here as soon as you can. We want also some round Knee buckles, white or yellow, and some Clasps for the men's stocks. Pray have the goodness to send me some patterns under cover to me with the prices.

I am ashamed to give you so much trouble and remain,

Dear Sir,

Your most obedient humble servant,

T. Johnes

To Robert Liston, in London   Liston MS. 5569, f.57

Hafod, Nov. 11, 1793

My dear Liston,

I was most exceedingly obliged to you for your kind Letter of the seventh of last month. As my movements were not very certain, I did not write to thank you for it before I could say something decisive of my time. Mrs Johnes & myself came here the 27 of last month, intending to return to Swansea as today. But Mr Nash my Architect who has been here all the time promises to stay a fortnight longer if we will remain, and will advance the building in a great degree. Uncomfortable as we are, this is such a flattering prospect of getting rid of such a set of rascals as I believe were never before collected together that I have consented. We therefore shall remain here till the 28 or 29th so as to be at Carmarthen the 30th. Now my dear friend if you will put up with the very wretched & confused accommodations we have to offer you, come here, and we will carry you to Swansea in your return to London, where you shall see your Young favorite. You have never seen the Glamorganshire Coast, and I think it superiorly [sic] beautiful.

We have had bad colds and cannot get rid of them.

I shall delay thanking you for all you say about Froissart until I have the pleasure of seeing you. Direct for me at *Hafod, Rhayader Bag, Radnorshire*, as I have at last got a post established from thence to Aberystwith which brings me my letters a day sooner; but I pay for it myself.

Pray let me hear from you to know when & where we may wish you a prosperous Voyage or Journey to Constantinople.[1]
Mrs Johnes desires her best Compliments.

I am Yours always,
T. Johnes

To James Edward Smith, in London   Linn. Soc. (Smith), 16, f.1

Swansea, May 12, 1794

My dear Sir,

I had the pleasure of receiving your two letters of the 25, and 2nd of this Month within a few days of each other, owing to the irregularity of the cross post, the last only yesterday and I beg you will accept of my best thanks for them both.

Mrs Johnes thinks herself highly obliged to you for the New Holland Flora you have sent to Mr Edwards & for the seeds of the *Dombeya* which I send tonight to Hafod. If it seeds you may depend on as many as you choose.

I have written about the *Pultenda*, but much fear if it is not out of Flower that some mistake will prevent it coming to you as I wish, but if I recollect it was going out of Flower. However as some of us will be always in future at Home, when we have the pleasure of seeing you, you have only to give your orders & they will be most punctually obeyed, I can promise you.

With regard to the Linnean Society, I much wished to be of it, and shall be very proud of being a Member of any Society of which you are

---

[1] Where Liston remained as Ambassador Extraordinary until February 1796.

President. But to speak out honestly, as I only shine in Botany but like the moon by borrowed light, or rather to please her who is dearer to me than the Light, I was ashamed of my Ignorance, otherwise I should have requested it of you. [1] At present I accept it most cheerfully & thankfully.

As for the Scandal of a Court, I hold it in complete contempt; and am only sorry that such a person as Deluc, whom for his Writings I esteemed should by his illiberal & bigotted servile conduct to you have sunk himself in my mind to the same level. There needs no other proof of Character, than the perusal of your Answers to his Letters, for to judge between an honest man & a Tartuffe. [2]

I have not heard from Liston since he left Ostend, and am happy to learn they have got safe to Vienna. I shall look for some interesting intelligence from thence if he has made the acquaintance I desired him to do with Jacquin. [3]

Mrs Johnes & my little Girl are exceedingly well & look forward with great pleasure to assure you personally how glad they will be to see you.

I am, my dear Sir,

Yours ever,

T. Johnes

[1] i.e. Mariamne Johnes. Both Mrs Johnes and Mariamne maintained gardens at Hafod in which they received the constant advice and encouragement of James Edward Smith. The gardens were of different style and content with Mariamne's occupying an elevated spot suited to alpine and sub-alpine species. By way of contrast, Mrs Johnes's garden was a formal affair embracing almost 2 acres alongside the River Ystwyth. Unlike her daughter's 'pensile' garden, Mrs Johnes's flower garden was open to visitors and excited much comment regarding its stark contrast with the surrounding forest and mountain scenery. [See, *inter alia,* C. Kerkham and S. Briggs, A Review of the archaeological potential of the Hafod landscape, *Ceredigion, XI(2), 1990.*]

[2] Jean André de Luc (1727-1817), Swiss geologist and philosopher. Clearly Smith and de Luc were in dispute, probably over some arcane aspect of religious dogma.

[3] N.J.C. Jacquin (1727-1817), Dutch botanist after whom Linnaeus named the genus *Jacquinia.*

To Bishop Thomas Percy[1]   J. Nichols, *Illustrations of the Literature of the Eighteenth Century*, VIII, 1817, p.303.

Swansea, May 15, 1794

My Lord,

I beg your Lordship will accept of my warmest thanks and acknowledgements for the very obliging letter you wrote to Mr Stirling, and which I had the pleasure to receive last night.[2]

I am very happy you approve of my undertaking, and shall labour as hard as I can to make it deserving of your Lordship's compliments.

I feel as I ought your liberal offer of assistance, which I shall take the liberty of availing myself of with with no small share of pride.

Your Lordship may, perhaps, not be displeased to know from what cause this Translation is attempted. At M. Paris' sale, I bought a fine copy of Froissart, and the finest printed vellum I ever saw; it came from the Prince de Soubise's library, and was unkown to Denys Sauvage.

Mrs Johnes one winter's evening, as I was reading part of it to her, offered to write for me if I would translate it, and give her the profits to build an habitation for six poor old men and six old women, and endow it afterwards at so much per week.

I wrote to my friend Mr Edwards, of Pall Mall, who directly accepted the proposal, and made the most generous offers. Idle and indolent as I am, when thus driven to the wall, I could not refuse, but, indeed, to use a French phrase, '*Si je n'avois pas peur, je tremblois*', and put it off as long as I could: repeated scoldings, &c. made me begin on it last year, and, to my surprise, it was approved of in London. This has now given me spirits, and I am now putting my shoulders to it in earnest, and shall do my utmost that my friends' partiality may not be blamed more than needs.

I inquired of Lord Lansdowne, but in vain, after Lady Pomfret's copy or notes; but as I must be in London again next week, I shall renew my inquiries after it.[3]

[1] Thomas Percy (1729-1811), Bishop of Dromore and author of the influential *Reliques of Ancient English Poetry* (1765).

[2] The Rev. Joseph Stirling had introduced Johnes to Bishop Percy in the hope that the latter might be able to assist him in deciphering some of the less obvious personal and place names in Froissart.

[3] William Petty, 1st Marquis of Lansdowne (1735-1805), better known as the unpopular statesman Lord Shelburne.

The Chateau d'Alquest is mentioned before the battle of Otterburn, which from the distance mentioned, *six miles* from Edinburgh, I put down as Dalkieth: but there will be many names of persons and places that I despair of, for Denys Sauvage in his time could not make them out, and Lord Berners adds confusion to confusion.

I endeavour to make my Translation as exact as possible, and I never look into Lord Berners' but when in *great* doubt. I consult Cotgrave's *Dictionary*, which I find invaluable, and Lancombe's *Dictionnaire du Vieux Language*. But I am here with my regiment, without the assistance I should have at home from my own library, and am reduced to make marks for future researches.

I am building a new room for my books, so that at present they are all in confusion, but Mr Edwards has my Catalogue of the Romances, which he bought from Mr Grenville, and I have desired Mr Stirling to inquire of him for it. [1]

My intention is to collate my printed vellum copy with two copies I have in MS. and with all the others I can find, for I believe few MSS. are the same. Those in the Museum I have seen with great pleasure, and we intend to have some of the best illuminations engraven on wood, by a young man of most promising abilities. [2]

With again thanking your Lordship for your kind attention to me, I am, my Lord, your much obliged, humble servant,

T. Johnes

To James Edward Smith, in London   Linn. Soc. (Smith), 16, f.3

Swansea, May 15, 1794

My Dear Sir,

I had the pleasure only last night of receiving your friendly letter about Lord Bute's collections and thank you most kindly for it.

I meant to have been a large purchaser at the Sale, but have been prevented by circumstances which I will relate to you. So Sir Joseph

---

[1] Thomas Grenville (1755-1846), statesman and book collector who bequeathed some 20,000 volumes to the British Museum.

[2] One John Harris of Penton Street, Walworth.

need not fear me, for I should never forgive myself if in any ways I was a hindrance to his pursuits. I have too many obligations to him personally not to say that I look upon him as one of the most publick spirited men we have, for alas they can be counted. [1]

But I shall have the pleasure of talking to you more of this sooner than I expected. The Message of the King's about all these Societies will bring me to Town on Monday. [2] I hope to remain no more than that week, and I have persuaded Mrs Johnes to accompany me so that if you will favor us with your Company at Breakfast on Wednesday I shall be very happy to introduce a real Lover of Plants, but a very ignorant one, to your acquaintance. However for family reasons I shall thank you not to mention this; otherwise we shall get into a Scrape, as she does not wish it to be known that she is in London.

I was going on merrily with Froissart, but this interruption will be a great hindrance to it.

I am, my dear Sir,

Yours ever,

T. Johnes

[1] Johnes and Sir Joseph Banks, the botanist and patron of science, do not appear to have corresponded, yet they certainly met at Banks's Soho Square soirées. Banks himself frequently visited Wales as a young man, his uncle having married Bridget Williams, heiress to the Edwinsford estate in Carmarthenshire. On one visit, during the summer of 1767 he dined at Dolaucothi from whence he inspected the Ogofau gold mines. [H.B. Carter, *Sir Joseph Banks, 1743-1820*, British Museum (*Natural History*), *1988*].

[2] In the early 1790s many towns and cities throughout Britain had their own reform societies, the largest being the London Corresponding Society. These were seen by a ruling class appalled by the excesses of the French Revolution as a potent threat to the stability of civilised society. In the spring of 1794 a number of leading reformers, including Horne Tooke of the Society for Constitutional Information, and Thomas Hardy and John Thelwall, respectively secretary and principal protagonist of the London Corresponding Society, were indicted for treason. But treason could not be proved and when Hardy, Thelwall and Tooke were discharged, charges against other suspects were dropped.

To George Cumberland, at Egham, Surrey   Add. MS. 36497, f.318

Hafod, July 28, 1794

Sir,

You have shewn so much partiality to the Country round the Devil's Bridge, that I shall make no apology for troubling you with this Letter.

It is to inform you that within these few days an apparently valuable mineral spring has been discovered close by the Devil's Bridge. It seems to be a very strong Chalebeat; as you may wish to taste some of it, I have ordered a small bottle of it to be sent by the Coach directed for you to the care of Mr Edwards in Pall Mall, and I shall write to him this post to desire he would forward it to you. If further Tunbridges or Cheltenhams should arise there, I trust that the beauties of Nature are of features too grand for any ornaments of Art to have other effects than to make the old Lady appear more beautiful.[1] ·

Perhaps I should not now have intruded upon you, if when I had the pleasure of meeting you at Mr Knight's you had not given me some hopes that I might have the satisfaction of seeing you here, and that I may take this opportunity of reminding you of it.

Indeed I am anxious to shew you, who have seen this place in its original wildness, that by *beautifying it* I have *neither shorn* or *tormented* it. I shall remain here from my Regiment as long as I can, but I much fear I must return to it the latter end of September. Any time between that time I shall be exceedingly proud to receive you here.

I am, Sir,

Your most obedient humble Servant,

T. Johnes

---

[1] Whereas Tunbridge waters had been enthusiastically recommended to their patients by seventeenth century doctors, Cheltenham only came into prominence following George III's five weeks of water-quaffing in the little town in the summer of 1788. [G. Hart, *History of Cheltenham*, Leicester, 1965]

To James Edward Smith, in London   Linn. Soc. (Smith), 16, f.10

Hafod, Aug. 30. 1794

My dear Sir,

I had the pleasure of your Letter from Bungay last post, and beg you to accept my best thanks for it.

You will believe me when I say we are all most exceedingly disappointed in being forced to give up the pleasure of seeing you here. For much as we wish it, yet it is absolutely impossible to request it after what you have said, and it would be a most unreasonable return for the friendship you have honored me. But remember next year I shall expect the pleasure of a longer stay, and as every day I am taking faster root here, I hope this present drumming life will not tear me away so that you may fix your own time.[1]

I hope this will find you in London quite recovered from your Sore Throat. We had many complaining this Season, and as my Lady Bountiful's medicines are not yet arrived, she is forced to administer from that not less bountiful dispensatory, y clepyed the Kitchen.[2] She desires me to return you her best thanks for your remembrance of her respecting Mr Wilson's seeds from New Holland. We have not been lucky this year as scarce any plants have succeeded. We have now a fine yellow hibiscus in flower from some seeds which you gave me. There are many of them. Shall I send you the flower or will you have any of the plants? My Garden is doing well, and those who used to rank that & a farm here among the impossibles begin now to change their minds. The late rains have brought us Grass and Turnips, but Cattle are very low indeed, which I attribute to want of fodder from the drought of last Summer in England.

I have not been to visit the Chalybeat, as I had flattered myself we might have seen it together. It appears from the Taste very strong; and from what Dr. Davies of Carmarthen writes me, the strongest he has met with in Wales. I sent him a bottle of it. It may in time do much good, but next Summer I trust it will be more fully known.

That wild Girl still continues as wild in her wishes to go to India as when I mentioned it to you in London last winter. Her sister having told her the reasons that would deprive us of the pleasure of seeing you, she is now at my Elbow begging I would write to you to know if

---

[1] Johnes refers here to his obligations with the militia.
[2] Johnes uses the archaic Middle English *cleped, clept, clepyt* (called).

Hafod: the meadow below the flower garden, by John 'Warwick' Smith
(by permission of the National Library of Wales)

Mrs Kindersley would be so good to let her go under her Protection when she sails for India, provided she receives the answers to the Letters some of my friends wrote for her last spring. It has given us all the greatest uneasiness, and when the time comes for her departure, as she is bent upon it, it will be a heartbreaking business to her Sister. I should have thought content might have been enjoyed among her relations who are eager to gratify every wish, instead of seeking it among Strangers & foreigners. But we are poor Creatures!!

Pray did you ever read La Fontaine's fable of the Pigeon that wishes to travel? If not, you will thank me for mentioning it. It has always struck me with great pleasure, and now perhaps (more so) from the Circumstance of this Girl's throwing herself with her Eyes open upon a World of which she is completely ignorant.[1]

Adieu, my dear Sir. The ladies all desire to send their best Compliments & regrets,

I am yours ever,

T. Johnes

[1] Charlotte, Mrs Johnes's sister, spent four years in India, possibly as a governess. Mrs Kindersley was the wife of Nathaniel Edward Kindersley of Sunningdale, Berkshire, for many years a civil servant with the East India Company. Their son, Sir Richard Kindersley (1792-1879) became a distinguished King's Counsel.

Hafod, Oct. 9, 1794

My dear Sir,

I should have sooner thanked (you) for your very kind letter of the 15th Sept. if Dr Anderson had not been here, who has made me more wild than ever about this place. For he is not only delighted with its romantick beauties, but says he never saw any Country in its natural state so fertile, or that was capable of such very great improvements with so few obstacles. You will find me at least six feet increased in height when I have the pleasure of seeing you, and if I am spoilt, I shall lay it at both your Doors. But I shall endeavour to deserve your good opinion and in a few years I flatter myself I may be worthy of it.

The poor Girl who is so wild to go to India has just brought me the inclosed letter, which as I said I was going to write to you, she desires I would send, to shew that all she requests is the protection of any Lady of Character who is going out to that Country.

Dr Anderson desires to be particularly remembered to you. Have you ever seen his scheme for avoiding lockwork in Canals? It is printed in his Agriculture Survey of Aberdeenshire for the Board. He is also about a most simple & portable water Level that promises to be in this *Levelling* age (pardon the Pun) of great utility. I am much afraid I shall lose him, and it will be like tearing something from me, as the more I know of him the more I respect him & feel honored by his friendship. [1]

I, who love in my heart building Castles in the Air have been most industriously employed, and hope I shall live to see some of them on more solid foundations and if I had my whole income, would very soon make amends for what have been stiled [sic] my follies, some indeed properly enough, but I will not allow of what I have done here coming under that denomination.

We have had very rainy & blowing weather, but it is now I hope clearing up and my woods & cascades are in high beauty. We wish

[1] James Anderson LL.D. (1739-1808), economist and agriculturist. He resided in Aberdeenshire until 1793 when he moved to Isleworth (Middlesex) to pursue agricultural experiments. The author of many tracts on economics, slavery and rural affairs he wrote, on behalf of the Board of Agriculture, *A General View of the Agriculture and Rural Economy of the County of Aberdeen*, London, 1794.

Hafod: the Cavern Cascade, by John 'Warwick' Smith
(by permission of the National Library of Wales)

much for you, but as that cannot be, I look to the Harcourt motto *Le bon temps viendra* —I fear, however, never again for that poor family. [1]

I see no end to this War, but fear that my friend Knight's note will be realized, and all Europe be thrown into a state of Barbarism. Peace would be the ruin of the Convention, for what could they do with the Hordes in arms? They have subsisted so long on plunder that they will not soon return to peaceable farmers. [2] As for ourselves, by the behaviour & insolence of the great towards the lower classes, and by the frequent prostitution of the word Patriot, the people have lost all confidence in any man and believe them all activated by the self-same motives, Avarice or Ambition. For my part I am quite tired of a

[1] The ancient Harcourt family of Stanton Harcourt, Oxon, were bedevilled with bad luck. Simon, the 1st Earl Harcourt had been drowned in a well in 1777 and both his sons died without issue in 1809 and 1830 [*Burke's Peerage*].

[2] The National Assembly, proclaimed in 1789, was succeeded by the Convention against whose government and citizen army Britain was to fight for over 20 years following France's declaration of war in February, 1793.

publick Life, and wish nothing so much as to fix my staff here, not to be removed until placed in the Black Box.

Mrs Johnes desires her best Compliments to you.

I am, my dear Sir,

Yours ever,

T. Johnes

To John Johnes, Dolaucothi, Carmarthenshire   N.L.W. Dolaucothi MS. Vol. 16, f.47

Swansea, Monday night, (n.d., 1794?)

Dear John,

I understand that all the effects of Glanbrane [sic] are to be sold on Wednesday, except what the young man chooses to keep. I am very anxious to have the *manuscript* Welsh music which I have heard Mr Gwynne collected and shall be much obliged to you if you could purchase them for me and if they are not to be sold, if you borrow them for a few days I shall be equally thankful.[1]

Jack is the bearer of this to Llandovery who goes with my Horse to bring Mr Morgan's son of Brick Grove here.

Your Sisters unite with me in every love to you all.

I am, yours ever,

T. Johnes

[1] Sackville Gwynne of Glanbrân, Llandovery (1751-1794), distinguished harpist, and patron of harpists and Welsh music.

To James Edward Smith, in London   Linn. Soc. (Smith), 16, f.18

Hafod, March 22, 1795

My dear Sir,

By the very heavy fall of Snow we have had, I did not receive your letter of the 15th until yesterday. I am exceedingly obliged to you for thinking of me at such a time, and wish from my heart that I could say anything that could in the smallest degree alleviate so just a grief. But in such melancholy cases there is but one resource; and of all the Evils the French are most deserving of curses is that attempt to take from the wretched their only consolation. But it cannot succeed unless Man becomes worse than a wild beast, for Providence has too kindly implanted Religion in our Breasts to be easily rooted out.[1]

Since my last we have been most seriously alarmed at our dear Girl's state of health. Insomuch that I wrote to Pitcairn, but suspecting he could not leave his Patients, Dr Davies came here from Carmarthen and remained the greatest part of a week.[2] I hope she is now in a fair way of recovery, as she daily improves. When we come to Town, she shall come with us, as change of air is strongly recommended.

Mrs Kindersley was so good to write to me and we shall be ready to set out at a moment's warning. But as I could wish to stay in Town as short a time as possible, I shall be very much obliged to you upon your return to let me know when it will be necessary to set out. I suppose a Fortnight will be sufficient to make the proper equipments for the Lady.

Everything is very quiet in this part of the Country and there needed no bustle at all if the Magistrates had not acted imprudently. There is certainly a scarcity, and we must import barley or there will be a famine before next harvest. I have got rid of the Cavalry, for as our poor eat oats I did not wish that two troops of Horse should be of their dinner partys, and two Companies of my Regiment marched in there on Fryday last. It is an ill wind that blows nobody good, for by this means I hope to pass all my Summer among my Mountains.

[1] The Convention passed a decree in February 1795 allowing general freedom of worship and severing the connection between Church and State. This confirmed an earlier decree and brought to a halt the growing tide of de-Christianisation which had been spreading rapidly throughout the various *Départments* of France.

[2] David Pitcairn (1749-1809), Scots physician and authority on rheumatic fever.

The latter part of your Letter gave us very great pleasure indeed, as it assured us your health was better. When I took my leave of you I was not comfortable, and Mr Kindersley's letter did not add to it. Mrs Johnes says she is sure this air will quite restore you, and if your other engagements will permit there will be a place in our Carriage when we return from Town. Change of air will be as necessary for you as for my little invalid.[1]

Mrs Johnes desires her best Compliments to you.

I am, my dear Sir,

Your sincere humble servant,

T. Johnes

To James Edward Smith, in London   Linn. Soc. (Smith), 16, f.30

Hafod, Oct. 17, 1795

My dear Sir,

I from my heart congratulate you on the intelligence which your Letter of the 13th conveyed to me, and most sincerely wish you every happiness. I know no one more deserving of it, & hope it will more than surpass your own expectations. I have been one of the few fortunate ones; but my opinion has always been that it is a state of reciprocity & no one liberty can be allowed to one party that the other is not entitled to. I agree with you in what you term old fashioned notions, and if they should be erroneous, which every sense & perception we have assures us they are not, they are errors on the right side, and our Lives here must pass more to the satisfaction of those whose Hearts are not displaced.[2]

Our little Girl is delighted with your Letter, and is preparing another letter, but she complains she has nothing new to send you.

---

[1] Smith journeyed to Hafod in August 1795 where he befriended the child Mariamne with whom he commenced a correspondence stretching over a number of years. Mariamne's letters to Smith are preserved in the Linnean Society Library.

[2] A reference to Smith's engagement to Patience Reeve of Norwich.

She used to come every post day to inquire if there was any letter for her. I have only mentioned the intelligence you communicated to me (& for which I feel myself very much obliged) to Mrs Johnes, as I consider her as my better half and I can assure you she participates in your prospects. I need not say she will be very happy in making this place as agreeable to her as possible. You see we look forward to next summer, that you will not come alone. She desires me to thank you for your intended presents, but she is fearful she is hurting your collection if she accepts them.

Dr Anderson is now here, and desires his best Compliments to you. The weather has been so boisterous & rainy that we have not been able to get out as I could wish. Our Cataracts and Cascades have been in very high beauty. I never saw the Devil's Bridge in greater Glory than a few days ago, when a very old friend & schoolfellow from Warwickshire came to see me. I suppose there could not be a greater contrast the [sic] the Warwickshire Scenery than what he saw.[1]

I am afraid I must come to London this month on my own business and then I dread being detained there. Oh, I long for the time as Falstaffe [sic] says when, 'I can live cleanly & like a gentleman'.[2]

We all unite in kind Compliments to you.

I am,

My dear Sir,

Yours very sincerely,

T. Johnes

[1] Johnes regarded both trees and water as being fundamentally important to his notion of the landscape ideal. Here he refers to the falls created by the confluence of the rivers Rheidol and Mynach at Devil's Bridge which continue to the present day to excite the fascination of visitors.

[2] 'I'll purge, and leave sack, and live cleanly, as a nobleman should do'. [*Henry IV Pt. I, v, iv, 168*]

To James Edward Smith, in London   Linn. Soc. (Smith), 16, f.41

Hafod, Jan. 11, 1796

My dear Sir,

I have had the pleasure of your two letters and least I may follow your example & forget to answer the part relative to Silk for purses, I will begin by saying that Silk etc. is to be had at Gardom's, St. James's Street, London.

I was not able to get here before New Year's Day late in the evening, & walked the last 12 miles which notwithstanding the darkness of the night, the rain & the muddiness of the roads, I performed in 3 Hours 35 Minutes. I was amply repaid by finding all I hold most dear as well as I could wish them. As for my health, after what I have said of the walk, I may be silent.

This Scene etc. is such a perfect contrast to London & what I suffered there, that I feel like one awakened from a frightful dream, and even now cannot sit quietly to any thing. Since I last saw you I have had such a Lesson that I shall remember for many years. It was perhaps necessary & to be sure I cannot plead undeserving of it. If

Hafod: the great fall of the Mynach, by John 'Warwick' Smith
(by permission of the National Library of Wales)

however it makes the impression & is followed by the effect that I trust will be the consequence it will be more to be thankful for than otherwise. When we meet I will (if I can, for I hate to think of it) inform you more particularly of it. This much I can say that it has made me look on Mankind with no friendly eye, and if my heart would let me, I should not hold much commerce with the world. But that is impossible. This place and its dearer inhabitants make me too happy not to wish to shew my gratitude in doing all the good I can to others. [1]

Dr Anderson has been most amazingly active here, and has done more than I can ever thank him for. Among others he has made, or rather began to make, the most singular garden for my little Girl I ever saw. The pensile Gardens of Semiramis will be a farce to it and it will equally surprize you as it has done me. I am very well satisfied with my Gardener & trust everything will go on well. We have the finest verdure here that is possible, all from my good Doctor's watering. [2]

I hear of everything being perfectly tranquil & quiet in this part of the Country. Our Bread is 6 lb wheat, 6 lb Rye & 9 lb of Potatoes which is equally good, to my taste, as yours at Hammersmith & that is saying enough. [3]

Mrs Johnes etc. unite in kind Compliments with me to all your family.

I am, my Dear Sir,

Yours very truly,

T. Johnes

[1] Summoned to London by his legal and financial advisers in the winter of 1795 Johnes had been confronted by the ugly spectre of his debts which he had chosen for some years to ignore. The bubble of credit upon which he had floated happily had suddenly burst and as he edged perilously close to bankruptcy so did many of his London friends and acquaintances choose to ignore and, in some cases, to desert him. To the easy-going and opened handed Johnes the discovery that friendship could be held so cheaply was profoundly shocking.

[2] The 'pensile' gardens and Mrs Johnes's flower garden are currently being restored (1989) by the voluntary efforts of the 'Friends of Hafod'.

[3] Alive to the harsh realities of recent events in France, Johnes and his fellow gentry were constantly aware of the consequences of winter hunger among the rural poor and took steps to ensure that cereals and other staples were imported at times of scarcity so as to prevent price rises and the possibility of food riots. It would be with some relief that he reported Cardiganshire to be 'tranquil and quiet'.

To George Cumberland, at Egham, Surrey   Add. MS. 36498, f.100

Hafod, Jan. 21, 1796

My dear Sir,

I am to thank you for two letters and for the excellent verses you were so kind to inclose. My little girl is very proud of hers, but what is to be done with the ode, is kept secret from me. She is most exceedingly improved in her music.

Mrs Johnes thanks you for the seed you sent. Is there any thing we can send you or to Mrs Cumberland from hence? You have only to say, and it shall be immediately forwarded.

The Salmon was ordered very long before I had the pleasure of receiving either of your letters, as a sort of tribute for your very warm attachment to Wales. You need not, at least in my opinion, make any apology for the verses, for they please me very much indeed.

I will now explain how I became acquainted that your account of Hafod was in the Printing Office.[1] I saw the advertisement just before I left Town at the end of Egerton's catalogue, and as I thought you might have made some trifling mistakes with our Welsh names, I offered to correct the Sheets in that respect and return them by the ensuing post. Mr Wilson sent me the whole at once, which I received on a Monday & returned them to him with a Letter on the Thursday following, *the very first post I could do so.* I am sorry it was printed before the copy I looked over was received, for in spite of Mr Lucas's accuracy there were several, though very trifling faults.[2] One inaccuracy ought to have been corrected; you say that the Cottage (now a most respectable Inn with better beds & Wines than at any other Inn, for they were both supplied from hence) at the Devil's

---

[1] G. Cumberland, *An Attempt to Describe Hafod, and the neighbouring scenes about the Bridge over the Funack, commonly called the Devil's Bridge, in the County of Cardigan. An ancient seat belonging to Thomas Johnes, Esq., Member for the County of Radnor*, London, 1796.

[2] Cumberland's work was printed by W. Wilson, St. Peter's Hill, Doctors' Commons, and sold by Thomas Egerton of Charing Cross whose business flourished between 1783 and 1837. Lucas probably read the proofs on behalf of the printers [P.A.H. Brown, *London Publishers and Printers, c. 1800-1870*, London, 1982].

AN ATTEMPT TO DESCRIBE

HAFOD,

AND THE NEIGHBOURING SCENES ABOUT THE BRIDGE OVER THE FUNACK, COMMONLY CALL-ED THE DEVIL's BRIDGE, IN THE COUNTY OF CARDIGAN.

AN ANCIENT SEAT BELONGING TO THOMAS JOHNES, ESQ. MEMBER FOR THE COUNTY OF RADNOR.

BY GEORGE CUMBERLAND.

Unvex'd with quarrels, undisturb'd with noise,
The country king his peaceful realm enjoys;
Cool grots, and living lakes, the flow'ry pride
Of meads, and streams that thro' the valley glide,
And shady groves, that easy sleep invite,
And, after toilsome days, a soft repose at night.
Dryden's Virgil.

LONDON:
Printed by W. Wilson, St. Peter's Hill, Doctors' Commons.
And sold by T. Egerton, Whitehall

MDCCXCVI.

Title page of George Cumberland's "Attempt"
(by permission of the National Library of Wales)

Bridge fronts Plinlimmon [sic]. That mountain cannot be seen from the House.[1]

I suggested in my letter to Mr Wilson that a good sale might be made of your work at the Devil's Bridge where crowds still increasing come every year. The work itself gave me very great pleasure, and considering it as the production of a Poet & Painter it has very few more embellishments than that good old dame, Nature, has herself given.

I wish you could persuade Long to accompany you once more to this place. It would prolong his life many years, and as yet I do not think Office has had its almost usual effect on him.[2]

My friend Anderson was here till late in the year & has been most active to serve me. Thro' his means my farm will be most respectable & all my Estates put on the best footing both for tenant & Landlord. My sole wish is to remain here, *Ducere sollicitae jucunda oblivia vitae.*[3] I never liked publick Life, and last winter I received such lessons on the score of friendship that I shall not soon forget. My heart will not suffer me to be a Misanthrope, but I find it too true that Mankind have but one Idol. I will therefore in order to be on a level, make myself a Priest of that Idolatory. I have not time to say more than that,

I am,

Yours always & ever,

T. Johnes

[1] On p.9 Cumberland had written of the Devil's Bridge Inn as 'a little public cottage built by the hospitable proprietor of Hafod'. A footnote, presumably added at the proof stage on receipt of this letter states that the author is now informed that the inn is 'comfortable' and 'enlarged'. According to the 1832 Hafod Sale Catalogue, Johnes spent some £2000 in building and stocking the inn and its appurtenances. The existing inn at Devil's Bridge, built largely under the direction of the 4th Duke of Newcastle, occupies the site of Johnes's building and incorporates some of the original features.

[2] Charles Long (1760-1838), Secretary of the Treasury and Paymaster General (1807-1826). Although a schemer and faceless functionary who it was said, '. . . used to slide in and out, and slide here and slide there —nobody knew where he went or when he came', he was widely acknowledged as a collector and man of taste. Cumberland and he had travelled together on the Continent and it was to Long that the former dedicated his '*Attempt to describe Hafod*'.

[3] Horace, *Satires, VI, 60;* [To drink in the pleasant draughts which make us forget life's troubles].

To James Edward Smith, in London   Linn. Soc. (Smith), 16, f.45

Hafod, Feb. 1, 1796

My dear Sir,

Many thanks for yours of the 21st. When I have the pleasure of seeing you I will inform you more fully of what I mentioned in my last Letter. It relates solely to my own personal affairs, but I found that whenever money comes in competition with what is commonly called friendship the last vanishes away like an airy vision leaving the Dross behind. I was more hurt & vext at being under (?) than at what concerned myself, for a few years must make them see clearly how much they have been mistaken.

We are exceedingly happy that you have settled everything so much to your satisfaction. I hope you will permit me to throw in an idea that may add some little to the money arrangements. You sometime since seemed to think of of writing a short Tour thro' those parts of Wales which are hitherto maiden, and of publishing them. Suppose you were to begin at Hereford, follow the Wye to Rhayader then take this place, the Devil's Bridge etc etc, and follow the Tivy down to Cardigan taking in, by way of Episode, the beautiful little valley down the River Irfon. If you approve of this skeleton Edwards will publish it for you, *and make no charges* except what it actually costs for Printing. I have some beautiful drawings by Smith, and can borrow more from Col. Greville, and from them we can select some which I must beg your acceptance of when engraved.[1] [2] So that I think with your writing & other embellishments I can answer for the sale being very great.

Mrs Johnes will execute your commission with very great pleasure & will order it to be sent by the first London vessel. I shall direct it to the care of our friend Chauntrell at the Custom House & give him a Line to desire he will inform you of its arrival in the River.

We have had fine weather, but very great storms of Wind & Rain & such thunder as I do not remember to have heard this season. I hear many Sheep have been killed by the lightening.

[1] John 'Warwick' Smith (1749-1831), landscape painter, who had visited Hafod several years previously with Robert Fulke Greville.
[2] The Hon. Robert Fulke Greville (d. 1824), equerry to King George III.

I am busy about my Garden & think I shall introduce some capital improvements in the oeconomy of forcing plants & fruits. I am as usual very sanguine. But my Gardener is as eager as I am myself, so that something I hope will come of it.

We wish for the summer that we may have the pleasure of seeing you & Mrs Smith; when all parties are determined to be pleased, nothing can prevent it.

Our united kind Compliments attend you, Miss Reeve and all your family.

I am, my dear Sir,

Yours very truly,

T. Johnes

To James Edward Smith, in London   Linn. Soc. (Smith), 16, f.49

Hafod, March 13, 1796

My dear Sir,

I have delayed thanking you for your last obliging Letter until I should have the pleasure of seeing your happiness announced in those faithful chronicles of the Times, (the) Newspapers. We all unite in every kind Compliment to you & Mrs Smith and wish you as much happiness as you yourselves expect. I shall only add as much as my own, and I have now had thanks to Heaven (and) enjoyed a tolerable spell of it.[1]

I thought once the events of this year would have thrown some alloy to it, but when I came here, I only laughed at what if I had been from

---

[1] Smith married Pleasance Reeve at Lowestoft on March 1st, 1796. Lady Smith was subsequently to survive forty-nine years of widowhood and live to be one hundred and three years old. The couple had no children.

home would have seriously affected me. I have nothing of any moment to reproach myself with, so I am content. You shall know all when we have the pleasure of seeing you here.

I have long ago read Zimmerman with great pleasure; but have you read Lavater's journal? Few will have the boldness to do what he has done. I only read a page now & then, for I appear in my own eyes so little and good for nothing. It is printed for Cadell in 2 small volumes.[1]

Mrs Johnes had ordered a Tureen before your letter arrived and it is on its way as the enclosed bill of parcels will shew. I ordered it to be directed to the care of Mr Chauntrell at the Custom House and have this post desired him to forward it to you at Hammersmith by water.

The *Strelitzia* and *Illusium floridanum* are in fine flower. The little Girl has drawn the first most incomparably well indeed. So much so that I mean to frame it.

When the Cabinet maker sends the Cabinet of Insects that you have been so good to promise her, I wish it may be sent by West & Goulding's waggon to Builth, directed to the care of Mrs Jones, Crown Inn, Builth, as that is the most speedy & convenient mode of sending things here.

My friend Liston is also married, and to an old flame also. I have not heard if he has brought us anything from Constantinople. I fear not by his silence. He is going Ambassador to America.

I wished for you here during the dry & sharp weather to enjoy one of the grandest sights I ever witnessed. I took the opportunity of the great dryness to set fire to some mountains covered with Furze. The wind was very high and the acres of Flame as they rapidly ascended must have been something like a grand eruption of Lava, for it ran up in streams of fire & flame. The wind dissipated the Smoke and when you went on the Top of the Hill to the windward side, you appeared as above the Clouds, which every now & then a sudden Gust divided

---

[1] Johann Georg von Zimmerman (1728-1795), Swiss philosopher whose *Uber die Einsamkeit* and *Vom Nationalstolz* were widely translated. Johann Kaspar Lavater (1741-1801) produced a number of indifferent and largely-forgotten poetical and mystical works. His work on physiognomy, *Physiognomische Fragmente zur Beforderung der Menschenkenntnis und Menschenliebe*, found enthusiastic admirers throughout Europe, more perhaps for its handsome appearance and quality illustrations than its rather desultory contents.

& gave you a Glimpse of Paradise below. The Smoke was grand & put me in mind of one of the lines of Virgil's description of Orion:

Ingrediturque solo, et caput inter nubila condit. [1]

We all unite in kind Compliments to you, Mrs Smith and all your family.

I am, my dear Sir,

Yours ever,

T. Johnes

To George Cumberland, at Egham, Surrey   Add. MS. 36497, f.98

Hafod, Sunday [1796]

My dear Sir,

I thank you much for yours of the 1st and am very glad your description was not printed before the few corrections I made arrived, as some were essential. I have not a doubt of its success, and will lay any wager the first edition is sold within twelve months.

I wish my six to be neatly bound, tho' not in the highest extravagance of the mode. And I will answer for the sale of 50, if you send them to me by the Shrewsbury Waggon, for the concourse of strangers to the Devil's Bridge is immense. Last Summer there were 40 in one day; some for the place, but more I believe for the *Wine.* [2]

I hope you are mistaken in Long, for I think he is the only man that office will not spoil. I have lately had a confirmation of my opinion in a letter received a few days since, which contained a great deal of very good nonsense, and I believe it was the first letter of the sort ever written from the Treasury Chambers. I have known many secretaries of the Treasury and really I think him as yet an exception to the general rule.

[1] Virgil, *Aeneid, X, 767.* [Walking upon the ground his head in the base of the clouds]

[2] Which was of the highest quality since it was supplied from the cellars of Hafod, to which Thomas Martyn's travel diary gratefully testifies [N.L.W. MS 1340c].

Hafod: Tylogau Bridge by John 'Warwick' Smith
(by permission of the National Library of Wales)

When your work is ready, if you will send him one he will frank it to me, by which means I shall have the pleasure of receiving it very soon. Those you send for me to dispose of, I think should be in boards, and let me know what price. I think if the people at the Devil's Bridge have six pence profit on each, it would make them more careful and more anxious to sell them.

Monday

I am hard at work on old Froissart, and think I shall have the first volume ready for the press by Christmas. But every fine day I cannot remain at home, as I am anxious to see my Garden & Farm. By the bye my friend Dr Anderson has been very busy in making a Garden for my little Girl, that is something in the pensile manner of Gardening that we have heard so much of in Semiramis's time. It will be very beautiful & very surprising. I am beginning this day on a new walk to it, and shall probably set about in the summer the walk up the river above the stone bridge, which so much pleased you. I must also change the walk over the Millbrook, to make it correspond with your description. [1]

[1] During the course of his description of the estate Cumberland inferred that Johnes proposed (at his suggestion) to erect a 'druidical temple' on the domed hill at

We have had such a continuance of Rain that I am all cascades, but this morning it is a very sharp frost. My fruit trees are in flower so I dread the consequences. The *Strelitzia* is also in flower, and most beautiful.

I am interrupted. The ladies desire their best Compliments to you.

I am,

Dear Sir,

Yours ever,

T. Johnes

N.L.W. Dolaucothi MSS. Vol. 16, f.19

Circular Electioneering letter. [1]   Cardigan, May 21, 1796

Sir,

At one of the most respectable & numerous meetings ever held at Cardigan for the purposes of nominating a proper person to represent the County at the next general Election, I had the Honor of being named.

I take therefore the Liberty of soliciting your Vote & interest. Although a Canvass has been carried on by Lieut. Col. Vaughan for a considerable time, I have never till this day canvassed one person. [2]

Pant Melyn. This artefact appears on Blake's map accompanying the text. Although Johnes had made enquiries of Harrison, the Chester architect, respecting both building materials and plans, there is no evidence for the 'druidical temple' ever having been built.

[1] There had been no poll in Cardiganshire since 1741 and when Lord Lisburne of Trawscoed retired there was considerable consternation at the threat of a contested election when Edward Loveden of Gogerddan and Thomas Powell of Nanteos united against the traditional Trawscoed/Hafod coalition. Despite Loveden's attempt to persuade his son to contest the seat, a candidate could not be found and Johnes gave up his Radnorshire seat to come in for Cardiganshire which he managed to hold unopposed until his death. [R.G. Thorne, *History of Parliament, The Commons, 1790-1820*, London, 1986].

[2] Vaughan, Lisburne's son, stood aside for Johnes in the county and was himself returned for the Cardigan Boroughs.

I thought it a respect due to the County, and was anxious that it might have its free choice on such an important occasion.

From the honorable manner in which I have been nominated, I have not any doubts but that the choice so loudly expressed this day will be confirmed on the day of Election. I shall make no professions of my attachment to this County, for my residence among you so many years must have offered many opportunities of observing it; even the Honor I have this day received cannot increase it. But I feel most sensibly the very strong proofs of friendship from so large a Body of independent gentlemen and nothing but Death can ever obliterate them from my memory.

I have the Honor to remain, Sir,

Your most obedient humble Servant,

T. Johnes

To George Cumberland, at Egham, Surrey   Add. MS. 36498, f.98

Hafod, June 17, 1796

Dear Sir,

I should sooner have thanked you for yours of the 27th May, had I not been in a continual bustle. Loveden seems to have completely done for himself. He has lost his own seat, & by his crooked politicks has enabled two to gain seats which he was most anxious to keep out. He was indifferent who came in for this County & Town, provided Mr Vaughan & myself were excluded.[1] No County ever behaved

[1] Edward Loveden Loveden F.R.S. (d. 1822) of Buscot, Oxon. and Gogerddan, Cardiganshire. Though described by Wraxhall as a man whose demeanour, '...bespoke a substantial yeoman rather than a person of education and condition' and elsewhere as an almost inarticulate and unknown country gentleman, he was in fact a classical scholar of some accomplishment and a correspondent with many of the leading figures of his time. [See, R. Mitchison, *Agricultural Sir John, The Life of Sir John Sinclair of Ulbster*, London, 1962; R.J. Colyer, The Pryse Family of Gogerddan and the decline of a great estate, 1800-1960, *Welsh History Review, 9, 1979*.]

more handsomely nor has any one ever received more personal marks of attachment, which as long as I retain, he may vent his malice, but can never carry it into effect. No one ever took less pains for a seat in Parliament than myself, and had I not been so honorably called on I should have remained here in quiet planting my Cabbages. Nor has any Election cost so little, considering there was a sort of Contest. A very few hundreds will pay for all. My opponent does not come off so cheap. But of this more when we meet.[1]

I shall hold my Parliament here, for I told my Friends I thought I might be more useful to the County at Hafod than at Westminster. Therefore if you take an Excursion this Summer I need not say we shall be all happy in seeing you.

We are in high beauty, tho' it is cold uncomfortable weather; and the Crops look well.

You will be surprised when I tell you there are two diligences as I hear coming to the Devil's Bridge & Aberystwith from Leominster & Ludlow by different roads. We shall be genteel, but *ware necks*, for I should think the Passengers underwent a service of danger.

The Ladies send their Compliments to you.

I am, Dear Sir,

Yours ever,

T. Johnes

[1]Geraint H. Jenkins, himself no mean cricketer, has elegantly summarised the local political scene in Johnes's day as follows : 'Welsh politics resembled a gentlemanly game of cricket, with powerful landowners occupying the crease for long periods, their agents or sheriffs acting as umpires, the lesser gentry tossing up donkey drops and enfranchised freeholders and tenants chasing leather in the outfield'. [*The Foundations of Modern Wales, 1642-1780*, Oxford, 1987]

To George Cumberland, at Egham, Surrey   Add. MS. 36498, f.112

Hafod, July 17, 1796

Dear Sir,

I had the pleasure of yours of the 11th yesterday and as I think I may be of some service to you in respect to the object of your journey into Wales I answer it directly. [1]

The only Map I know of Pembrokeshire is a very old one which you may get at any Mapsellers. It is comprized in a large Map of South Wales, and another on a reduced scale from it, but too old to be of any use in pointing out late improvements.

The Ground about the new Town of Milford belongs I believe to Sir Wm. Hamilton; & his supposed Heir Charles Greville is laying it out for him. I do not believe you will get any bargains from either of them. However you will do well to see it, and you will then form your own observations on the spot. [2] But I would recommend your staying a day at Carmarthen, which you must pass thro' whichever road you come from London, and examining the Country round about. Dr Anderson is wild about it, and says he never (saw) such a situation for Trade, on a fine tide navigable river, & a beautiful plentiful Country with Coal & Lime round about. He says it does not at present know its own value, but in time must find it; and is not well pleased with my offering for Sale an Estate close to it. [3] The fact is; I bought that Estate in order to get another in this County which is as convenient & contiguous as that is distant, and mean to dispose of it. I have offered it by private Contract but whether from the Scarcity of money my

---

[1] Cumberland had shown interest in purchasing a modest estate in Wales.

[2] Sir William Hamilton had come into his Pembrokeshire properties by way of his first marriage to Anne, daughter of Richard Skrine of Wansley in 1768. While serving as Envoy Extraordinary at Naples he appointed his nephew Charles Francis Greville as agent in charge of the development of Milford harbour, for which he had obtained an Act of Parliament in 1790. [D. Miles, *Portrait of Pembrokeshire*, London, 1984]

[3] Carmarthen had been an important port and trading centre since medieval times serving as a point of entry for foreign luxury items and for the export of fleeces, hides, corn, cloth, slates, bark, timber, etc. With the growth of tin and iron manufactures and of the printing trade, it maintained its commercial importance throughout the nineteenth century. [J. and V. Lodwick, *The Story of Carmarthen*, Carmarthen, 1972]

price has not been accepted. I shall sell it in parcels this Autumn by Auction, and I would recommend you looking at it. The name of it is Penybank, and Mr Herbert Lloyd at Carmarthen will give you all particulars. There is much wood at Penybank farm, and a fine situation for a House.[1] Why I advise Carmarthenshire to Pembroke, is this; for what reason I know not the estates in the Vale of Towy which are all very rich Land sell for under 30 years purchase.

But as you will probably come to Llandovery & go down that Vale to Carmarthen, I am but 40 miles from Llandovery (and) 45 miles from Carmarthen so I hope you will let us see you, and if I can be of any Service to you in your intended purchase you may command me. Lands in this Country sell for 30 years.[2] There is a pretty Estate to be disposed of near Llanelly, and as there is Coal underneath & near the Sea, & the navigable river Loughor, I do not think the price asked dear.

I know of no good account of any county of Sth. Wales. Monmouthshire has just been published by Mr David Williams, with engravings by the Rev. Mr Gardner. They are not worthy the Book, or the places.[3]

Dr Anderson is not come here yet, and I much fear he will be delayed longer.

I shall be very happy to see your brother here, but he will find Sheep & stock of all sorts immoderately dear. I never saw such a rise in two years; more than double. It must be owing to the increase of Luxury.

There have been many strangers here, and at the Devil's Bridge— it is all the vogue—and from those I saw I heard universal praises of your book. But our weather is so bad, it must be bad tour making.

I shall order your Book, and am sure to read it with pleasure.

I must now conclude,

I am, Dear Sir,

Yours ever,

T. Johnes

---

[1] Penybank, near Abergwili some two miles from Carmarthen, subsequently became the property of the Morris family, the Carmarthen bankers.

[2] i.e. thirty times the annual rental per acre.

[3] David Williams, *A History of Monmouthshire*, London, 1796.

To George Rose   P.R.O. 30/8/148, ff.170-1

Cardigan, Aug. 12, 1796

My dear Rose,

I came here to the Assizes two days ago, and from a Conversation
I have just had with Mr Vaughan he tells me his father Lord Lisburne
is exceeding ill, and I believe from his Conversation dangerously so.
Should this be the case & he dies, I shall hope that my former request
to succeed him, that the Honors he holds in this County may devolve
to me will be granted. Pray have the goodness to mention this to Mr
Pitt, least he may have other applications.[1]

Ever & ever yours,

T. Johnes

To James Edward Smith, in Norwich   Linn. Soc. (Smith), 16, f.63

Mr Knight's, Whitehall

Sunday, Feb. 19, 1797

My dear Sir,

In my hurry at leaving Hafod, I fear I left behind me your last
Letter. However as I was writing to Dr Anderson when it came I sent
yours to him in mine and I hope you have had a satisfactory answer
from him.

Our dear Girl was getting so much better about a fortnight ago,
that her mother & myself thought we might go to Hafod for ten days
as I had much to do & accordingly your letter was forwarded to me

---

[1] Johnes's application was successful and on the death of Wilmot, 1st Earl of
Lisburne, in 1799 he became Lord Lieutenant and Custos Rotulorum for
Cardiganshire.

there from Bath. Just as I was in the midst of my business I received such letters from my friend (at whose house I am) who has acted a very friendly & manly part, and from Mr Troward my Solicitor, that I was obliged to set out directly & came here Fryday early. My business was to prevent the destruction of *all* the Timber at Croft, which perhaps you may have seen advertised. I am sorry to say our attempts by consiliatory measures have been ineffectual, and altho' the most extraordinary calumnies have been told & believed of me, yet I left nothing undone before I was forced to file a bill in Chancery & tomorrow an Injunction will be moved for.

This may perhaps cause my offers to be accepted, which in fact are their own, but they would not accept of my security. 'I could such a tale unfold'.[1] It has had this effect that it has restored ease to my mind on this Subject, which I confess it has not enjoyed a long time, and I have the satisfaction of thinking that I have been forced into these measures in justice to myself & Child. If I live Time will shew the justice of the portrait they have drawn of me.

I saw Sir Jos. Banks very well this morning, & shall go there tonight.

Dr Anderson is very well. He had sent me a lock of the *Golden Fleece*, which I suppose you have seen the account of in the Papers. It is very curious & just the colour of raw silk, a bright gold colour.[2]

My time has been so taken up by the Grimgribber gentlemen that I have not had time to see anyone else.[3]

I beg my Compliments to Mrs Smith & all your family.

I am, my dear Sir,

Yours ever,

T. Johnes

---

[1] 'I could a tale unfold whose lightest word,
    would harrow up thy soul, freeze thy young blood...'
    [*Hamlet, I, V, 13*].
[2] A reference to the order of knighthood rather than Jason's celebrated acquisition?
[3] i.e. by lawyers and attorneys.

To Matthew Boulton, in Birmingham   N.L.W. Fac. Vol. 77, f.25

Hafod, Rhayader Bag,

Dec. 2, 1797

Dear Sir,

I am exceedingly obliged to you for your letter of the 13th Nov. But you made a mistake in directing it to me at Dolecothy, by which means I had not the pleasure of receiving it until a few days ago.

The person who wrote to you about the ore at Dolecothy, which is my brother in law's place (Mrs Johnes' brother) is a distant relation of mine. I am very sorry your opinion of that ore agrees so completely with that of Dr Pearson to whom my friend Mr Long gave some last summer. That place is however very worthy of the visit of some other miner. It was worked by the Romans, and must have been of very considerable importance from the appearance of the Hillocks, from their having carried the River Cothy for many miles by a small canal probably to wash the ore, and from their having a military station near to it. Last year there were many gold ornaments discovered in ploughing a field, which I gave Mr Knight of Whitehall and they are in his Museum. Before I parted with this Estate to my Brother in Law, I granted a lease to the late Alderman Townsend of these old works.[1] His death put a stop to their working, but they found Cobalt, tho' in small quantities not more than a few pounds, before they forfeited the Lease from want of a sufficient quantity of Workmen employed. Sir Joseph Banks has seen this spot frequently & would be able to give a much better account of them than I can. The name of the Hill where they are situated is called Cogové.[2]

I shall be very sorry if any Tax is laid upon Iron; and as I always thought you have done more for the prosperity of this Country than all the orators of the House of Commons, I shall on all occasions wish to serve you as by that means I think I am serving the country.[3] But

[1] Chauncey Townsend, M.P. and mining entrepreneur [see W.J. Lewis, *Lead Mining in Wales*, Cardiff, 1967].

[2] For the Ogofau (Cogové) Mines see, *The Dolaucothi Gold Mines; a Report from the Archaeology Unit, St. David's College, Lampeter in collaboration with University College, Cardiff and the National Trust,* 1984.

[3] Pitts proposal, in 1796, to impose a tax on coal at the pit head and an excise of 20/- per ton on pig iron in order to raise money to finance the French wars, upset the

I am detained here by the long illness of my only Child. Thank God however she is better, tho' she recovers very slowly. I am under great obligations to your neighbour Mr Galton Jnr. whose kindness in respect to her I shall never forget. He will tell you of my hermitage here.

I am, dear Sir,

Yours ever,

T. Johnes

To George Cumberland, at Egham, Surrey   Add. MS. 36498, f.214

Hafod, March 25, 1798

My Dear Sir,

I had the pleasure of your Letter a few days ago.

I am very little acquainted with the Country about Carmarthen, as to its owners, or its value; indeed I know not where Abersannau Estate lies. I expect however a friend of mine who lives at Carmarthen this week, when I will make every inquiry from him & let you know the result.

The House & farm of Penybank is now to be sold. The present rent is 112£ and there is a good deal of Timber on it. But Mr Herbert Lloyd of Carmarthen will give you further particulars. There are other farms also undisposed of. But the situation in Penybank is very pretty & within 2 miles of a most excellent market Town. You will however find very few Estates to be sold with old rents. The times, however miserable in other respects, have been excellent for Farmers.[1]

I agree with you on the madness of persons investing their money in the Funds for one per Cent more than they can have from Land.

industrial interest. After intensive lobbying he was dissuaded from this measure and as an alternative caused a heavy duty to be levied on imports of iron, thereby affording additional protection to the ironmasters [T.S. Ashton, *Iron and Steel in the Industrial Revolution*, London, 1924].

[1] With the eventual falling-in of the early eighteenth century leases for lives, landowners, aware that the value of money was now falling, were tending to offer

Land must be more durable than paper, and for this miserable one per Cent they risque their principal. I speak feelingly for from the difficulties of borrowing on Land, I may probably be a considerable loser in some purchases I lately made. When you see your Broker I wish you would ask him if he knows any of the great insurance offices or other bodies who lend money on Mortgage that will advance from 40 to 50,000£ on an Estate with a *net* rental of 3200£. Or if that cannot be had, if any of his Employers choose to change their Security from the Funds to Land, on covenanting to replace it there in a fixed time etc.

Hafod flourishes my dear Sir, in spite of these eventful times, and added to them our domestick misfortunes; for our dear Girl has been ill these 18 months with a Curvature of her Spine. We have been in very great distress, and have remained with her ever since last May; Thank God at present we again indulge our hopes & look forward for warmer weather with the greatest anxiety.

As she is certainly much better within these last 2 months, I am indifferent to other plagues. I should then more sensibly feel my Mother's conduct, who urged on by her advisers are endeavoring to pillage me as much as possible, and perhaps also should be more sensible of the present dangerous state of publick affairs. They are very bad indeed. Nor do I see how we can get out of them without suffering such losses as we shall never be ourselves again.

I have been busy planting & farming; by tomorrow I shall have planted upwards of 600,000 Trees this season. I am more & more attached here, and only wish to preserve my Wife & Child & then never to move from hence, for I am quite sick of Publick affairs in every sense of them.

Mrs Johnes etc. desire their best Compliments to you.

I am, my Dear Sir,

Yours always,

T. Johnes

leases of 7, 14 or 21 years, or, in some cases, annual tenancies. By creating agreements of relatively short duration, they were enabled to effect regular rent increases and thereby to enjoy a share of the substantial profits earned by farmers throughout the Napoleonic Wars. Johnes here implies that estates sold with the 'old rents' could be purchased more cheaply than those where high rent, short-term tenancy agreements prevailed.

To James Edward Smith, in Norwich   Linn. Soc. (Smith), 16, f.79

Hafod, Thursday [May, 1798]

My dear Sir,

You will probably see Mr Abernethy as soon as this Letter, for he went away from here very early and I gave him your direction.[1] He has also that of young Jones as he thinks he can give him some useful hints about the Stays. Dr Davis came to us Monday night and he is just gone.

We have been very much pleased with Mr Abernethy, who encourages us to hope our poor Girl will do very well. Should it not disperse of itself he will return to make the Puncture, but that may be two or three months, so my dear friend there is an end of our Castles in the Air respecting Matlock. I wish you & Mrs Smith would content yourselves with *our* waters, and keep the engagement here instead of Matlock.[2] It would make us all very happy.

I hope Jones will come as soon as he has seen Mr Abernethy for a new Stays is much wanted.[3] I say nothing of the Child, for you will have it so much clearer from Abernethy. He has left us written directions which we must rigidly follow. I hope everything will turn out well. Pangloss's doctrine is a fine one.[4]

The issues were healed in time, or they would not have been allowed. However the poor thing does not gain much for she is to have a perpetual blister near where they were. But Abernethy will tell you all this, and the *pourquoi*.

Mrs Johnes is not well, but would not own it when we had advice here. She says she shall soon get well when her daughter recovers.

[1] John Abernethy F.R.S. (1764-1831), anatomist and surgeon, among whose various contributions to practical surgery was the introduction of a method of opening lumbar abscesses without the admission of air. Hence Johnes's interest in securing his advice in the treatment of his daughter's spinal condition.

[2] For much of his life Smith suffered from inflammatory disorders from which he sought relief in the waters of Matlock. The Johnes family had seemingly been planning to join the Smiths at the Derbyshire spa.

[3] Without her spinal stays Mariamne was unable to walk at this stage of her illness. Writing to his wife from Hafod in October 1797 Smith noted that, 'The machine has done wonders. Jones the maker is here & has managed her very well, but he is a drunkard....'. [Linn. Soc. (Smith), 16, f.73]

[4] See Voltaire, *Candide*, 1758. Against all evidence to the contrary Candide's tutor Dr Pangloss steadfastly maintains the optimist view that everything is arranged for the best in the best of all possible worlds.

I am desperate stupid myself; and it all appears like a frightful dream which I cannot unravel.

I write to Pitcairn & Knight this post. They have both been very kind.

It is a great comfort to me, that as those from whom I had a right to expect kindness fall off, I find others who make ample amends, and the more flattering to self-love because one hopes it may be owing to personal qualities. Among all, my good Friend I can never forget your great kindness & affection, *Dum memor ipse mei, dum spiritus hos regit artus.* [1]

All our kind Compliments attend you.

I am, yours very truly,

T. Johnes

To James Edward Smith, in Norwich   Linn. Soc. (Smith), 16, f.81

Hafod, Monday [June, 1798]

My good friend,

Our poor sufferer continues the blisters which have created more irritation than they should have done had Mr Williams not been so conceited, but attended to them as he ought to have done. They are now reduced; the ointment much lowered, and tho' they discharge very well have not much pain. But she cannot wear the Stays and without them she cannot walk. Young Jones will return here in about a Fortnight or three weeks when I hope she may again experience their benefit. She has been down these last two days to dinner.

This year will be a memorable year to me for independant of all our sorrows on our poor Child's account, and the heavy pressure of my own affairs, we are now in the greatest distress least I may be ordered to Ireland, for my Regt. I find has offered itself, and being at Liverpool will I suppose of course be sent over. If so, I must go, for disgrace attends on one side & worse than death on the other. I was

---

[1] Virgil, *Aeneid, iv, 335* [While I have memory and breath governs these limbs]

not even consulted; for tho' I disapprove exceedingly of the measure as being the total destruction of the Militia, and of the principles of its constitution, yet under the *existing circumstances* I should have been puzzled how to have acted.[1] That Lord Buckingham and Lord Hertford who have such large possessions in Ireland should wish to go there to preserve them with their Regiments I can easily conceive, but why my Officers who have not a foot of Land there should be so eager I know not. They will be kept there during the War and sufficiently repent of their rashness. I shall throw up my commission the very first moment I can without incurring disgrace, for surely nothing could have happened more unfortunate in my present situation. The little Girl does not know it & if I do go I shall say I am only going to join my Regt. for a month at Liverpool, so I hope she will be ignorant of where I am.

I cannot write more, for I have many letters to answer that I have suffered to Remain too long in hand.

Mrs Johnes etc unite with me in every kind Compliment to Mrs Smith & all your family.

I am yours very truly,

T. Johnes

---

[1] The *Militia Act* (1757) emphasised that the local militias were to be deployed solely for the purposes of home defence, hence Johnes's disapproval. In 1798, however, numerous militia units volunteered to serve against the insurrectionists in Ireland. Moreover, throughout the Napoleonic Wars militiamen frequently volunteered to serve in the regular army and in 1813 it was enacted that militia units could henceforth serve overseas alongside regular troops.

To James Edward Smith, in Norwich   Linn. Soc. (Smith), 16, f.85

Hafod, July 7, 1798

My dear Sir,

I thank you much for yours of the 2nd which I received on Thursday. My plots begin to thicken desperately, and I am now in very great distress about my Regiment. I have this moment a letter from my Lieut. Colonel to say that out of 960 men only 300 would embark and that out of the rest 200 had mutinied on their march to Ormskirk!! Genl. Grinfield marched against them with the Garrison, all the Cavalry & 2 field pieces which soon made them go on. Many were in Irons and tried by a Court Martial, but he did not know the result. He himself was returned from bad weather to a bay in the Mersey & the other transports to one at the mouth of the Dee. All this business has been most wretchedly conducted, and after having commanded the Regiment for 20 years (I believe with credit), I must probably leave it disgraced. I fancy Mr Ravenscroft by never sending me the proposal to serve in Ireland to forward to his Royal Highness the Duke, which in my opinion he should have done, wished to have all the *Glory* himself, and a fine Glory he has made of it!!![1]

I really have no patience with the folly of mankind, nor what wretchedness they cause by it. I am fit only to live like a wolf among my Mountains. I had prepared everything to set out for Dublin, but I suppose now this *detachment* will disembark, for what is to become of the refractory two thirds on shore?

Fortunately I had written last Monday to the War Office to know if my Regiment was to embark or not, as I was totally in the dark and expect very impatiently the answer today. If anything particular is in it you shall know.

Dr Davies came here last night. He only saw her by candle light but thinks she is not worse. He has not seen her this morning. Thank God for this, but this has been a famous year for me. Croft is *en train*, so there we brighten a little, notwithstanding it lowers in other quarters.[2]

[1] Frederick Augustus, Duke of York, commander-in-chief of the armed forces 1795-1809. Ravenscroft was Johnes's lieutenant colonel and Fenwick (presumably) a War Office functionary. By this time, the Irish rebellion was running out of steam so that there was little need for Johnes's regiment to cross the Irish Sea and its commander could remain at home with minimal loss of face.

[2] i.e. the sale of Croft Castle.

The little Girl thinks I am only going to be reviewed at Liverpool and this almost distracts her. I hope the regiment will not go. I shall certainly resign the Command the very first moment I can without discredit.

Pray read Mr H. Walpole's correspondence. It delights me and raises him most exceedingly in my opinion. He is (from) Norfolk too.

Adieu for the present. All our united kind Loves attend you.

I am,

Yours always,

T. Johnes

Fenwick has never given my letter to the War Office—Why I know not, unless to add to my vexations.

To James Edward Smith, in Norwich   Linn. Soc. (Smith), 16, f.87

Hafod, Monday, [July 1798]

Thank you my dear Sir for your short letter enclosing the old Drunkard's which I got on Saturday. I have had another more impertinent, in which the rascal offers to pay for the wine he drank here!!!

I have had no news about my Regt. so my distress still continues. I hope that the detachment will be countermanded. As the Militia is completely ruined, at least the principle on which it was originally founded is destroyed, I shall resign the first moment I can without discredit. I fear we are got into an inextricable Abyss, and the further we go on the the more we shall sink, until we are overwhelmed.[1]

I read yesterday Mr Fellowes' book, and like it much. But particularly from what he says of St. Paul & his Epistles.[2] I never

[1] Despite the protestations of the King, Johnes resigned his command early in 1799.

[2] Probably a reference to *A Picture of Christian Philosophy or Illustration of the Character of Jesus*, by Robert Fellowes (1771-1847). The work appeared in 1798 and rapidly went through four editions.

could comprehend them, and regret much the whole of recorded religion was not simply confined to the Four Gospels which are fully adequate if you follow them for your happiness in this & to ensure it in another world. I have been always delighted with their Simplicity, and was happy at seeing what I feel so very well expressed.

Our weather is now very cold & heavy Showers. This is good for my Turnips, but my Hay will suffer.

I have had an excellent letter from Mr Galton. I will copy in my next what he says of you, but I have left writing too late today & must conclude.

Dr Davies went away Saturday. He does not think our poor Child worse, but rather better. He wrote a very long letter to Abernethy. The Tumour in the thigh is much lessened but has gone higher up, under the Belly, and I fancy from what dropt from him that the Abscess will form there. A young boy is to have a similar one opened in Carmarthen this day who also has a Curvature of the Spine, but the Dr says his health is not so good as our Girl's and seemed doubtful of the event.

Our united kind Love attends you all.

I am, my dear Sir,

Yours ever,

T. Johnes

To James Edward Smith, in Norwich   Linn. Soc. (Smith), 16, f.92

Hafod, Sept. 2nd, 1798

My dear Sir,

I had the pleasure of yours yesterday inclosing Mr Voght's letter to you. I am exceedingly obliged to you for it; but, my good friend, you have painted us with the Colours of friendship indeed. His prices of Wine are very satisfactory, and in the course of a post or two I will return you his Letter & one which I shall thank you to inclose to him containing my orders.

I was very sorry Mr Gurney made so short a stay for I was never better pleased with any one at so short an acquaintance. I liked one of his daughters very much, but it was all such hurry I could scarce speak to all of them. They travelled in the proper stile, determined to be pleased with everything, the only mode that could have made their number of Travellers any way comfortable.[1]

I am afraid poor Dr Anderson's health is but very indifferent. He complained much in his last Letter, and I have not heard (for) some posts. I am exceedingly sorry for it, and wish anything I could do or say would relieve him. He will not come here, tho' I have repeatedly asked him, and I am sure it would do him good. I have had a very handsome letter from Mr Pennant inclosing one to Dr Anderson which will probably bring me an answer this or the next post to forward to Mr Pennant.[2]

Mr Warner seems as rapid a publisher as he is a walker & I have no doubt but next Spring will produce an account of his Summer Travels.[3]

I did not much like the Company he brought with him. However, they staid but one day. I really think you should hasten your Tour, or indeed you will be forestalled. You must press young Anderson for I do not think he seems ever satisfied with his own performances which is not the way to get forward.

We have been quite alone since the 16th, as the two Sisters are gone to Dolecothy, but have seen different parties, some pleasant, others to the contrary.[4]

Did I mention that many of our Russian seeds were come up? I hope we shall have some nutmegs as Charlotte brought us some fine seeds.

We have had the finest harvest weather possible. Yesterday it rained a little, but from the Barometer I fear we shall have a great

[1] The Norwich banker John Gurney and his seven daughters were holidaying at Aberystwyth. The daughter to whom Johnes appears to have taken a fancy was probably Elizabeth who, as Mrs Elizabeth Fry, would eventually achieve celebrity from her philanthropic activities among the women in Newgate prison.

[2] Thomas Pennant (1726-1798), antiquary and naturalist. Pennant's health was by now rapidly failing and he died on 16 December.

[3] Rev. Richard Warner (1763-1857) of Bath, antiquary and divine among whose voluminous writings on topographical, religious and antiquarian subjects were included *A Walk through Wales* and *A Second Walk through Wales*, both enjoying considerable contemporary popularity.

[4] Charlotte and Eliza, Jane Johnes's sisters.

deal. I hope it may clear when Mr Knight comes here. He has lost his Mother. I expect him and the D. of Norfolk this or next week. I look to it with pleasure & hope not to be disappointed.

Our poor Girl goes on much as usual. Dr Davies & Williams think her general health mended. The Back is flatter but the Tumour remains in *status quo* and she cannot walk tho' she constantly wears Jones's machine. I hear of many recovering, but we seem to stand still. That confounded Journey to Bath instead of London was our ruin. I meant it for the best & was every way disappointed.

Should the French get a footing in Ireland we shall be near neighbours.[1]

Our united Compliments to Mrs Smith etc.

I am, my dear Sir,

Yours most truly,

T. Johnes

Have you ever read Eton's survey of Turkey? It has amused me much. What a set of rascals they must be!!![2]

---

[1] A French force, organised by Wolfe Tone and commanded by General Humbert had landed at Killala, Co. Mayo on August 22 only to surrender after several skirmishes. On October 12 another French unit of some 3000 men under the direct command of Tone was defeated by a British squadron in a naval battle on Lough Swilly. The capture and suicide of Tone brought down the final curtain on the rising of the United Irishmen. [John Ranelagh, *Ireland, an Illustrated History*, London, 1981]

[2] William Eton's *A Survey of the Turkish Empire* was published in 1798 by Cadell and Davies of London. A French translation appeared the following year.

To James Edward Smith, in Norwich Linn. Soc. (Smith), 16, f.94

Hafod, Sept. 22, 1798

My dear Sir,

I am very much obliged for yours of the 14th. I have not yet had a satisfactory answer about my wine in Bottles, and the moment I have I will return Mr Voght's letter, and one to him which I shall request you to forward. I used to import all my French wines in Bottle, and it appears very strange that wines from Hamburg should be excepted. They say it is but I have written for further explanation. The duty indeed [sic] of 4 Shillings per dozen is indeed a prohibition except for very extravagant fellows like myself.

My little Girl desires her best thanks for the biscuits which in *due time* will I dare say arrive here safe. She continues much the same as when I last wrote, but Mrs Johnes said yesterday she thought the Tumour much abated. She cannot however walk without support in the smallest degree. I look to good dame Nature's operations with great anxiety & hope.

Mr Galton has been with us these two or three days. The more I see of him the more I like him. He leaves us tomorrow. We have had many Visitors, among the rest the Duke of Norfolk & Mr Knight so that assessed Taxes and all the associations armed and unarmed do not keep people at home. Indeed Aberystwith has been fuller this Summer than ever known.[1]

Pray have you seen the *Philosophical Magazine*? It is a new one, and seems a very excellent collection.[2] Among other discoveries it mentions a method to create Germination in Seeds ever so old, by oxygenated muriatick acid. Jacquin at Vienna has made grow seeds of 100 & 120 years old. 20 or 30 years is nothing to this powerful acid. I wonder they do not try it on the human species. Who knows what effect it may have. Pray look at this magazine & see it. I shall certainly

---

[1] Charles Howard, 11th Duke of Norfolk (1746-1815) was celebrated principally for his profound aversion to soap and water and clean linen. That 'damned dirty devil Jockey of Norfolk', despite (or because of) his habitual slovenliness, was a close friend of the Prince of Wales and the Dukes of Clarence and York.

[2] *The Philosophical Magazine, comprehending the various branches of Science, the Liberal and Fine arts, Agriculture, Manufacturers and Commerce*, ran from 1798-1813, and continued under various other titles into the present century.

try it (in) the Spring & doubt not of raising tomatoes and Nutmegs in Abundance. I wish you would inquire from some of your Chemical friends if this discovery could be made cheap enough for us common farmers to besprinkle our Turnip seeds with, as it would effectually I should imagine prevent Fly or Slug.

If it should be applied to the Human race, will the Male or female require it—or both? You will see also in one of Roses (?) magazines that a Frenchman thinks he can make people live to the ages of the Patriarchs. If so, these two discoveries united will be an admirable remedy to make amends for all the late depopulations in various parts of the World.[1]

Mrs Johnes & Min unite with me in best Compliments to Mrs Smith.

I am, my dear Sir,

Yours ever,

T. Johnes

To George Cumberland, at Egham, Surrey   Add. MS. 36498, f.272

Hafod, Jan. 21, 1799

My dear Sir,

I am very much obliged to you for your friendly Letter which I had the pleasure of receiving a few posts ago. I have been here two years next May constantly nursing our poor Child, and very happy am I to inform you that every prospect of success now seems likely to attend it, for we flatter ourselves that she is daily gaining ground, so that we

[1] Hypochlorite, oxygenated muriatic (hydrochloric) acid would assist in the germination of old seeds (especially those with thickened outer coats), by abraiding the seed coat thereby facilitating the entry of water and oxygen. It would, moreover, curtail the depredations of bacteria and other inhibitors on the emerging shoot. The effects of its application, in whatever form, to the human race are beyond imagination!

now look for a complete recovery. This has been our only misfortune, for tho' my own family have done all they can to pillage & distress me, yet with patience those matters must come round, and I must be thankful for the uncommon share of happiness we have enjoyed.

As for publick affairs, I never wish, if possible to think of them, for I very much fear we shall never again see Peace, and not having any of the common sort of Ambition I do not envy those who have the management of them. I find the days too short, for what with farming, planting & reading etc. I have more employment than I have time for.

I wish I may be able to answer the latter part of your letter to your satisfaction, but so much is included in *substantial* comforts that the meaning is understood differently by every one.[1] There are two places you may have in this Country & I think you should not lose time to see them, for according to two different scales each would suit you. The first is a farm of 200 Acres upon the River Tivy, very beautiful, & well cultivated, the House comfortable & convenient, (and) a most excellent farmyard, which is to be sold. I imagine the price will be about 4 or 5000£. There is wood upon it.

Upon a smaller Scale, I have a House which I built some years ago for a bathing House, but did not put my plan into Execution, thinking a lodging for the short time we should want it would be more convenient at Aberystwith. This is about 3 miles north of Aberystwith close on the sea; a good comfortable small House, but no land. The ground rent is 7£ a year. If this would suit you, it is very much at your Service if you will do me the favor to accept of it. A Tenant at present inhabits it. But it is absolutely necessary you should see this as well as the other place, and if you come here I have a Horse to carry you to each.

I must conclude for the post is come in & I cannot keep him.

Ever yours,

T. Johnes

---

[1] Presumably Cumberland's concern with 'substantial comforts' refers to the house he proposed to buy.

To Arthur Young[1]   Add. MS. 35128, f.100

Hafod, April 15, 1799

Dear Sir,

As this was the usual time our Society of Agriculture published their annual report, I trouble you with this to account why you have not received one according to my promise.

This Country has had a very severe loss in the sudden death of our worthy Secretary, the Rev. Mr Turnor; and I have lost a very sincere friend.[2] In his last letter to me he complained much of the non-attendance & non-payment of the Members; I very much fear this favorite Child of mine, which he so kindly nursed, will not succeed as I have ever wished it. However no exertions of mine shall be wanting for its support.[3]

Ever since I last saw you I have been at this place attending the long illness of an only Child. Thank God, notwithstanding the very great severity of this Winter, we have now a fair prospect of her recovery. My chief amusement has been my Farm & planting, and should you ever make an excursion near this Country I shall be very happy to shew you both. Much has been done, but more remains.

Should any of your friends want to purchase a very magnificent place, I have such to dispose of. It is called Croft Castle, 5 miles from Leominster & 7 from Ludlow. The Castle is in excellent repair & fit for the possession (of) a large family directly. The demesne is near 1400 acres and has upon it upwards of 20,000£ of the finest Timber in England. Two advowsons and two manors. Possession may be immediately had; 20,000£ may remain as a mortgage.

This has been a very hard Winter upon us Mountain Farmers. The losses among the sheep & lambs are very great indeed. I know not

[1] Arthur Young (1741-1820), the celebrated agricultural pundit and Secretary of the first Board of Agriculture.

[2] The Rev. David Turnor of Wervilbrook, Llangrannog, Cardiganshire (1751?-1799). With Thomas Lloyd of Coedmor he wrote, *A General View of the Agriculture of the County of Cardigan*, London, 1794.

[3] Johnes was closely involved in the founding of the Cardiganshire Agricultural Society, for which see R.J. Moore-Colyer, Early Agricultural Societies in South Wales, *Welsh History Review, 12,(4)*, 1985.

when to expect an end of it, for it snows & hails as fast (as) if it was the middle of December instead of April.

I am, Dear Sir,

Your very obedient humble Servant,

T. Johnes

To James Edward Smith, in Norwich   Linn. Soc. (Smith), 16, f.98

Hafod, April 27, 1799

My Dear Sir,

I had not the pleasure of receiving your Letter of the 19th before last Thursday. It has got some very long postmark upon the Cover which I cannot make out, to say where it has been travelling.

We are very sorry you send us so very indifferent accounts of your Sister. I hope you will take care of your own health, for without that all is indeed vexation of spirit. Seeing our dear Girl do so well has been our sole support. These last 18 months however have given me more knowledge of Mankind than 18 years before. I am more & more determined not to quit this place, tho' the cruelty of this winter, for it is not yet gone, would have frightened any less determined Farmer. My losses of Sheep will be very great. I have sold 330 skins already. What then must the poor hill Farmer suffer? I am afraid Corn will be scarce & Bad. I have not yet sown my Oats, not owing to any fault of mine but to the wet. I bar the pun upon *wild* ones for I hope they have been sown some time, yet *you* have known when Wine & Spirits fill my head, I can act Tom Fool with the most foolish.

My Girl sends you in another cover a flower from the *Conchium*, which she says you wished for. Pray could you get me at Bristol this famous oxygenated muriatic acid that gives such a powerful stimulus to seeds. I have some old Seeds that have been too sluggish to grow.

Todd is going on vastly well, tho' his Garden has very severely felt the weather.

I see Dr Thornton has done wonders with Dr Beddoes airs. [1]

They will make a new & grand epoche in Medicine, and surely he deserves more thanks than this ungrateful nation will give him. [2] Pray would they do any good to our Girl in reducing the tumours she has near the Chin & on some of the Glands? Her back is almost flat, and she looks the picture of health. She is now wondrous busy in improving herself and is really doing wonders.

Mrs Johnes's Sisters left us yesterday for Dolecothy so now we are quite alone. I hate to say anything of my own affairs when I cannot say anything pleasant, but I know you will expect to hear if there is any improvement. I think indeed tho heavily pressed at this moment, that the prospect rather brightens. Davies still wants Croft. He is a poor devil & not deserving of it, but it may suit me. And I have a proposal for another Estate which if it succeeds will make me quite comfortable. But that is in Embrio [sic] as yet, & I fear will miscarry. You see *qu'avec des Loups, on apprend à heurter.*

Adieu, my dear Sir, wishing you every success in all your undertakings & every happiness.

I am yours always,

T. Johnes

My wife & daughter send their kind Compliments to you.

---

[1] Robert John Thornton (1768?-1837), botanical and medical writer. He succeeded James Edward Smith as lecturer in medical botany at St. Thomas's Hospital.

[2] Thomas Beddoes (1760-1808), physician, radical and polymath. In 1793 he moved to Clifton near Bristol where, with the assistance of the young Humphrey Davy, he established a 'Pneumatic Institute' for the purpose of investigating means of curing disease by inhalation. It was at the 'Institute' that Davy elucidated the properties of nitrous oxide. Beddoes himself was an interesting man of broadly ranging talents who was much in demand as a physician and whose passing in 1808 was much lamented. [See, for example, K. Curry (ed.), *New Letters of Robert Southey*, I, Columbia, 1965]

Dr. Thomas Beddoes
(by permission of the National Portrait Gallery, London)

To James Edward Smith, in London   Linn. Soc. (Smith), 16, f.103

Hafod, June 23, 1799

My dear Sir,

Your letter contained the following words. 'I cannot tell you how long I shall stay in London nor where to write to me.' Otherwise I should not so long have delayed assuring you that we all participated in your affliction for the loss you had at Clifton. Her disorder however was such that you were prepared for such events which at all times & in all cases must be terrible.

I had another reason for not writing sooner for as I must from the fullness of my heart have said something of myself, I did not wish that you should share my troubles also, as I know you would do. I have been unfortunate in my sale of Croft. It has been minus 10,000£ at least to what I was always taught to expect and what is worse from the neglect etc. of Lawyers I fear I shall be sometime even unpaid what I am to receive from it. However was it to do again & I had no more information on the subject than at that time, I know not how it could have been done better. I have myself alone to thank; for I should have exerted myself & depended on myself alone, and it would have succeeded.

I must make large sacrifices in this Country for I am determined to be free from this hanging on Tenterhooks, and if I am granted health & Life my Child shall not have any reason to accuse me of having lessened her Fortune.[1] I do not mean to perform it by sordid avarice, for tho' I have of late learnt more concerning Mankind & Money than in all my life, I trust my heart whatever it may feel will never harden nor my purse close for any deserving Objects. My sinking fund will be in Larch plantations. I am even more wild about them than my good friend Anderson, and intend every year after this ensuing season to plant out a million as long as I live & have ground for it. Todd has been very fortunate this year in raising from seed which was thought too bad to send me, from one to 3 millions.[2] At least the seed beds are

[1] These sacrifices principally involved selling extensive tracts of land in Cardiganshire and Carmarthenshire.

[2] James Todd, the head gardener at Hafod; formerly of the Edinburgh Botanic Gardens.

as full as they can hold. So now my stock is begun I will take care not to lessen it.

It is with the greatest pleasure I can send you excellent news of our dear Girl. Jones has been here with a much improved machine. She has walked without crutches since last Wednesday. She drinks three half pints every day of the Llanwrted [sic] waters, which Dr Davies advised instead of going there.[1] They are Sulphurous and have done miracles in several cases. I believe & hope they agree very well with her. She is certainly much improved in all respects; and Jones has not a doubt of her perfect recovery if we keep her out of the hands of Surgeons.

Our weather has been uncommonly hot and I never saw the foliage so magnificent as this year, nor the Hawthorns nor Crabs in such high beauty. Our woods are like flower gardens, & many have flowered which I never remember before.

My paper forces me to conclude. Mrs Johnes & our Girl send their kind Compliments to you & Mrs Smith.

I am,

Yours ever,

T. Johnes

---

[1] The 'much valued medicinal wells' at Llanwrtyd (Brecknockshire), '. . . are said to possess similar qualities with those at Llandrindod, and alike difficult of access and destitute of accommodations'. [G. Nicholson, *The Cambrian Traveller's Guide*, Stourport, 1808]

To William Owen[1]   N.L.W. MS. 13222C, f.631

Hafod, Oct. 3, 1799

Dear Sir,

I have just finished *A Cardiganshire Landlords Advice to his Tenants* consisting of extracts from the best Authors and facts from my own observation. I wish to have it printed in Welsh & English to give to my Tenants only. I shall be very much obliged to you if you could inform me what would be the cost of translation and printing. The Size is three of those paper Books that contain Froissart which you were so good to letter [sic] the back of the case which contains them. But to be more particular the 4to Books have 45 pages and 21 lines. The writing is the same as this.

Should you know of any person wishing to buy Land in this Country, I shall thank you to say. I shall have a good deal to dispose of the latter end of next month and there is a most desirable Estate called Stanage between Ludlow and Knighton of 1400£ Rent that I must also sell to make up for the deficiencies caused by my Mother's unexpected Claims. Perhaps Mr Owen Jones could help me to purchasers. When you see him I shall thank you to mention it, and also to enquire the price of a Fine Black Foxskin as I wish to make Mrs Johnes a present of one.[2]

I hope you will excuse all the trouble & believe me to remain, Dr Sir,

Your most obedient Humble Servant,

T. Johnes

[1] William Owen (Pughe) (1759-1835), lexicographer, grammarian, poet and antiquary. His numerous published works included *The Cambrian Biography* (1803), *The Myvyrian Archaiology of Wales* (1801 and 1807) and a Welsh translation of *Paradise Lost*, uncharitably described by Iolo Morganwg as 'Milton Lost'. Although he provided valuable assistance to English authors working on Welsh and Celtic subjects, his lexicographical ventures led to considerable confusion in nineteenth century Welsh grammatical studies.

[2] Owen Jones (Owain Myfyr) (1741-1814), wealthy London currier and patron of Welsh letters. For over 20 years the guiding force behind the *Gwyneddigion*, he promoted a number of literary and publishing projects including the *Myvyrian Archaiology*.

To James Edward Smith, in Norwich　　　Linn. Soc. (Smith), 16, f.111

Hafod, Dec. 8, 1799

My dear Doctor,

I have had the pleasure of your two Letters the last two posts and thank you much for them as well as for the Seeds. The last indeed Mrs Johnes claims & desires me to say everything for her.

Had I not heard I should have written to you as this day to inquire after you, & to desire you would thank your Brother for the best of fearnoughts.[1] It comes very acceptable to our poor. I wish for the same quantity *every year*. I have hitherto had it every two, and pray assure him I will very shortly send him proper remittances for the two.

My good friend, not only my *worldly* matters are improving but everything else. This I know will give you pleasure. First & foremost, my Girl I hope is daily improving in health, wisdom, Stature & Beauty. She is *now* a woman, everything well & agreeable. Jones came here yesterday & is quite surprized at her recovery. *2nd.* My wife has had a very severe cold, but is recovering fast. *3rd.* I am myself in such health as I never enjoyed. Your friend Mr Voght has behaved most handsomely as to Wines, & to them & temperance I owe my health. Pray when you write say as much for me of him as you have been kind enough to say to him of me. He is a precious Correspondent. He has got me samples of Hungarian wines,—I must not call it Tokay or I shall be thought lost beyond redemption—and I believe can get me the Wine I have so long hunted for from Gottenburg. *4th.* My Farm is answering amazingly. A few years ago I had my meat from Knighton & Newtown. This year I shall fat for sale 50 head of cattle. I am now building the most complete feeding House that ever was. *5th.* All my sales in this Country have gone beyond even my Calculations. *6th.* I hope & believe I shall get better terms from my kind Mother to sell Stanage than I did for Croft, & should this sell to my expectation, I shall be clear.[2] So without running into more

---

[1] Stout woollen cloth made into jackets and trousers. Often used for sailor's garments, fearnought was also known as 'shepherd's cloth'. Smith's brother Francis (1764-1815) had succeeded his father in the family wool business.

[2] Johnes thus hoped that his mother would release the share of her life interest in Stanage in order to leave him free to sell.

particularities about self, which want of other matter forces me to I think you may congratulate me. My sole wish now is to keep my comforts. Upon the thought of this I shall wake old Froissart from his sleep on the first day of the new Century.

There is a dirty dog of a parson called Lloyd who I believe has a curacy in Norfolk & this must be the man who told the Lie of this place being sold to Mr Crowe. Pray thank Mr Crowe for me, but I should certainly sell myself as soon as this place.

My Girl desires her best Compliments to you, & thanks you for the small plant. She says she hopes to be able to accompany you a-botanizing when next you favor us with your Company. Mrs Johnes unites with me in kind Compliments to Mrs and Miss Smith.

I am, my dear Sir,

Yours ever very truly,

T. Johnes

To George Cumberland, at Egham, Surrey   Add. MS. 36498, f.375

Hafod, Jan. 30, 1800

My dear Sir,

I am much obliged to you for your last letter; but more so for the drawing of your mode of draining. I think exceedingly well of it, especially in those Countries that can make bricks. Here however Nature (tho' so kind in other respects) has precluded me from trying it. I hope that your mode of flat roofing & draining will be fairly and fully tried. As for myself I have no doubts of either, and the publick ought to be thankful to you.

With regard to the political part of your Letter, I am much obliged to you for it; and wish the War at an end as much as you can. It appears singular to me that none of the opposition have taken notice of the great change in the publick mind this new Century, from what it was at the beginning of the last. We had then a long and expensive war, solely and avowedly to prevent two Princes of the House of Bourbon from occupying the Thrones of France & Spain. Now we have a long war apparently for the very purpose of establishing these two families on those Thrones.[1] The follies of Mankind would be laughable if they did not use such cursed instruments in the execution of them. The Abbé de St Pierre's dream was that of an honest man that will never be realized.[2]

The World has had an irreparable loss in the death of Mr Washington, for I look upon him as the greatest man of any Age whatever, and the only example (melancholy enough indeed) of one that did not abuse absolute power, & was not spoilt by it.[3]

I think you blame Dr Anderson unjustly, for I am sure he will think himself highly flattered by any communications from you. Underneath is what he wrote to me some time since.

'I have been much out of my duty to Mr Cumberland. The truth is, I read his communication only once in great haste and put that & another paper I valued from a friend at Manchester carefully by until I should have more leisure, but where they have been put I have never been able to discover. I never lose a paper when I give it the common run, but when I am at more than ordinary pains I frequently mislay them so as not to lay my hands upon them perhaps for years. I shall certainly find it, but I have made so many ineffectual searches that I have now determined to wait till chance brings them to hand. I cannot think of writing to him under these Circumstances, nor could I, if I would, as I have lost his address. But if you should have occasion to write to him, I should take it as a great favour if you would try to apologise for me'.

Pray send me your Brother's address as I want to write him a few lines respecting my farm. I have recommended my translation of old Froissart with the ardour of renewed Love. It will be the better for having lain by, as I take now much more pains; and begin to hope it may be valuable. I only mention this, as you will judge from it that I

---

[1] The Treaty of Utrecht (1713) ended the War of Spanish Succession in which Britain had engaged herself in 1702. She had done so in order to protect the Protestant succession and to eliminate the prospect of a Franco-Spanish dynastic alliance. Even so, the House of Bourbon was established in Spain in 1713.

[2] Charles Irenée Castel, Abbé de St. Pierre (1658-1743), author of *Project for a Perpetual Peace*.

[3] George Washington had died from a pulmonary disorder the previous autumn.

think my Girl in a fair way, otherwise my attentions would have been occupied by her illness, that swallowed up everything else.

Mrs Johnes sends her Compliments to you.

I am, my dear Sir,

Yours ever very truly,

T. Johnes

To William Owen N.L.W. MS. 13223C, f.681

No. 6, Sion Hill, Clifton. June 5, 1800

Dear Sir,

I have taken the liberty of sending you the first sheet of my Advice to my Tenants in another cover by this days post, which shall be regularly continued as fast as I receive them from the Printer. I shall beg of you to have it translated into Welsh, for which any recompense you may think proper I shall be happy to allow, and to have 400 copies of it printed. I will send you the Engravings when finished so as to be half bound up with it. You see I make no ceremony in accepting your very friendly offer and hope you will excuse it.

We have been here for 5 weeks. Fortunately a severe pleuristic fever attacked my daughter. I say *fortunately* for if that had not been the case we should not have come here, where I hope & believe we shall find that health we have been so long in search of for her. Dr Beddoes has shewn great skill & attention, for she does not drink the waters, and she is already so much recovered you would not know her again.

I hope to return home early in July, and shall be exceedingly happy if you make any Tour thro' Wales to have the pleasure of thanking you in person for all the trouble I have, and am about to give you.

I am, my dear Sir,

Yours very Truly,

T. Johnes

I should be very much obliged (if possible) if I could take the advice home with me to give away at my rent meeting.

To George Cumberland, at Egham, Surrey   Add. MS. 36499, f.341

Hafod, Jan. 19, 1801

My dear Sir,

I thank you much for remembering me in your letter of the last Century, and I should not have allowed it to have remained so long unacknowledged if I had not put it by so carefully I could not lay my hands on it before this morning.

I give you joy of your Mendip acquisition which I had before heard of. You will have near you a most excellent farmer in Mr. Billingsley of Ashwick Grove. It will be a loss to Agriculture his declining that pursuit, which I hear he intends doing.[1] You will not regret turning farmer; at least I know from experience that it has been the saving of me, for my farm turns out a very sincere friend. In such times ruin must oppress anyone who has not such a resource to fly to. And I would encourage you by all means to follow it, but with prudence with regard to Sheep. I can give you very little information for I have been sadly cheated about them. However that has been my own fault for not attending to them more. I am now about following a new plan this Spring which will reduce the prospect to a certainty, as well as the number of Sheep I have, for ridiculous as it may seem I really do not know their exact numbers. Our shepherds think it very unlucky to tell them. My plan is this. First I change my Shepherds, and I have the new one(s) from Scotland. I buy in May 1000 Ewes & Lambs, which are then sold according to the Lambing Season being good or bad, from 7/- to 10/6 per head. I wean the lambs as soon as I can, keep the Ewes in good pastures & milk them 'till the first week in September when they are turned to the aftermath, and sold to the Butcher in October or Novr from 10/- to 12/- per head. I have by this means the lamb, and 2/- profit, besides the wool which I estimate at 2/- and their milk which is very valuable.[2] The lambs are turned to the mountain.

[1] John Billingsley of Ashwick Grove, Somerset (fl. late 18th/early 19th centuries), farmer and writer on local agriculture [*V.C.H. Somerset II*, p. 538].

[2] Sheep milking, for the purposes of cheesemaking, hitherto a widespread practice in Wales, was becoming less common by the early years of the nineteenth century. [R.J. Colyer, Aspects of the Pastoral Economy in pre-Industrial Wales, *Journal of the Royal Agricultural Society of England, 144, 1983*.]

I continue this proceeding every year, but after the second year I bring the first year lambs to better grass, or early rape, and sell them to the Butcher in the Summer, for they will all be castrated. So that after the 2nd year I sell 2000 sheep, which besides their wool & milk, will produce from 10/- to 12/- the Ewes, and from 12/- to 15/- the Wethers.

This is the plan I intend to follow. I do not believe it has ever been done before, and I confess I do not see any objection to it. Should the Ewes & Lambs be too dear in a course of years, I can then return to breeding from a larger stock than these countries afford, as by that time I hope my farm large as it is will all be brought under Culture.

I agree with all you say respecting my worthy friend Dr Anderson, but he will *not* be taken up in the manner he ought by the present Ministry. His mind is too independant [sic]. The public will have cause to regret it, but so it is.[1]

Railroads will supersede Canals, for they can be travelled on in frost & in drought, and the expense of making certain. I long for one in this Country to bring us Lime.[2]

Long corresponds with me. He is a worthy fellow & too good for where he is. Have you seen his Pamphlet on the Scarcity? I too have written a book of Advice to my Tenants. It is translated into Welsh for them & I hope it will do good. This has not been any interruption to Froissart who goes on merrily. This & farming have been my great resources for I have had a share of vexations & troubles. I wish you would come here when we could talk these & other matters more fully over together. I have done so much since you were here, you would not know parts of the place again.

Let me know to whose care I shall send your Salmon to [sic] in London, and one shall go by the following carrier after I have your directions.

---

[1] Pitt had employed Anderson in 1784 to undertake a detailed survey of the state of British fisheries. His subsequent failure to secure state patronage may have been due to official disapproval of several of the articles critical of government which appeared in *The Bee* between 1790 and 1794.

[2] Johnes's various references to railways presumably imply rails along which horse-drawn carriages could be conveyed. Trevithick's steam locomotive first operated in 1804, and the Stockton-Darlington line, specifically designed for steam traction was not opened until 1825. Even then horse-drawn carriages continued in use on the railways until well into the 1830's.

Mrs Johnes desires her Compliments to you. Thank God I can send you good Bills of health. I have not paper to say more, but I had a Frenchman with me last summer, *one in office*, so I know more of that country than you do.

Ever yours,

T. Johnes

P.S.
We have completely succeeded in making Parmesan!!!! Come and taste it.

To George Cumberland, at Egham, Surrey   Add. MS. 36499, f.7

Hafod, Feb. 21, 1801

My dear Sir,

I hope your Salmon will arrive safe, & prove as good as all his brethren we have eaten. I sent it to Shrewsbury where it arrived, or ought to have arrived, last Thursday & to be conveyed according to your directions to London by the first Waggon.

After what my Master in Farming Dr Anderson has said to you, it would be too much presumption in me to contradict him. I still think, judging from myself now, that a farm is most desirable, & tho' there may be very many drawbacks, I should be miserable without one. However a common sort of Farm would not do for me, but it is a great delight to see Ground which was a waste now bearing luxuriant Crops.

All he says of Scots shepherds is perfectly true, as I know from experience, and you would like all beginners be miserably cheated.

It would be doing great injustice to the Parmesan to have sent you a sample, and we are not yet rich enough in them to spare a whole Cheese. But you may depend on what I say, and when you begin farming I will give you a copy of my 'Advice to Tenants' which I have had translated into Welsh to give to those deserving among them.

Your copy will be in English, & contain all our dairy receipts, [sic] which are valuable, as having *all* succeeded.

My good Friend no man feels fewer sorrows than myself, and I hope I am grateful for a very uncommon share of happiness. But when public affairs seem running headlong to destruction, your Poor starving & emigrating by hundreds to America, with smaller troubles to make you feel you are mortal, they must now & then make one growl for the perverseness of Mankind.

I thank you much for your offer of Head and Tail pieces for Froissart. They will be very acceptable. I cannot print it here from the trouble & great expense it would cause me. Remember in this insulated [sic] spot I must have every material & apparatus sent at a vast cost. Mr Roscoe might easily get his work done in such a town as Liverpool, but remember where I am. I shall let the Booksellers manage this as they please. I have been much flattered lately by the praise it has received from a very old friend, whose abilities are equal to his honesty. I am now satisfied about it and am going on *con amore*. This call of the House however will be an interruption, for I must attend, but I do not mean to remain more than one fortnight. I shall be during that time at my friend Edwards's in Pall Mall.[1]

If you can spare a day let me have the pleasure of seeing you during my stay there. We can then more fully discuss your farming scheme, which I cannot (?) in such miserable times. Have you seen the Doctor's essay? I hope the *old* Corn Laws will now be renewed, and all Adam Smith's doctrines & of such speculators [sic] be annihilated and that we shall trust to experience & fact alone.[2]

Vast emigrations are going to America from this County; we can but ill spare them.[3]

[1] He proposed, presumably, to be present at the continuing debate over the question of Catholic relief.

[2] The eighteenth century Corn Laws had encouraged the export of grain by a bounty when home prices were low and permitted imports at low rates of duty when prices were escalated by bad harvests. Whereas this had tended to benefit the consumer, the Corn Law Act of 1791 tended to favour protection for producers [J.D. Chambers and G. Mingay, *The Agricultural Revolution, 1750-1800*, London, 1966.]

[3] Depressed social and economic conditions among the poor had caused widespread emigration from West Wales to America. Shipowners regularly advertised their willingness to transport emigrants from harbours like Newquay, Cardigan and Aberaeron to Liverpool whence a passage to New York could be secured for as little as £4. [J. Ballinger, Local History from a Printer's File, *West Wales Historical Records, IX, 1920-23.*]

Thank God my daughter is so well recovered. I really do not know what infinite improvements Dr. Beddoes will introduce into the Art of healing with his Acids & Gasses.

Mrs Johnes sends you her best Compliments.

I am, my dear sir,

Yours very truly,

T. Johnes

To Charles Taylor,
Secretary,
Royal Society of Arts.

Transactions of the Society for the
Encouragement of Arts,
Manufactures and Commerce, XX,
1802, pp. 182-4.

Hafod, September 25, 1801

Sir,

I shall shortly forward to you the particulars of the Timber-trees which I have planted between the 1st of October, 1797, and the 1st of May, 1799.

My plantations are generally made on such land as I cannot plough, that my best ground may be reserved for grain and grass. I plant the sides of mountains, which are almost universally composed of argillaceous shistus, or slate rock; the surface of which is decomposed by exposure to the atmosphere, and admits the roots of trees to penetrate therein, and to grow luxuriantly. The land betwixt the mountains consists of peat-earth, which, when well drained and limed, produces good grain, potatoes, yams, or grass. I am at present engaged in a course of experiments to ascertain what kind of cows will answer best in this country. A gentleman farmer, who was here last week, insisted that though the Guernsey cows gave but little milk, yet that it contained more butter and cheese than other cows milk. I therefore made a trial, and found the following result :

Devon cows............	gave of butter	................7⅞ oz.
Small Scotch cows...	do	....................6 oz.
Guernsey cows.......	do	................5½ oz.

Devon cows............	gave of cheese	............1 lb. 8 oz.
Small Scotch cows...	do	..............14½ oz.
Guernsey cows.......	do	................13 oz.

I have sent my friend Dr Anderson a sample of my Wheat grown here; and those to whom he has shown it said it was the finest they had seen. My crop is supposed to be thirty bushels per acre; and yet there are persons, pretendedly knowing, who declared that Wheat could not be grown here. [1]

This crop was on very high exposed ground.

I am, Sir,

Your obedient humble Servant,

T. Johnes

To George Cumberland, at Axbridge, Somerset   Add. MS. 36499, f.53

Hafod, Oct. 3, 1801

My dear Sir,

I should be very happy if I was able to give you the advice you ask for. But as I am quite ignorant of the Country where you are it is not possible for me to say any thing correctly on the subject. I think however the rent is very high for such land, particularly in the wild

---

[1] From the time of Henry VII various efforts had been made to standardise weights and measures, yet local variations persisted. Assuming that Johnes refers to the standard bushel of 8 gallons and not to a local variant, his yield would have been approximately 1800 lbs per acre, given a weight of 60 lbs of wheat per bushel. On the other hand, bushel weights varied widely according to variety and the conditions of the growing season.

state it is in, and when I consider the low price for our Hilly ground
I am more surprized. Mr Davis is an exceedingly able, and I believe
a very honest man; you have besides Mr Billingsley at hand, so that
it would be highly impertinent for me to pretend to advise you, not
having seen the spot, when you have two such excellent judges at your
Elbow, as I may say. This is not a put off, for indeed if I thought I
could say any thing to the purpose you should instantly have my real
sentiments.

I thank you for your obliging intentions of coming here when we
will fully discuss every subject. You shall see all I have done, & intend
doing, and if I can any way assist you, you shall command it.

My Farm amply repays me, and I really do not see how far it may
be carried. But you must remember my Land was not ten shillings the
acre. Lime does wonders here, as the soil is schistous, but on yours
which is calcareous I should think a mixture of Oil of Vitriol & Water
would have the most beneficial effects by causing a fermentation. I do
not know if this has ever been practised, but if I had such a Soil I
would certainly try it, in the proportion of about 5 to 1. We are as yet
very ignorant in Agriculture.[1]

I have just sent for a set of Cooke's implements, as my Tenants
have all too much land, and I wish to shew them what a small quantity
will produce.[2] My Dairy has answered very well. I have sold 1200 lbs
of Butter at 8d and four Tons of Cheese at 6d, after having kept a
sufficiency for the House & School. Next year I propose having near
a hundred cows, if I can get money to buy them. We mean to have a
winter dairy this year as a trial. If it succeeds, as I think it must, I will
never suffer a Cow to be out of the House, except during night in the
Summer time.

---

[1] While the addition of sulphuric acid to a calcareous soil would help to neutralise
it, it would also wreak havoc with soil fauna to the ultimate detriment of soil
structure. Yet 'diluted sulphuric acid may also be employed as a means of increasing
the fertility of all calcareous soils in the growth of whatever crops are benefitted by the
action of gypsum'. [Rees, *Rural Cyclopedia, IV*, 1847.] Thus was the reaction of
sulphuric acid on soil chalk viewed as an inexpensive means of applying gypsum
(calcium sulphate).
[2] The Rev. James Cooke of Red Lion Square, London, manufacturer of farm
equipment, especially cup-fed, gear driven seed drills and ploughs. [G.E. Fussell,
The Farmers Tools, 1500-1900, London, 1952] Details relating to the plough invented
and marketed by Cooke appear in *Patents for Inventions, A.D. 1783,* January 13, No.
1349.

Adieu, my dear Sir. I wish you every success, and hope it may turn out as well as it has done to me.

I am, Yours very sincerely,

T. Johnes

To James Edward Smith, in Norwich   Linn. Soc. (Smith), 16, f.131

Hafod, Dec. 26, 1801

My dear Saxon,

It is only against those of your Countrymen that expect everything, and who give themselves airs when they come here that I am vexed at. But indeed to say the truth I am very sorry at the repeated Complaints I have had of the avarice of my Housekeeper and shall indeed thank you to put me in the way to avoid it. I have two or three plans, but like none. I believe the shortest will be to shut up the House, for if it is open to all I shall be overrun by the Canaille of Dowkers from Herefordshire, Radnor, Montgomery and Shropshire & I am quite tired of living my lot *pot au feu*.[1]

I have neither heard nor seen anything of Symmons since he has returned to Wales. I suppose he is now gone to London for we have had two months incessant wet. He has had many workmen, and will I dare say after he has improved it, sell it again for you know he cannot remain long in one place.[2] I have a small bantling coming out from White. But he seems to charge us poor authors most exorbitantly. I pay all the expenses of printing (and) when the book is sold at 5/- he

[1] The previous month Johnes had complained to Smith that 'Saxon' visitors to Wales regarded the place as '*un pays conquis*... and think everything may be had and done here with impunity'. Ignoring the objections of some visitors he had allowed his housekeeper to accept 2/6 from individuals and 5/- from groups wishing to view the house and offices. [Linn. Soc. (Smith), 16, f.128] Of this the traveller Barber sourly commented, '... that such emoluments are taken into account of a servant's hire, and in some measure contribute to the support of the great man's establishment... and in that view I consider the *Grandee* as somewhat of a mercenary showman, however magnifique'. (J.T. Barber, *A Tour through South Wales and Monmouthshire*, London, 1803.]

[2] Charles Symmons (1749-1826), son of John Symmons of Llanstinan, MP for Cardigan. A Whig cleric, author and friend of William Windham, Symmons held the rectories of Lampeter Velfrey and Narberth in Pembrokeshire together with a prebendal stall in St. David's Cathedral. Symmons's father was occupying the the

quickly accounts to me for only 3/-. This is an easy way to get rich, and yet they can combine so much together that you cannot help yourself. This instance is very trifling & is well paid, for it cost me but a week.[1]

This, however, does not say much for the book. I am ready with Froissart, so as not to delay a printer, but I wish to see how this harbinger is received. I sent it out, to sound the world, and indeed to give some little information, for I am sorry to say that 18 out of 20 know no more of my old Gossip than the Man in the Moon.

I propose being in Town early in February (for I am tired of waiting for reversions) to sell a sufficiency to pay everyone, as I am both ashamed and tired of the life I have led. I wish it may suit your conveniency to be in London at the time for I do not mean to remain more than one month. My Farm is now on such a Scale that it will require constant attention.

My old Schoolfellow Windham seems willing to undo all he formerly did, & from being a steady Whig is become a determined Tory.[2] I do not think Peace will last long but I am thankful for it as is, and mean to take my advantages of it.

Every one ought to attempt to alleviate our infernal debt. I have drawn up a plan which to me seems, as to all Schemers *perfect*. I have hinted it to a friend who I dare say will write me word it *is all nonsense*. It destroys all patronage, so it will not do.

This letter is but a bad return for your gay one. *Mais, que voulez-vous?* I cannot make a silk purse from a Sow's Ear.

Our kind Compliments to Mrs Smith etc.

Yours ever,

T. Johnes

mansion of Buwchllaethwen (Carms) in 1804. In the first decade of the 19th century a completely new house superseded the original mansion and it may be to this that Johnes refers. [See F. Jones, *Historic Carmarthenshire Houses and their Families*, Carmarthen, 1987.] The Symmons family seat of Llanstinan (Pembs) was purchased 'in decay' by Sir John Owen of Orielton in 1811. [T. Lloyd, *The Lost Houses of Wales*, Save, 1986.]

[1] i.e. the Froissart *Memoirs*.

[2] William Windham (1750-1810), Secretary at War under Pitt and Secretary for the Colonies under Grenville's administration. Despite his enormous wealth, charm and social grace, the inconsistency of his views and his unerring tendency to change his stance according to the direction of the political wind earned him the sobriquet of 'Weathercock Windham'.

To Robert Liston, in London Liston MS. 5598, f.48

Hafod, June 21, 1802

My dear Liston,

I am very much concerned that you give us such small hopes of the pleasure of seeing you & Mrs Liston here. I was very anxious to shew you that though I had expended much money it had not been *thrown into* the water, but on the waters and was now returning again. I had also many other reasons; and hope if possible you will find a few days to come here. If I can settle my affairs, which the delays of these confounded lawyers seem determined I shall not, we will return your visit at the Hague, but it will require your Eloquence to induce some of my party to cross the Sea. [1]

I will write to Freeling this post, and you shall have his answer, but if you can secure Ld. Auckland the business will be done, for he having interfered in it & with so plump a negative, I fear my friend will not determine without his sanction. [2]

I am very happy you can give such good accounts of Foreign goodwill towards us. Our Insolence has been too long, and I hope we shall be more humble in future & look more to our resources at home. But people I fancy like going far for those things they may have better at home. For instance all this Country is full of Peat; nothing is so excellent a manure when lightly mixed with lime, and it is never thus used. I am myself much to blame but I shall in future stick more to it than I have done.

My Dutch ladies I expect here today. [3] They have been very long on the road, owing as I hear to their poor state, so I suppose I shall see nothing but skin & Bone. I never expected much from them *this* year & therefore am not disappointed. We are going on well with the dairy, tho' from want of Cows, and my Vetches failing we shall fall short of

[1] Johnes alludes to the complex legal wrangles being conducted by his attorney Hugh Smith of Bloomsbury to resolve his financial difficulties.

[2] With his usual generosity Johnes seems to have been interceding on behalf of Liston for a favour from the authorities. Sir Francis Freeling (1764-1836), the postal reformer and book collector, occupied an important position in the General Post Office while William Eden, 1st Lord Auckland (1744-1814), served as Postmaster-General in Addington's cabinet.

[3] In 1802-3 Johnes imported 40 heifers from Holland which were to form the basis of a 100 cow 'winter dairy'.

Tonnage in Cheese. However, what is made is superior to any we have yet made.

I am up every morning at 5 and hard at Froissart till breakfast. All the rest of the day I am a gentleman idler.

Pray give our kind Compliments to Mrs Liston, and I shall look to her for making you perform your promise of coming here.

I am, my dear Liston,

Always yours,

T. Johnes

To James Edward Smith, in Norwich   Linn. Soc. (Smith), 16, f.135

Hafod, July 27, 1802

My dear Sir,

We are exceedingly sorry to hear you have been so ill, and sincerely hope this may find you perfectly recovered. I did not write before, as tho' I had not electioneering bustle you & your friends seem to have had enough and besides my House was so full that I have not had a moment's quiet before now. This County has behaved exceedingly handsome for they not only re-elected me but made up their dislike of Mr Vaughan & re-elected him to prevent even a possibility of any disturbance in the County. This is very flattering and the only way I can now wish to be in Parliament for I am more & more tired of the public & public Life.

We have had some very pleasant people here this Summer, if it may be so called. The Edwards's, Rogers, Douce, Liston & his wife, and Roger Wilbraham was on his way when he was sent for to your County Election.[1]

---

[1] An interesting gathering; although one can only speculate as to how the gossiping poet Samuel Rogers might have got along with the doleful Francis Douce (1757-1834) the antiquary and collector who features as 'Prospero' in Dibdin's *Bibliomania*.

Sinclair let Windham know your sentiments pretty clearly, tho' I do not like Smith whom you have exchanged for him. He is too much the opposite and I have no opinion of politicians who under the pretence of patriotism or alarm would sacrifice everything to their faction. *Est modus in rebus* etc.[1] Windham & I were formerly very intimate friends —7 years in the same room at Eton, but since his commencing Politician I know him only to bow to. This is not as it should be.

Mrs Johnes & my daughter are both well. The last is grown so stout you would not know her again. But this sad weather is much against my Invalids.

I expect Dyke here early in the ensuing month to view the Estate I intend to dispose of, and I hope he may sell it well.[2] If it is sold near to my expectations I shall be a made man, but then perchance there may come some devilment worse than money which I find I have always held too cheap, to let me know what poor things we are.

Pray let me know how Fearnoughts sell this year? for if not too dear I shall want some for my poor people. They are excellent things.

Mrs Johnes & Mariamne desire to add their best Compliments with mine to Mrs Smith & your family.

I am, my dear Sir,

Always yours,

T. Johnes

[1] *Est modus in rebus, sunt certi denique fines,*
Quos ultra citraque nequit consistere rectum.
[Horace, *Odes, XII, 106*]
[There is a measure in everything, and fixed limits beyond and short of which right cannot find a haven]

[2] Of Dyke & Co., surveyors and valuers. Dyke was to earn Johnes's displeasure by valuing the property he proposed to sell at a figure well below that which he, Johnes, had anticipated.

To Edward Williams[1]   N.L.W. MS. 21281 E, f.215

Hafod, Sept. 30, 1802

Dear Sir,

I have been favored with your letter of the 14th and have delayed answering it in hopes some of our Manufactures would have been returned from the Weavers etc., but have not heard anything of them. If you will let me know when you set out, or when you shall be in London & where to direct to you I will be sure to forward to you specimens. This Country & its worth is perfectly unknown. It was said & even firmly believed I could not grow Wheat here; well, this Harvest I have 30 bushels an acre of the cleanest wheat I have seen, and the ground destined for it not in the condition it shall be. When thrashed I will be exact as to quantity & weight.

The greatest drawback I experience is in the price of Lime; it costs me 10d per bushel delivered here and from a late emigration to America carriers are become very scarce. I once talked with Marment at Pill and I think he said he could supply me with as many bushels as I pleased at 1d per bushel burnt.[2] Now the difficulty is to transport it in this state to Aberystwith. On the East Coast of England lime is constantly carried burnt and what is done in one place may be done in another, & I shall think myself very much obliged to you if you would make inquiries of the price of burnt Lime on your Coast and if any persons will undertake to deliver a quantity at the Port of Aberystwith and how much per bushel. Should it be moderate I will contract for 10 or 20,000 bushels. A premium shall also be given to the three first vessels of 10£, 7£ & 3£ that shall enter Aberystwith Port with the burnt Lime. Of course the nearer the Coast is to our

[1] Edward Williams (Iolo Morganwg) (1747-1826); poet, antiquary and stonemason. An extraordinarily versatile man, Iolo was closely associated with the London Gwyneddigion, and travelled the length and breadth of the Principality collecting materials for the *Myvyrian Archaiology*, of which he was one of the editors. His notorious forgeries appeared in that work and in *Barddoniaeth Dafydd ab Gwilym* (1789) and *Y Greal* (1805-7). With respect to his contribution to Welsh life and letters and his role in the arcane world of druidism and the eisteddfodau, Prys Morgan has concluded, '. . . that he was in many ways crazy, misleading and wrong-headed, but he has . . . to be considered the true spiritual father of modern Welsh nationalism'. [Prys Morgan, *Iolo Morganwg*, in M. Stephens and R. Brinley Jones, (eds.) *Writers of Wales*, Cardiff, 1975.]

[2] Y Pîl or Pyle, Glamorgan.

Country, the freight will be less, and I am certain it will meet with much encouragement as we are at present in the sole hands of the owners of Lime rocks & Culm in Pembrokeshire. I hope you are now quite recovered.

I am, dear Sir,

Yours very truly,

T. Johnes

Edward Williams (Iolo Morganwg); by Elijah Waring and engraved by Cruikshank
(by permission of the National Library of Wales)

To Robert Anderson, in Edinburgh   Adv. MS. 22.4.12, f.197

Hafod, Nov. 29, 1802

Dear Sir,

I had the pleasure of your very flattering note respecting Froissart last post; and very sensibly feel all you so kindly express relative to it. Your praise shall serve to stimulate me to be more deserving of it. I have made many Corrections in the sheet you had, *discrete* is now *discreet* but I see Ld. Berners remains with its original sin. Edinburgh is so distant otherwise I should take the liberty of soliciting your advice on several topicks, more especially those facts which regard Scotland. I was advised not to print a larger Edition than 200 4to & 20 folio, for the admirers of *large* paper; the books will I fear be too expensive for a quick sale even of this small quantity. I hope it may answer, but no author has so indifferent an idea of his own works as I have. It has at all events much amused me.

I beg my best compliments to Ld. Buchan & am,

Dear Sir,

Your much obliged humble servant,

T. Johnes

To William Roscoe, in Liverpool   L.R.O. (Ros) 2216

Hafod, Jan. 3, 1803

Sir,

As I have not any acquaintance with you but from the pleasure I have had in perusing your writings, & being very intimate with your friend Mr Edwards of Pall Mall, I have many apologies to make for thus troubling you. I write also this in confidence as I should be sorry if by my impudence I should hurt the credit, which is so delicate, of commercial men. Not to make a further preamble, my cause of writing to you, is this : a Mr Worthington & a Mr Holland came here in the Autumn of 1801 and brought the produce of my dairy, offering at the same time their services at Liverpool, as Agents, which I gladly accepted of, for at that time I had been ill used by others who had become bankrupts.

They transmitted various things tolerably well, until late this last summer four Boxes of Tokay & very old Hock was sent to me from Hambro' to their care. By their neglect these were seized, but I sent them a letter from Mr. Olmius one of the Commissioners of Excise, to point out their fault, telling them how to act; at the same time the Board ordered a stop to be put to the business.[1] Since then I have repeatedly written to him, but have not had any satisfactory answer, nor received the Wine. There has also been shipped from Cadiz a Butt of Sherry, the bill of lading of which has been sent to Mr. Worthington, & I wrote to him also, but have not had any answer. Now, Sir, I shall be very much obliged to you if you would act in this business as you in your prudence shall judge right, in order that I may receive these Wines without loss; for their conduct appears to me very odd & mysterious.

I cannot offer you any assistance towards the *Life of Leo the Tenth* which I hear you are about. But if Mr Sheppard [sic] who has published the *Life* of Poggio, should come thro' this County I can shew him two manuscript Volumes of his letters on Vellum.[2]

I am Sir, your most Obedient Humble Servant,

T. Johnes

---

[1] As subsequent letters reveal, Johnes's wine from Hamburg had been seized by excise officers pending the payment of duty, which Worthington had failed to do. John Luttrell-Olmius, third Earl of Carhampton (d. 1829) had been appointed a Commissioner of Excise in 1784.

[2] William Shepherd (1768-1847), Liverpool dissenting minister and poet. A regular visitor to Hafod, Shepherd's enthusiasm for civil and religious liberties was united to a wide range of scholarly interests, notably in Italian literature. His *Life of Poggio Bracciolini* appeared in 1802 and was eventually translated into several languages.

To Robert Anderson, in Edinburgh   Adv. MS. 22.4.12., f. 205

Hafod, March 4, 1803

My dear Sir,

As my Printer says he cannot nor will not do more than 3 sheets a fortnight the matter is settled. But by the bye it is only since I made some inquiry after an abuse of paper that this resolution has been taken. I think therefore I have had a lucky deliverance, at least I hope I shall have.

Now I shall trouble you to find me out a good Compositor, and a press man, who are fully equal to the business, and who will undertake completing 4 Sheets per week of 300 copies of 4to and 25 folio. I would rather pay them so much per sheet, as finished. I wish it, of course, as well done as possible, and if they give me satisfaction you shall settle the present I am to give them on completing the work.

They will have a Cottage & Garden rent free & as they will find many of the(ir) Countrymen here it will be more agreeable to them. I have the letter for 5 Sheets besides notes, one Press mounted, and another that may be so in a very short time. They shall have everything they can want and I shall leave the terms for you to settle. I give the present man, who has no-one to help him 1-14-0£ per week. I am convinced it is too high, & that from the ease he had this agreed to, he wants to raise his price, for he never had, according to his own acct., money in his pocket until now which has made him saucy.[1]

I hope you will forgive my thus troubling you, but I know no-one who can so well assist me.

I am,

My dear Sir,

Yours very truly,

T. Johnes

[1] Johnes had written to Anderson on March 2nd enquiring as to whether 'good and honest workmen' were to be found in Edinburgh since his present printer had been provoked into making unreasonable demands by his wife 'who has been used to the Chandlers and Gin shops in London (and) finds the situation melancholy'.[Adv. MS. 22.4.12., f.203]

To Robert Anderson, in Edinburgh   Adv. MS. 22.4.12, f.207

Hafod, March 18, 1803

My Dear Sir,

I had the pleasure of both your letters of the 11th & 12th yesterday. I really know not how to thank you for the warmth & ability with which you have kindly executed the commission I troubled you with. I am now quite easy, & thank you most sincerely for it. The fellow I have here, has been a sort of Blister for some time and as I shall part with him immediately, I could wish no time was lost by his Successors in coming hither. I should imagine their best mode would be to buy a good one Horse Cart, & a useful Cart horse that would convey the Wife, Children & furniture. The Cart etc. would serve me afterwards on the Farm.

In answer to your questions, there are many corrections made in the sheets, for though I have carefully looked over the Copy, I send a proof to my friend Mr Edwards in London, & another to an old schoolfellow settled in this Country almost 40 miles off. When they are returned I carefully collate them, for one strikes off too much & the other too little, but as I always write *currente Calamo*, I have some alterations even to make in the second proof.[1] All this takes time & plagues. I do not think I could manage more myself than four sheets per week, and this would forward the work sufficiently. I estimate that the whole will require from 4 to 500 Sheets and should this succeed I will then go on with Monstrelet, as I have made preparations for it. Now my dear Sir, I shall beg of you to settle every term, for I shall subscribe to whatever you agree to, only let every particular be put on paper & signed by them, so that no misunderstanding may arise. I wish to have 4 Sheets of the quarto per week of 300 Copies and 4 Sheets of the folio of 25 copies, and independent of a present such as you yourself shall recommend at the close of the work, a Cottage & garden. I agree to whatever arrangement you make. Of course I pay the expenses of their Journey hither, & back again if they require it. In the Cottage there will be one very good Bed, a small Table & 3 or 4 chairs. Their shortest road is thro' Carlisle, Lancashire, to Welshpool. Newtown distant 12 miles. Turn thence to Llanidloes, 12 miles; to Hafod 22 miles.

[1] *Currente calamo*; with running pen, off-hand.

Froissart alone will take them between 2 & 3 years, for I doubt if more than 20 sheets are done, and Monstrelet not quite so many, supposing I am encouraged to complete these historians.

If you shall have leisure in the course of the Summer, you will complete the obligations I am under to you if you will allow me the pleasure of thanking you personally for them here. It is a wild spot, and we have our 'rumbling Brigs,' also, which we dignify with the grander appellation of Devil's Bridge. For he seems to have been the architect of all that seemed supernatural to our Ancestors.[1]

Your printers will find themselves at home for my Bailiff, Gardener, head ploughman & two Shepherds, with a head workman are all Scotsmen. Your people are certainly purer & better than ours. God send they may long continue so. And this I attribute to your excellent Church policy & able Ministers.

I am, my dear Sir,

Your much obliged, humble Servant,

T Johnes

To Robert Anderson, in Edinburgh   Adv. MS. 22.4.12, f.215

London, May 23, 1803

My dear Sir,

I had the pleasure of yours of the 17th two days ago, and am concerned you have been so unwell. If you have the same weather as we have here, I fear your convalescence will be retarded. It is more like the beginning of March than end of May. I propose returning home the latter end of this week.

[1] A reference to Rumbling Bridge, near Dollar, Kinrosshire, where a spectacular gorge on the River Devon carries bridges of 1713 and 1816. The lowest of the three bridges at Devil's Bridge, on the periphery of the Hafod estate, was locally reputed to be the work of the Devil himself [For details see E. R. Horsfall-Turner, *Walks and Wanderings in County Cardigan,* Bingley, 1905, pp. 48-52.]

I fear war is inevitable, and as you have no doubt read the correspondence, I do not see how with such a Madman it can be avoided. Ministers seriously wished for peace, as their forbearance shows, but Buonaparte is intoxicated by power. I am truly sorry for it, as the event is uncertain and so much mischief must ensue before it will be over. The die is now cast, and I hope his usual good fortune will be tired out.[1]

I can send you no publick news but what you will see more detailed in the papers. But as a private intelligence I can tell you the Duchess of Gordon has succeeded. The Duke of Bedford is to marry Lady Georgiana immediately!!![2]

Inclosed I send you a Specimen of the engravings. It represents the battle of Crecy, & is a facsimile of the illuminations in the finest MSS in the National Library at Paris. My friend Mr Edwards went thither this spring & chose out eighty which will be finished like the one sent you, so the work will be splendid at least. But I hope it may please otherwise. Mr White of Fleet Street has bought the whole impression. It is to be delivered to him in London as the volumes are printed and he is to pay 700£ per volume, in all 2800£. My expenses will be great, but I am glad I have had the trouble of disposing of them taken off my hands.

I must conclude as I am interrupted. Wishing to hear that you are quite recovered I am, my dear Sir,

Yours very truly,

T. Johnes

[1] The Peace of Amiens had been signed in March 1802. Nevertheless Napoleon's apparently unquenchable ambitions continued unabated and as he acquired Louisiana, Elba and Parma from Spain, annexed Piedmont to France and meddled in the affairs of Switzerland and Holland, it became clear that French expansionism would have to be halted. Angered by Britain's refusal to surrender Malta, as agreed in the terms of the Peace, Napoleon prepared to resume hostilities with the result that Addington, despite his desire for peace, was obliged to declare war in May 1803.

[2] Francis, Duke of Bedford had become engaged to Georgiana, daughter of the Tory Duchess of Gordon the year before his death. With what appeared to the Whig ladies to be unseemly haste, Bedford's heir and younger brother Lord John Russell, now a widower, stepped into the breach and married the lady. The young Duchess of Bedford, on a visit to Hafod with her husband, assisted in printing the title page of the second volume of the Froissart translation [Adv. MS. 24.2.12, f.237].

To Robert Anderson, in Edinburgh   Adv. MS. 24.2.12, f.216

Hafod, June 9, 1803

My dear Sir,

On my arrival home last Monday from London I had the pleasure
of finding your very obliging letter, the same I presume which you
had mentioned in yours to me in London. I hope by this time you are
entirely free from all illness, and that the Influenza has returned to
France, where I could wish it to remain. From the papers before the
House it seems to have affected the Consul's brains for I never heard
of such conduct as was repeatedly told me of him when in London by
several well informed persons who had returned from Paris. This war
has vexed me much, both as a public & private calamity, but I cannot
see how with such an irritable & suspicious Character, whose
ambition & hatred for us are unbounded (it) could have been avoided.

I am concerned you say so much about the Printers mode of
travelling for I am exceeding thankful to you for all the trouble you
were so obliging to take about them. And they are such excellent men,
especially Henderson, that had their expenses been twice as much
more I should have been perfectly pleased.

The account of the praises of my book from Edinburgh are highly
gratifying to me indeed, and I shall study more to deserve them.
During my stay in London I disposed of Froissart to White for eight
& twenty hundred pounds, or rather for 700£ per volume as
delivered. He takes the *whole* impression, and to him your friend
should write to bespeak a Copy, for if I may trust to what I heard the
whole will be instantly sold. I must beg you to favor me with the
acceptance of a Copy as a small token of the obligations I feel myself
under to you. I hope you received the proof print; there will be about
80 of such and one or more Maps. I shall endeavour to make it as
perfect & splendid as possible. Whenever any very interesting part
turns up I will send you a Sheet. I am very much satisfied indeed with
my Printers; their parts will be very well done.

I was quite happy to return hither, for I find myself less & less
calculated for the meridian of London. I read on the road part of
Ritson's dissertation; the Bishop need not be hurt by such very
blackguard abuse. Before anyone attempts to throw stones, he should
carefully examine his own conduct, for such language loses its effect

and fortunately very few know how to use irony. The best I ever saw (it was strong!) was Dr. Dunbar's of Tucker. [1]

I am, my dear Sir,

Your much obliged Humble Servant,

T. Johnes

To James Edward Smith, in Norwich   Linn. Soc. (Smith), 16, f.144

Hafod, July 29, 1803

My dear Sir,

I am much obliged to you for yours of the 19th. You have e'er now received mine by Mr Shepherd & heard all how & about us from him. We are exceedingly happy your Lectures turn out so much to your advantage which will I hope induce you to renew them every year. Liverpool is I believe one of the most liberal commercial Towns and Mr Roscoe's taste & knowledge in Italian literature will have made it fashionable. [2] So much depends, & so much can be done by individual exertions when properly seconded. I am glad his *Leo* is finished. It must be an interesting work, & is a suite of his *Lorenzo*. Lord Cork I believe, had some curious papers of that period which I suppose Mr Roscoe has seen, or at least inquired about. I regretted much I had nothing here to help him, but Mr Shepherd found some curious letters of Poggio, as you know.

Mariamne is fonder of her Gardens than ever and is the picture of health. She danced the greater part of the evening of the 30th which

---

[1] Several of John Ritson's antiquarian writings were charged with personal abuse of other writers. His *Ancient English Metrical Romanceës* of 1802 opened with a censorious dissertation on Bishop Percy while in the preface to his *Select Collection of English Songs* (1783) he was highly critical of the latter's *Reliques of Ancient English Poetry*, accusing Percy of including garbled (or forged) versions of ballads.

[2] Early in 1803 Smith had been invited by William Roscoe to give a course of botanical lectures in Liverpool where Roscoe had recently founded a Botanic Garden. The two men eventually became close friends.

is saying everything as to her health. She desires me to say you have never yet sent her the *real* name of the plant she sent you. As for Todd he is an Idiot, but as he seems wasting away, in spite of his appetite which is become voracious, I shall hope he may be carried off. It is a melancholy spectacle, but here he will not want for anything. I only insist he does not enter the Garden, where he has played the Devil. [1]

I had a narrow escape of having all my farm yard burnt down last Saturday. But from the great exertions of my poor Labourers I came off with about 150£ loss, but neither Man nor Beast nor Cock of Hay were damaged. My daughter was quite angry at my Philosophy and saying it was a sublime spectacle. The Country have made a story more to my credit, that I was only anxious least anyone should be hurt, and when assured of that not being the case I sate down quietly to read the Newspaper. I had a narrow escape of losing 2000£ at least.

Yesterday I had the news of gaining a very long Chancery Suit concerning a large estate near Cardigan. [2] It is a very considerable gain; & this puts the matter at rest for 700 years. I hope the Wheel is now turning. If I could but get rid of my Estates which are on sale for any tolerable price so as to pay off (the debts), I shall be rich. Every thing here is doing vastly well in spite of Attornies & Stewards, who to be sure have done all the(y) could to ruin me.

I hope my first volume will be printed by Christmas; we are hard at it. This is the paper the folio edition of 20 is printed on. The quarto of 300 is not much inferior.

Today it rains for the first time this month. I never remember so long a drought. The country wants it, for we are burnt up.

My wife & daughter send their kind compliments to you. Remember me to Mr Shepherd.

I am, my dear Doctor,

Yours always,

T. Johnes

[1] Todd appears to have had some sort of breakdown, set into motion by a fall from his horse in the spring of 1802, 'which had affected his head'. Writing to Smith in March the following year, Johnes suggested that 'Jealous whims added to it but I trust they are gone with the blood the leeches took from his head. I should have had a great loss, as he is an honest man . . .' [Linn. Soc. (Smith), 16, f.142]

[2] The Priory Estate, Cardigan.

To George Cumberland, at Axbridge, Somerset   Add. MS. 36499, f.249

Hafod, Sept. 12, 1803

My dear Sir,

I was very glad to have the pleasure of seeing your handwriting once again. Your letter came here a few days ago; and though your farming scheme did not answer *your* expectations, yet as I hope you have found it out early enough not to be any great loser in pecuniary matters, it will have been so much experience gained. A farmer's life is a laborious one, and unless it is constantly attended to, must fail. This I know from myself and always endeavour to reduce things as much as possible to a certainty; yet in spite of all, disappointments will arise, and the doctrine in Law of *qui facit per alium, facit per se* may be good there.[1] It is the reverse in farming.

My farm is now but beginning to repay, for at this moment I am not half stocked with Sheep. I imported last year 40 Heifers from Holland and we made near 5 tons of the finest Glocester, Cheshire, Stilton & Cheddar Cheeses, not one drop of cream taken from them. But we could not get a market anywhere for I tried all places in vain, and now have 2500 lbs and sell them to the workmen at 5d & 6d per pound!!! Of course we make no more such fine cheeses but turn to butter & skim milk Cheese, which always finds a market.

I have done much out & in doors since I had the pleasure of seeing you, and having sold Froissart to White, I am busily printing it here, and hope it will add another laurel to Hafod. The first volume will be done by Christmas or very soon after. This war has prevented my having the tracings from the MSS in the National Library, at least in time for the 1st Vol. I propose to give 20 per Volume.[2] I am to deliver the whole copy 300 quartos of 4 volumes, and 20 folios to White free of all expenses, and he is to sell them in any way he chooses. They tell me the price is too low, but I am satisfied for I should never have sold them myself.

I was most exceedingly disappointed last spring in not selling the parts of my Estate you probably saw advertised by Dyke & Co. Could I have disposed of them, I should have been at my ease, & free from

[1] i.e. he who does anything by another, does it by himself; thus is responsible for that which he authorises.

[2] i.e. the Bibliothèque Nationale at Paris.

all debt. Fortunately I have met with a friend in the law who is taking me out of the fangs of an Attorney & Steward in this Country who though obliged to me for their [sic] existence have done every thing they could to ruin me.[1] They most narrowly escaped doing so. But now I see all clear, even in spite of this War, which must last until the death of the Consul, or that France will in earnest leave off her damned plundering politicks. I hate the subject so I shall not say more. I hope this being blocked up at home will drive him mad.

Mrs Johnes & my daughter desire their kind Compliments to you.

I am,

My dear Sir,

Yours always very truly,

T. Johnes

I will mention what you say to Dr Anderson.

To James Edward Smith, in Norwich   Linn. Soc. (Smith), 16, f.146

Hafod, Sept. 22, 1803

My dear Sir,

I now sit down to answer fully your two letters of the 26th & 31 August. You will have received Dr Ford's letter with Mr Roscoe's certificate.

I have never seen Burleigh [sic], though this is among the many places I intend visiting, but which I suppose I never shall. The pictures I have always heard highly spoken of. When at Loretto,[sic] the monks said the late Lord Exeter had offered to cover a Raphael with guineas if they would sell it, but they refused. To do so at this

---

[1] Herbert Lloyd of Carmarthen.

time would be a cheap way of buying his pictures, compared with present prices. [1]

When I see you I will detail to you the history of the Chancery suit. It is curious, but you will *perhaps* stare, when I tell you I owe it entirely to *my friend* Symmons; 'and Brutus is an honorable man; so are they all, all honorable men'.

I wish I could advise you how to act with regard to your *Tour*. I would however certainly try the effect of this Winter, by advertising as soon as I could, & by every means. If I recollect, White said 35 had subscribed. Now surely 15 more could easily be raised, if this would be enough to pay charges, and trust to the other 50 for profit. I have never answered Bowyer's letter, but he is enterprising and his things are in general tawdry & badly done. [2] I allude more particularly to his *Views etc of Egypt & the Levant*. But as Loutherbourg was in Wales about 12 or 15 years ago, though not here, he has carried away you may be sure sketches in abundance. [3]

I have had another Tourist since my letter to you who intends publishing his Tour thro' South Wales, a Mr Malkin who lives near Hackney. [4] If I may judge from what I remarked of him the world will not be much enlightened, but he means to attempt it in one or more volumes 4to with well engraven prints. Anything now sells with prints. You see you have not any time to lose in order to prevent being forestalled. You may be assured you have my warmest wishes for success in every line & if I could point out to you the surest way of obtaining both that & profit I would do it. White will be your safest Counsellor, for the sale will depend on his activity, and I do not think there is *now* any other man who could undertake such things with the credit he can.

[1] If the acquisitive 9th Earl of Exeter had proposed buying the so-called 'Madonna di Loreto' in the pilgrimage basilica at Loreto he would have gained a fake since the original disappeared without trace in 1618 to be replaced by copies in 1741 and 1759 [L. Dussler, *Raphael; A Critical Catalogue of his pictures, wall-paintings and tapestries,* London, 1971.]

[2] Probably R. Bowyer of Marlborough Place, Pall Mall, publisher of prints [S. Houfe, *The Dictionary of British Book Illustrators and Caricaturists, 1800-1914,* London, 1978.]

[3] Phillipe Jacques de Loutherbourg's influential *The Romantic and Picturesque Scenery of England and Wales* appeared in 1805.

[4] B.H. Malkin's, *The Scenery, Antiquities and Biography of South Wales,* with views by Laporte was published in 1804, being followed by a two volume octavo edition in 1807.

Viganoni leaves us Tuesday. His improvement of Mariamne's playing & singing is wonderful, but I believe her talents for drawing are equally good.[1] She has begun on Heads and her progress in 6 lessons has been extraordinary. Poor Banks who is now here is very much surprized at it. You may not perhaps have heard that he has had a paralytick stroke in one arm. I fear it has affected his whole frame, for he is now a sad wreck.[2] Todd has been received into St Lukes, but he can never be trusted again. However I shall take care of him, though he had most shamefully neglected my Kitchen garden and destroyed seeds without number.[3] If you can send us any new Botany Bay seeds we shall thank you.

Mrs Johnes & my daughter unite with me in kind compliments to Mrs Smith & your Sisters.

I am, my dear Doctor,

Yours ever,

T. Johnes

---

[1] Guiseppi Viganoni, Mariamne Johnes's singing teacher, appears in none of the standard musical dictionaries nor does he feature on any of the contemporary Covent Garden playbills. He was, however, active in the King's Theatre, Haymarket in the seasons 1781-1783. [*The London Stage, 1660-1800.*] William Hawes, great great grandfather of the composer Malcolm Arnold, recalled in 1835 that Viganoni, Bauti and Rovedino 'were in their glory' in the Haymarket during the 1790's. [*Royal Opera House Archives, William Hawes Correspondence*]. Two engravings of Guiseppi Viganoni (1754-1823) are listed in the *Harvard University Catalogue of Dramatic Portraits*. According to Johnes, 'His taste is that of a manly and pure sort very uncommon for an Italian'. Moreover, he noted approvingly, when the Italian first heard the *Hallelujah Chorus*, '. . . his hair stood on end and he was not himself for several hours. [Adv. MS. 22.4.12, f.222]

[2] Thomas Banks, the sculptor.

[3] A reference to Todd's breakdown. While he may not have worked again in the kitchen garden, he seems to have recovered sufficiently to work in the forestry department to which his correspondence in 1805 with the Royal Society of Arts bears witness.

To William Roscoe, in Liverpool   L.R.O. (Ros), 2218

Hafod, Oct. 4, 1803

My dear Sir,

I had the pleasure of receiving yesterday your very obliging favor of the 29th Sept. and beg you will accept my best thanks for it. In another cover I send you Worthington's last account, and a letter from Mr Olmius one of the Commissioners of Excise. I sent Worthington 127.13.0£ on the 4th of June, by a draft *at sight* on Martin & Co. This ought to have paid the whole of the duties according to the statement in their letter before the additional one was imposed. I am afraid the wine will have been tapped, or suffered damage, by passing through so many hands and I suspect Worthington must have been *particeps criminis*. At all events his conduct has been so disgraceful I will never have anything to say to him again. Either himself or the Excise ought to reimburse me my expenses which I think amount to 80£, for it was very old wine, particularly chosen by a friend of Liston. The freight I now find of a Hogshead of Port to Bristol is 6£ so that as I shall fear some mischief having happened to the Wine, I had rather have my expenses & costs. This has been the second attack of the Excise at your ports which will force me to return to Bristol. [1]

I am very happy you are pleased with our Doctor Smith; he is a particular favorite here, and it would make me happy if you would contrive to meet him in this wild spot, that I may return you personally my thanks for all your friendly attentions. When Mr Shepherd was here, we looked but in vain for books that might have induced you to come hither, but he thought you had everything I had that could interest you in your pursuits.

You will have at your two First Concerts Viganoni. If you are not acquainted with him, I beg leave to recommend him to your notice; for his conduct here has been such, that I could wish by every means to make him a return in attention, since he would not accept of any other. I never had a pleasanter visitor, and the pains he took with my daughter will be very visible whenever I may have the pleasure of seeing you. He was so much pleased with my Hermitage that he promises to return early next year & make a longer stay.

[1] Where presumably the Excise authorities were less vigilant.

Since Mr Shepherd compares this place to Paradise, I must say that Adam & Eve are perfectly contented with it, and that we have no Cain. Pray give my Compliments to him.

I am, my dear Sir,

Your obliged, Humble Servant,

T. Johnes

To Edward Williams   N.L.W. MS. 21281 E, f.216

Hafod, Dec. 9th, 1803

You must not think, my dear Sir, that I have been insensible to the two excellent letters I received from you, by my delay in answering them. The Truth is, at the moment they came I was very much employed about the defence of the Country & laid them aside so carefully I could not find them again. I am indeed very much obliged to you for the pains you have taken respecting *burnt* Lime being imported into this Country. I adopt your idea; to say the truth I forestalled it before I had come to it in your letter.

I think however subscriptions would fail, and the moment I shall succeed to my whole fortune I will make the experiment in my own bottom. I the meantime I shall thank you to turn your thoughts on the best sorts of vessels for the importation, and lining them with Copper would perhaps be as cheap, certainly lighter, than with Tin. The Experiment, if I live, shall be tried & I hope under your direction. For it will be of the most importance to this Country, when Lime is so essential & becoming daily dearer. [1]

I am busy at work on Froissart, and inclosed send you one of the last proofs; the first volume will be ready by Christmas.

---

[1] This rather dubious project never materialised.

When will Mr. Davies' survey of our Wales come out?[2] Should any business or pleasure bring you to these parts I need not say I shall be very happy to see you.

I am, dear Sir,

Yours very truly,

T. Johnes

To Robert Liston, in Copenhagan   Liston MS. 5605, f.181

Hafod, Dec. 10, 1803

My dear Liston,

I only write two (lines) for I know they will give you both pleasure, to inform you that my friend Hugh Smith has just wrote me word he has disposed of so much of the Estates as to warrant him in saying I shall be freed from all my difficulties by Lady day. Viva!! *We* shall go to London sometime in March, and I will take care never to put myself again in a similar disgraceful state. We are all well & unite in every kind Compliment to you both.

I am,

My Dear Friend,

Always Yours,

T. Johnes

[1]Walter Davies (Gwallter Mechain) (1761-1849), antiquary, cleric, poet and agriculturist. Besides his various Welsh literary works, Davies's *A General View of the Agriculture and Domestic Economy of South Wales* (2 Vols., 1814), was widely influential.

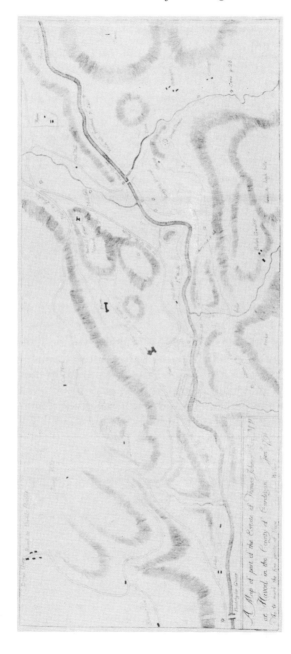

The Hafod demesne showing the various walks etc., as delineated by William Blake
in Cumberland's *An Attempt to Describe Hafod* (1796)
(by permission of the National Library of Wales)

To Robert Liston, in Edinburgh   Liston MS. 5606, f.60

Hafod, Feb. 3, 1804

My dear Liston,

It is so very long since I had the pleasure of hearing from you or from Mrs Liston, that I fear one or both of you are unwell. We have had the dampest winter I ever remember, but excepting colds we have all continued well. As for Mariamne you will guess how well she is when about ten days ago she & her aunt walked to the Devils Bridge & back again. They were caught in a snow storm returning which gave them slight colds.

The first volume of Froissart is now with White, but I believe he does not publish before he has the second or perhaps the whole. I wish it were better, for I see on reading it all together hundreds of faults that must now go with all their sins on their head. I trust that the general amusement it must give will serve as a passport for its errors.

I intend going with my family to Town the 19th or 20th March for two months. Poor Mary has formed such expectations of the opera, that I am afraid she will be disappointed. That seems to be the sole pleasure she looks to & the improvement of herself. I told you in my former letters that Viganoni was here last summer, who has improved her so much in music you would not know it again. She had likewise a drawing master, and promises to make an equal proficiency in that as in music. Some of her performances are extraordinary.

I have also told you my misfortune with the Butt of Sherry, which my rascally agent in Liverpool sold, and I begged you would inquire concerning Sherry that had been in the East Indies at Gottenburg.[1] I hope my letters have not miscarried. I have never heard of your American Madiera. You see that all this fuss of invasion does not alarm us. I wish he would come out of his Cage, for I should like the Tyger was sent [sic] on David Jones' locker, but his prudence in this one instance will prevent it.[2]

[1] As Anglo-French economic warfare intensified, the Swedish port of Gothenburg became a vital entrepôt for British exports and re-imports into northern Europe.

[2] Napoleon's sole hope of total victory lay in the invasion and ultimate conquest of Britain. To this end he assembled an enormous invasion force at Boulogne so that by the middle of the summer of 1805, one hundred thousand men and the necessary transport facilities lay in preparation. Ultimately the planned invasion was abandoned as Napoleon was obliged to turn his troops against Austria and Prussia.

I have just finished a new walk far superior in grandeur & variety to any I had. It even surpasses *my* expectations. You will be delighted when you see it for it is indeed beautiful & completes the circuit on each side (of) the river. I mean to have a swing bridge of Chains from Rock to Rock, so do not be surprised if you read in some Tourist of my having caused the death of several by fear or drowning.

The Dutch Cows turn out wonderfully. They are now in good condition & calving. Two of them gave for one day 10 gallons of milk each & now they give 8. *A propos*, this brings to my mind Mr Meerman's library. I hear from the distress caused by the French, it is to be disposed of. You have some correspondents in Holland; I shall be infinitely obliged if you will *instantly* write to know the truth of this, and should it be so to let me have his lowest price for it *en bloc*. I should wish it delivered in London & paid for there, but I am very anxious to have it, if possible on any terms. Pray write about this as soon as you can. I shall be enabled when in London in March to pay for it.[1]

My Wife & Girl unite with me in every kind Compliment etc. to Mrs Liston.

I am, my dear Liston,

Yours always,

T. Johnes

To Robert Anderson, in Edinburgh   Adv. MS. 22.4.12., f.231

Pall Mall 77, April 19, 1804

My Dear Sir,

I am exceedingly obliged to you for your two letters, the last just received, and for the trouble I am continually giving you respecting my Printers. I wrote to Henderson to say his brother would not do from incapacity, and I fancy I received a letter from Edinburgh from the brother to him, which I inclosed on Tuesday. But there was no

[1] Johann Meerman (1754-1815), collector and bibliophile.

letter with it for me, only the direction. I must still trespass on your friendship and beg leave to desire you would arrange the whole as you shall think best, for I see unless you take the management I shall fare but badly. Henderson himself seems both indolent & selfish. To please him I gave a brother an ensignsy in the Cardigan Militia, who I am sorry to find has not done me much credit.[1]

I could wish to hasten the work, which can only be done by making exertions in the Summer, for the weather & shortness of Winter days prevent it. And from July to October, much may be done in these four months. I am now at my 248 page of the 2nd volume, and if I could finish that & the 3rd by about Christmas, the rest would be easy enough. White is impatient to publish the first, which I suppose will come out the first week of May with the Chimney Sweepers. We wait for the Engravings. Where we shall I send your Copy? To Heriot's Green?[2] I fear the Gentleman who brought me your *Life* of Smollet, for which pray accept my best thanks, will be returned before then, as on his card he said he should only remain a fortnight. I hope you may like it, but the more I look at it, the greater & more numerous errors I see. *Iacter alea est.*[3] It must therefore take its chance.

With regard to Lord Buchan, I thought it right to send you his Lordship's letters, and I am happy I did so. His conduct seems very strange & to me unaccountable. We have long corresponded, though never had any personal communication. I was however somewhat astonished some time ago to hear that he claimed what merit there may be in having urged me to translate Froissart, for he never knew anything of the matter until Dr James Anderson informed him of my intentions & of having made some progress.[4]

I can send you but little news except what you see in the papers. Party runs high and I think it very probable the present Ministry may be overturned, but it is not easy to say who shall succeed. The Grenvilles have offered themselves as I hear to Fox, *mains liées*, except in the article of reform. Fox has *I hear* offered himself to take any place under Pitt, who I hear also stands aloof from all parties. It is a

[1] Henderson appears to have attempted to use his position at Hafod to gain favours and posts for others of his family.

[2] Anderson's address in Edinburgh.

[3] Or, more accurately, *Alea jacta est*: the die is cast.

[4] David Steuart Erskine, 11th Earl of Buchan (1742-1829), antiquary, agricultural improver and eccentric. A fussy and rather tedious patron of arts and letters, Buchan had the irritating habit of claiming close association with literary and artistic projects with which in reality he was only peripherally involved.

melancholy business that when the Enemy is at the door there should be such scrambling for power. A more efficient Ministry we should have; but all parties ought now to unite for the common good.[1]

On Fryday will be the first trial of Pitt's friends respecting his motion about the army of reserve. He has now a slight attack of gout, & on Monday is Fox's motion to endeavour to unite the whole of the various oppositions.[2]

My daughter has been very seriously indisposed with cold & fever. The last is I hope abating, but she has alarmed us both exceedingly.

I trust you will keep your Engagment with Martin, for if you are fond of Music I shall be able to give you very good as Viganoni & Cramer will both be with us in August.[3]

I am, my dear Sir,

Yours very truly,

T. Johnes

[1] The country as a whole had little confidence in Addington's ability to stand fast against Napoleon and his resignation led to Pitt's second Ministry in May 1804. Although Fox had agreed to serve under Pitt, the King, Fox's sworn enemy, vetoed any appointment so that Fox, the Grenvilles and their supporters coalesced into a strong Whig opposition. This grouping became a source of embarrassment to Pitt by persisting with the question of Catholic emancipation which issue Pitt had promised the King not to revive.

[2] Pitt's motion on the matter of the Army of Reserve on April 25th resulted in a government majority of a mere 37 and the probability of a mass-desertion of pro-ministerial backbenchers led many to think (rightly) that Addington's ministry was close to collapse.

[3] Johann Baptist Cramer (1771-1858), pianist, composer, music publisher, and friend of Haydn and Beethoven. In June Johnes explained to Anderson that besides Cramer and Viganoni, Dragonetti, 'who plays on his tremendous double bass like on a fiddle', would be at Hafod [Adv. MS. 22.4.12. f.235]. Dragonetti (1763-1846) had been living in London since 1794. He was renowned both for his superlative bass playing and the enormity of his fees. [*The New Grove Dictionary of Music and Musicians*, V, p. 608]

To Robert Liston, in Edinburgh   Liston MS. 5608, f.21

May 1, 1804, 77 Pall Mall

My dear Liston,

I have this moment your letter of the 28th from Glasgow, & very truly do we condole with you & Mrs Liston on your loss. Pitcairn, who has just left us, says he was his old schoolfellow & an excellent man. Indeed we condole with you.

The danger is now over, but last week I despaired of our poor Girl. She has been very ill with a bilious fever for 16 or 18 days, caught by her own imprudence in not following a Mother's advice. However that is over, and she has suffered most severely for it. Pitcairn has behaved most kindly, but he would call in Dr Baillie, who has this day taken his leave. The fever is gone, but she has not yet quitted her bedchamber. However, as [sic] I trust she will gradually recover, so as to be well enough to see you both when you come to Town. We propose when able to bear a journey to carry her for a few days out of Town, then return for a fortnight to look about her, (for hitherto she has been but to two Operas) & then retire to our fastness.[1]

There is no one we would sooner go & see, but how will my work go on? The first volume with all its imperfections will probably come out in 8 or 10 days. *Je n'ai pas peur mais je Tremble.*

I long much to see you both, & hope you will arrive before we make our excursion.

In such times you would never forgive me if I was silent on politicks; last week I was indifferent if the world was at an end; now I am more alive.

Three parties have attacked the Doctor, & I suppose dethroned him, but who is to succeed is not so easily settled.[2] Perhaps this is the beginning of our difficulties. I voted for Mr Pitt, for I should have been the most ingratful [sic] fellow possible to have refused when he asked. Sorry I was to see those who owe him their all desert him.

[1] Matthew Baillie F.R.S. (1761-1823), nephew of John and William Hunter and Physician Extraordinary to George III. His *Observations on Paraplegia* (1822) indicated his interest in diseases of the spinal cord and hence his involvement in Mariamne Johnes's case. An earlier publication, *The Morbid Anatomy of some of the most important parts of the Human Body* (1795) was dedicated to his friend David Pitcairn.

[2] 'The Doctor': Henry Addington, Prime Minister (1801-1804).

The papers will inform you what passed in the Hse. of Lords. Mr Pitt was with the King all this morning. I hear he is unfettered from all parties, so he has a grand card to play if he does not lose the opportunity. There is much talk of a Regency, but I do not see how this can be after the conduct of the person who ought to be regent.[1] I called on one today who knows all, but he was silent, & only said Pitt was with the King and that Pitt could not form a Ministry without the Grenvilles or Fox. I confess I had rather the last, however much I have hated parts of his misconduct. I am promised news from the quarter I called on, & if any thing particular will send it to you. I do not expect you will be unemployed, but in the contrary earnestly sought for. It is no compliment to compare you with the Signories of Diplomacy who are now abroad.

Our kindest Compliments to Mrs Liston.

I am, my dear Liston,

Always yours,

T. Johnes

---

[1] In November 1788 George III had succumbed to a severe attack of porphyria, an hereditary condition exhibiting many of the symptoms of insanity. Fox and his allies, seeing the opportunity of seizing power under the patronage of the Prince of Wales, attempted to obtain an unconditional Regency for the Prince. Pitt, however, managed, early in 1789, to push through his Regency Bill which limited the powers of the Regent and protected the future interests of the King should he return to health. In so doing Pitt safeguarded the interests of himself and his supporters and as the King recovered, the Foxites' opportunity to oust Pitt began inexorably to ebb. By 1804-5, the King was once again suffering increasingly frequent bouts of porphyria, hence the discussion of the Regency matter.

To Robert Liston, in London   Liston MS. 5608, f.72

No. 6, Sion Hill, Clifton, Bristol

June 11th, 1804

My dear Liston,

I have the pleasure to say we arrived here the better for the journey on Tuesday last. I have been so vexed with the infamous conduct of Herbert Lloyd that I could not write sooner. Bad & infamous as I think of him I could not believe that even *he* knowing the dangerous state of my Child, & that his whole demand would inevitably be paid within the month, would have sent an execution to Hafod. But so it was, and the first I heard of it was last Tuesday from the undersheriff of Bath. This is a pettyfogging Scoundrel & fool who declared he would sell the Books etc. This enraged me, & I swore if he touched one thing I would sell every inch of property & quit the Country. This I believe alarmed him. He went for London on Saturday when all was paid. So there is an end of this rascally business. But this is not all; my friend Smith desired Mr Shute, who has for 20 years professed a great friendship for me! to pay one third of his purchase money (the whole of which he must pay this month) just as I was leaving Town in order to prevent Lloyd's malice, but strange to say he refused!![1] There's friendship for you. Oh, I am sick of such. I begin to think I have been dreaming & that it exists only in poetry & romance.

Well, our dear Mary is daily gaining health & strength. She has walked out leaning on my arm these two days and I trust we shall get home as I proposed, with her in perfect health.

I did not return you the Dane's letter about Madiera, wishing to keep it until the samples arrived. Pray have them sent to me at Clifton. Have you ever done any thing about the Hungary wines? I may talk now, but I can assure you had those rascals threats been put into execution we would all have left the Country, for my Heroines were as willing as myself. Aye Mary too, without a sigh, though Hafod is so dear to her.

---

[1] Shute, whose identity is not clear, was presumably among the purchasers of Johnes's sales of land the previous year. A John Shute of St. David's, Exeter, features in N.L.W. Crosswood Deeds, II, 615.

I fear everything bad is coming on us, & that the people seeing no Ministry can command more than 40 majority will take the management themselves. Being armed they may now say like the Irish,————or else.

Our kind loves attend Mrs Liston.

Always yours,

T. Johnes

To George Cumberland at Axbridge, Somerset   Add. MS. 36499, f.469

Clifton, June 24, 1804

My Dear Sir,

We had hopes of seeing you before we left this place which we shall do tomorrow with good bills of health, but shall not reach home until Fryday sennight.

I have found you a companion for Plinlimmon that you will thank me for; an excellent man & scholar, & as great an enthusiast for his own Country, Wales as you are. He writes, speaks, & reads Welsh, Greek, Latin, Italian & French. He is to be in Cardiganshire the latter end of next month and you may fix with him to meet you at Hafod, at any time but *the Cardigan Assize week*, from whence you may undertake your Pilgrimage. This gentleman is D. Jones of Redlands. [1]

My ladies send you their Compliments.

I am always yours,

T. Johnes

[1] Possibly David Jones of Llandovery, Unitarian Minister and Barrister.

To R.F. Greville   Add MS. 42072, f.65

Hafod, July 16, 1804

My Dear Greville,

I am sure you will be happy to hear we are returned home, & that our dear Girl is daily recovering. Just after I saw you we went to Beddoes at Clifton who as usual did her every good. We then made an excursion for a few days to Hampshire, but I did not think that air agreed with her. She is now visibly better every day.

We are in high beauty as to foliage etc. for we have not suffered any way from blight; it has been very severe in several parts of England, particularly in the New Forest. I never saw the Trees make such shoots as this year. I wish I could prevail on you & Lady Mansfield to come to us; we have room for you all, and you would see much done since your last visit. Indeed you know it is a place, like to Women & miles *où il y a toujours quelquechose à refaire.* [1]

I made last winter a new walk, so far surpassing my old ones that I almost repent having done it, for to use a nursery phrase, it puts their nose out of joint.

My farm is going on vastly well, and as I have now Shepherds I can depend on, I could wish to try a cross with the Spaniard. I was not sufficiently prepared when I before attempted it. Has the King any Rams to sell or dispose of? Should he have such, pray let me know and their prices. I want two only. [2] By degrees I shall reduce my Cattle & keep to Sheep, for they are most profitable & easiest managed.

We are happy at the good accounts of His Majesty's health, pray God it may long, very long, continue. As affecting a sight as I ever saw was my parishioners the first time our Parson prayed for him.

Mrs Johnes unites with me in compliments to Lady Mansfield.

I am, my dear Greville,

Your always,

T. Johnes

[1] Greville married Louisa, Countess of Mansfield in 1797.
[2] Of the Merino breed.

Hafod: the river Ystwyth above the first bridge, by John 'Warwick' Smith
(by permission of the National Library of Wales)

To Charles Taylor,
Secretary,
Royal Society of Arts.

Transactions of the Society for the
Encouragement of Arts, Manufactures
and Commerce, XXIII, 1805, pp.27-28

Hafod, Jan. 7, 1805

Sir,

I now enclose you such an account as I hope will be satisfactory, and entitle me to the Honorary Premium of the Society, either for my Oaks, Larches, or Timber trees in general. In December, 1802, I wrote to inform you that my gardener had raised for me 922,000 Oaks, and which were then two years old in the nursery: of the above 58,600 were planted out last winter and last spring, agreeably to the Accounts and Certificates I have transmitted to you. They are now in a thriving state. From the 24th June, 1801, to June, 1802, 220,000 Larches were planted in the manner I have formerly mentioned, by making holes and covering the roots. All of which were planted on land not fit for the plough, and are well secured by good fences.[1]

I am, Sir,

Your most obedient servant,

Thomas Johnes

To Robert Anderson, in Edinburgh   Adv. MS. 24.2.12, f.245

Feb. 8, 1805

My dear Sir,

As you desire I would give you my opinion on the criticism in the *Edinburgh Review* I shall very freely do it, though to criticize a criticism is dull work indeed.

I confess myself very much disappointed; not indeed with what regards myself, for in that respect I am well pleased, but from the expectation of better writing & more knowledge. For this I am convinced it has not been done by the person you mention, for assuredly better things should come from him. I never met with greater ignorance or neglect. Before a book is reviewed facts should be known, and such positive assertions and blame thrown on me for not doing what I had done. I am much dissatisfied with my *Memoirs* for trusting to others who had promised to correct them, my indolence never attended to the corrections before or when at press, and literally this Memoir was written within the week. I do not say it but to depreciate what little merit it may have.

I suspect your reviewer is some young man who has not read much, nor is very learned in books but, smitten with the love of Black letter, sees nothing beautiful but in that. When he talked of Lord Berners' style, he must have been ignorant of the *English Bible*, that was printed about the same period, and for style & sublimity of writing all others must hide their heads. But, my dear Sir, 'Who shall decide when

[1] Johnes's letter was accompanied by notes of confirmation from James Todd, gardener, David Richards, gardener and the Rev. Lewis Evans, Minister of Eglwys Newydd.

Doctors disagree'.[1] The *British Critic* is warm in my praise because I have made a new translation, and quotes Chapters from Lord Berners and me that the publick may judge. The worthy Bishop of Dromore proposed my republishing Lord Berners' edition, but I believe I convinced his Lordship what a patchwork thing it would be; 'a thing of threads & patches'. I never could have done it. But what may perhaps surprise you still more is the avowal I now make to your own ear (for it proves my indolence too glaringly) that I have never read Froissart, but literally as I proved in the translation, nor can I were you to put me on the rack, say what the next page contains to that I am now translating. It is this novelty & uncertainty that urges me on. But to return to the *Life* of Froissart. The reviewer perhaps never looked into your worthy namesakes *Bee*.[2] There is in that work, a life of Froissart by me also, from what I could pick up, as I had not then *Les Mémoires de l'Académie*. It was without any names like several other trifles he was so flattering to praise. I have never read it since, nor can I say what volume it is in.

The reviewer makes a pompous description of Lord Berners' binding. It may be true but I never saw such and I have in my library a great many books in *their original binding*, that belonged to Diane du Poitiers which are uniformly bound in red or green Velvet with massy corners of *brass*, & clasps of the same. There is none of the embossings he talks of, and I should suppose from the rank she held in the world, she would have had her library most superbly bound. I merely mention (this) because when a person is incorrect in one circumstance, other assertions cannot be depended upon. Had he seen my *Memoirs*, he would have known there were editions of Froissart that even M. de Saint Palaye never saw, though the magnificent one I allude [sic] was at Paris in the *Bibliothèque de Soubise*. And he seems in perfect ignorance of the MS in Breslau that has made so much noise in the world, as well as of the intentions of the French to publish a new edition at the Louvre press as a continuation of their Historians. M. Dacier, whose talents are well known, was to have undertaken it, and I have now by me the only part of the edition that

---

[1] Pope, *Moral Essays, III, 1*.

[2] *The Bee*, launched by James Anderson in December 1790 was a literary and scientific miscellany which continued to appear until January 1794. Among its contents were included essays on the political progress of Britain, some of which (despite Anderson's personal conservatism) from their liberal nature provoked criticism from the establishment.

was ever printed, which does not conclude the first Volume. Nothing more will be done for I am in treaty with him for his MSS of the various readings.[1]

I must leave off now, for I lent Mr Henderson your extract, which came here yesterday and when I read it over again will answer any parts that I think may require it.

But all this is *between ourselves*. I wish they had waited for the whole, as would have been just. I am no Herald, & submit to the correction of the *first* arms of Douglas. But I now refer almost all that I do not clearly understand to my friend Mr Lodge, Somerset Herald, who is too intelligent to suffer their barbarous Griffins etc to go into the world unexplained.[2]

I wish the reviewer had compared me with the original French instead of Lord Berners, for I do not think it quite fair, as no translation was ever more slovenly made and whenever he comes to a difficulty, he cuts the Gordian knot, by skipping it over.

Feb. 10th.

The reviewer is I believe wrong in his costume of Henry the 8th Court. 'The buff coat, slashed sleeves and trunk hose', were I fancy introduced long after, but I have not time to look. I have no time to look either after the expressions of 'sheering off—making off' and 'shewing their heels', but I believe similar expressions will be found in the *French*.[3] I hope we shall look for them together this ensuing summer. I want to be compared with the original & then to have decided how such expressions should *now* be translated.

As I said in the beginning I am very well pleased with what has been said of me by the reviewer, but he seems to have compared it solely with Lord Berners, and desirous when he gives a blow to add a speedy plaish (?). In short it reminded me of Tubal's dialogue with Shylock.[4]

Adieu,

[Letter ends here]

[1] Bon Joseph, Baron Dacier (1742-1833). *Conservateur* of the Bibliothèque Nationale in 1800, he was elected to the Académie Francaise in 1823.

[2] Edmund Lodge (1756-1839), biographer and genealogist.

[3] Such 'quaint' expressions were considered by the reviewer to degrade Johnes's text.

[4] *Merchant of Venice, III, 1.*

To George Cumberland, at Axbridge, Somerset   Add. MS. 36500, f.143

Hafod, April 7, 1805

My dear Sir,

I am very happy your minerals are arrived safe, but as for your plan of hanging shelves in the Colonade, why that is occupied all summer long with bird cages. [1] And Babilon [sic], as you are pleased to call my *well arranged* appartments will not be soon ready to be given up, for I want an architect to dispose of them properly as a China closet. Viganoni thought of having it done, but his architect says he must see the spot, so that the planning will go far to equal the beautifying of it in expenses.

I am come tolerably well out of the Edinburgh Reviewer's claws. He has shewn consummate ignorance, for which probably he will be repaid by those he has before scratched. It is fair game, though rather ignoble in hawking to fly at Kites. They are always *Craven*, or *Cravant*—I know not which is the word, nor have time to look.

The *British Critic* has behaved handsome; the *Gentleman's Magazine* is very ignorant. These are all the criticisms I have seen. I can find many more faults than they have urged, and serious ones too, but these monthly critics I am convinced never read an Author through and it is miserable that the publick should be savaged by such.

We are coming into fine beauty and the first green of spring is enchanting, though it may not be picturesque. My Mountain farm is licking, like a Bear's cub, into Shape, and I hope in the course of the summer much of the bareness between here & the Devil's Bridge will be done away.

My wife and Girl are both well & send you their best Compliments.

I am,

My dear Sir,

Yours ever,

T. Johnes

[1] Over the course of a long life Cumberland assembled an impressive collection of minerals from various parts of Britain. Johnes had dispatched to Bristol a package of minerals from the lead workings in the locality of Hafod [Add. MS. 36500, f.115].

To Robert Liston, in Edinburgh   Liston MS. 5609, f.82

Hafod, July 17, 1805

My dear Liston,

You promised to write on your arrival at home, and not having heard from you makes us uneasy lest you or Mrs Liston may be ill. Do, therefore, if it has been owing to your laziness, conquer it and write on the receipt of this.

We have had a great variety of Company since you left us. The birthday was brilliant & went well off.[1] Mrs Liston's painter, Williams, has been here, but I find she never saw him. If she had, I do not think she would have given him so strong a letter of recommendation. I asked him to dinner twice when he called & when I met him in the walks. His ideas of Landscape & mine are somewhat different, for he complained of *too much* wood in Glamorganshire!! I saw only two slight Scetches [sic], of the Devil's Bridge & part of Chepstow Castle, & to judge from them I do not think he will make a great figure.

My chain bridge is up, and more than answers my expectations. It suits the place admirably, which is lower down than where I at first intended it, and the effect is delightful. I wanted Mr Williams to draw it, for it was a maiden view, but he preferred another spot, that could not include it, but which admitted some *naked* hills.[2]

I am busy at my hay harvest, & the weather is delightful for it. I say nothing of politicks for you will see more than I know in the papers.

We are all well & unite in every kind compliment to Mrs Liston.

I am,

Yours ever,

T. Johnes

[1] i.e. Mariamne Johnes's coming of age, June 30th, 1805, celebrated, as was her birthday each year, with a party at Hafod for the estate tenants and other countryfolk.

[2] Mrs Liston's protegé was probably Hugh William Williams (1773-1849), the widely-travelled Welsh painter who had made his home in Edinburgh. Johnes's comments once again underline his belief in the supreme importance of trees as elements in the "picturesque" landscape of Hafod.

To George Cumberland, at Axbridge, Somerset   Add. MS. 36500, f.220

Hafod, Sept. 24, 1805

My dear Sir,

I fancy Buonaparte has now fully sufficient employment without troubling our coasts, and that you will not soon have occasion for Gunboats nor any other implements of War. I hope this social war may be attended with good success and introduce a lasting peace among Mankind, although I rather wish it, than expect it.

My hill farming has been greatly checked, first from want of parers and burners, and from want of weather to dry the sods. I am convinced the speculation will be a good one, and I hope open other people's eyes who have similar land. Next year it will make some appearance, for if I can get hands I shall go on with it lustily. My plan is paring, burning, sow rape & fold it, then lay down with grass under oats. I believe you are perfectly right in what you say of the disease of Wheat.

I have thrown my swing bridge over the river, & it answers my expectations. I have likewise added a fine painted window to the Church, and shall erect the Obelisk as soon as the workmen come. [1] They were to have been here yesterday sennight.

We have had a miserable season, scarce two days dry together; how the corn has been got in is somewhat miraculous.

Mrs Johnes & our Girl have both been ailing & the first is now not well.

Aberystwith has literally overflowed; people have been forced to sleep in carriages. They are going to erect a Theatre and a self-appointed master of the Ceremonies of the tribe of Levy [sic] means to commence his operations of Coupée and Bourée next summer. A Mail Coach runs once a week from Ludlow, and you will see on the cover of this we have a post office at the Devil's Bridge. I never remember so many *curious* travellers as this year.

Mariamne is making great improvement in her drawing under an

---

[1]The obelisk, designed by W.F. Pocock (and currently under renovation), commemorated the services to agriculture of Francis, 5th Duke of Bedford, who had died in the spring of 1802.

old acquaintance of yours, Stodhard [sic], who is now here. He is very deaf and, as the Scots say, *colded.* [1]

My ladies send you their best Compliments.

I am, my dear Sir,

Yours always,

T. Johnes

To Robert Anderson, in Edinburgh   Adv. MS. 24.2.12, f.265

Hafod, Nov. 10, 1805

My dear Sir,

Your letter of the 15th October followed me to the lower part of this Country where I was paying some visits. I can assure you the not having the pleasure of seeing you this summer was a serious mortification, but I hope the French proverb will be proved by you true that, '*Ce qui est deferé n'est pas perdu*'.

I am very happy you are pleased with the 3rd Vol. The 4th is not yet published from the fault of the engravers, and the negligence of those who undertook to see the plates done. I suppose it will come out in a short time or the new edition will get the start of it.

Inclosed I send you a note for 1.1.0£ for the carriage, but I must remain the 4d. in your debt. I thank you for your obliging attention in paying it.

I am sorry to confess I have been very idle indeed all the summer, but Joinville is not so pleasant a travelling companion as Froissart; and I have been in vain expecting the additions from the Breslau MS. I have as yet but those of the first volume, and do not intend to begin until the whole arrives, when I shall print the original text in with the translation. I think they will make two 4to volumes. Monstrelet is not

[1] Thomas Stothard, R.A. (1755-1834), painter, illustrator and associate of Blake. Besides decorating Burghley House, the Advocate's library in Edinburgh and elsewhere, he undertook several commissions for Johnes at Hafod.

advanced. When the printers come, then I must work, but I believe I must desire them to prolong their stay until June instead of February, for probably I shall go *en famille* to London in March or April & not return before the middle of June, when I will work lustily. I ought however to say as some excuse, that I have for these last 4 or 5 weeks had a violent attack of Bile, what [sic] I never had before. I am now a convalescent, but have an indolence that prevents me applying to anything with assiduity. I shall try to begin this week & continue on Joinville *con amore* if possible.

What a glorious victory we have had that contrasts grandly with Mack's dastardly conduct. We have paid however dearly for it in the loss of our Hero, whose good fortune seems to have left us on his death when Storms arose, that I fear may have hurt our fleet, & prevent(ed) the enemy's from gracing our Ports.[1] 20 Sail of the line taken or destroyed with a much inferior force of Ships & guns, is equal to any thing of romance, and Amadis himself need not have been ashamed of such deeds, when every sailor was a Hero.[2] We are a wonderful people when left to our own exertions!!!

My paper forces me to conclude.

Always yours,

T. Johnes

[1] General Mack's Austrian army had been defeated at Ulm on 7th October. Waning British morale was given a boost by Nelson's dramatic victory at Trafalgar on 21st October although celebrations were muted following the news of Nelson's death.

[2] Amadis was the eponymous hero of a long romantic Spanish novel, incorporating tales of travel and love, which Johnes may have read in the 1540 French translation by Des Essarts.

To George Cumberland, at Axbridge, Somerset   Add. MS. 36500, f.277

Hafod, Feb. 9, 1806

My dear Sir,

Peace is a fine thing, if to be had, but I believe this world to be in a state of Warfare from the greater shark Buonaparte to the lesser and innocent one of the Sea. I was never a very wise politician, and the Science has taken such a new flight from all that was and to be esteemed in Morality, Virtue and good faith, that I am less inclined than ever to trouble my head about it. I shall go on here just the same as if we were the most flourishing of Nations, & like Sterne's Dutchman when he planted Burgundy Vines at the Cape, did not look for Burgundy Wine from them but some sort of wine.[1] Just so I hope there may be those to benefit by my labours when I am no more.

I have seen so much of the *real* face of Mankind within the last two or three years, that I look on all, or at least the greater part as sharks, & think myself fortunate when they do not quite devour me, but are contented with a good Collop. What with false & professing friends & determined Enemies I have been miraculously saved from Ruin, and shall have an ample sufficiency in spite of them, both for ourselves and Child. But all this will not make me the less desirous of obtruding my person, nor more anxious to see the human face divine. What I have witnessed, & *quorum pars magna fui*, has formed my opinion that this world is a state of Warfare and that Man is *animal pugnax*, who sooner than not do mischief will tear his professed friend to pieces.[2] [3]

Don't think I grow misanthropical; my nature will not allow it, but I wish for as little communication as may be with my fellow animals.

I have but one Froissart for my own Library. The 4to Edition has been out of print since last spring, and I hear the 8vo that is now selling as fast as printed will be soon in the same state. Another is talked of without prints, at a cheap rate. Had I a copy of my own Edition which will be the only valuable one, it should be at your service. I dare say if you ask Dr Beddoes he will lend you his.

[1] Sterne's Dutchman trusted to chance and hoped for the best. [See, *A Sentimental Journey*]

[2] *Quaeque ipse miserrima vidi, Et quorum pars magna fui.* (I myself have witnessed these miserable events and played no small part in them). [Virgil, *Aeneid, II, 5*]

[3] Johnes had clearly read Hobbes : 'The condition of man. . . is a condition of war of everyone against everyone'. [*Leviathan*, Pt(1), Ch.4]

I am continuing my labours, for I find that is the only means to prevent musing & growing peevish on the present miseries.

Thank God we are all well and I think my daughter will succeed in drawing as in music. They send you their Compliments.

I am, my dear Sir,

Yours very sincerely,

T. Johnes

To George Cumberland, in Bristol   Add. MS. 36500, f.281

Hafod, Feb. 23, 1806

Do not be afraid, my dear Sir, it is not in my nature to turn Misanthrope. I may perhaps growl now & then when such flagrant instances of ingratitude and roguery as I have met with appear, but the storm is soon over, and the milkiness of human nature returns.

I should be very sorry that you thought yourself neglected by me, in not sending you a copy of *Froissart*. The state of the case is this, and you will see it was not in my power to do it, without giving away the whole. There were but 300 copies of Quarto & 25 of folio printed. Of the last I was to have for myself 5 copies, of the 4to none, but by paying. Of the folios I gave one to Lord Thurlow, one to Mr Edwards and the three others were for Mrs Johnes, my daughter, & my own library. The rule I laid down was to give copies only to such as had assisted me in the business, and to this plan I strictly adhered excepting for two Physicians who had more carefully attended my daughter, and frequently refused fees. Had I given copies to my friends in general, there would have remained but little for sale, and this plan was adopted in consequence of the agreement with Mr White who was to fix what price he pleased for the sale of the Edition, giving me a certain sum per Volume delivered to him. And I can assure (you) on the winding up of this business the balance in this respect was much against me.

I have entered into agreement with Longman for the 8vo Edition, but without stipulating for any copies for the reasons of not offending; but which I am much concerned to see has been a vain attempt. I have not a copy of the first Edition, nor is there one unsold, but if you wish for an octavo one, which will assuredly be the most correct, I shall be very happy to send you one.

I am, my dear Sir,

Yours very sincerely,

T. Johnes

To Robert Anderson, in Edinburgh   Adv. MS. 24.2.12, f.281

Hafod, April 18, 1806

My dear Sir,

I answer your letter of the 9th which I had the pleasure to receive yesterday, without loss of time, first to thank you for the continual trouble I am giving you, & next to protest against binding myself to any conditions whatever of providing for the Henderson who was forced to quit the Cardiganshire Militia. It is a mere trick, formed by the Elder brother, who has written me a letter that I shall enclose with the one of the Poet's, expressing his satisfaction and not a word of this brother, but brother Isaac is brought forward to insist on it as a condition *sine qua non.* [1] Now I had a promise from Lord Hawkesbury of a commission in the new South Wales Corps, but the change of

[1] In March Henderson had expressed his intention (against Johnes's wishes) of bringing his wife, child, maid and younger brother to Hafod. [Adv. MS. 24.2.12, f.277] Johnes had already obtained a place for another brother ('The Poet') in the Cardiganshire Militia, although such was the latter's incompetence that he had been asked to surrender his commission. While Johnes seems to have been prepared to help the younger brother Isaac to a commission in the South Wales Corps, Isaac's persistent demands for patronage appear to have upset him.

Ministry prevented it taking place.[1] I have very little acquaintance with Lord Spencer who I did not think attended to an application as he should have done when at the Admiralty, which has made me shy of making any applications to him. Indeed had it not been for my unfortunate loss, I should have been now in London, when I intended doing it personally. But this *demand* of Brother Isaac's has cooled me completely as to the business for when the wages I give are so handsome, I should suppose printers would be glad to come.

You have discriminated the Characters as I have done. I have always found Lhind most willing & open, having my interest at heart, but the others sneakers & hypocritically sentimental or impertinent.[2] I gave them 20£ to carry them home, & as that was fully sufficient I cannot think of giving more now, for if Henderson brings his family it is to oblige himself & not me. I almost dread the Sentiments & gentility I am to encounter.

Lhind has been very active in procuring me paper as good, and on much more reasonable terms than I have hitherto had it from a Mr Balfour, and he it was who proposed another Compositor. In short I have always had great comfort with him, but have been forced to keep his Companions at arms length which is what I dislike much. I must therefore my good Sir beg you will have the goodness to settle these matters, including always a sheet per day, or if that cannot be done with such intruders to whom if you give an Inch will require an Ell, I dare say your friend can find others as willing to come as the Hendersons.

I have had (between ourselves) a curious letter from Ld. Buchan which, as I hope to see you in the course of the Summer for we shall not go far from home, I shall shew you.

I am, my dear Sir,

Your much obliged,

Humble Servant,

T. Johnes

[1] Lord Grenville succeeded Pitt as Prime Minister in February 1806 whereupon, with the exception of Charles Long and Lord Spencer, one of the Post Masters-General, no member of Pitt's government was asked to stay in office.
[2] William Lhind, assistant printer at the Hafod Press.

To James Edward Smith, in Norwich   Linn. Soc. (Smith), 16, f.156

Wednesday [April 25 1806]

My dear Sir,

I had the pleasure of yours yesterday, & we all thank you for your friendly condoleance [sic]. The Blow has been most severe, and more so from being so very unexpected. It will be long before any of us recover (from) it, and he is very ill indeed.[1] But no more of this.

You may be assured I shall be happy to do every thing to assist you in the publication of Hafod etc. But my circle is now become so small from defalcations of summer [sic] friends & other incidences that have torn off Masks, I see few, and am not over anxious to increase it, nor have any further knowledge of the World. The longer I remain here the more I take root, and I do not think I shall be in a hurry to quit it again. I am not therefore so much surprized at Mr Salisbury's Conduct as I should have been some time ago, but am now rather inclined to think it natural, and was I to begin life again, I would follow Ancient Pistol's maxim.[2] That I have so many open & concealed enemies and more damned good natured friends, I am convinced of, but as my guardian angel Hugh Smith has so nearly brought all my affairs to a happy conclusion, I suspect you have been misinformed. However that may be, as I wish now to be always *en garde*, I shall beg of you to let me know by an early post the subject of your intelligence. In regard to rogues, I hold the maxim of *Trompeur, Trompeur & demi*, perfectly just.[3] At least it is one I would follow whenever I thought an honest man in danger.

I am glad you like Malkin's book. He is a very particular friend of mine who has proved his worth in numberless instances. Mariamne is quite well , & when I say she walks from 5 to 7 miles a day, you will

[1] Johnes's sister Elizabeth Hanbury Williams had died the previous month.
[2] Richard Anthony Salisbury (1761-1829) the Edinburgh-trained botanist had previously been intimate with James Edward Smith. In 1802, however, the two men fell out when Smith criticised Salisbury's advocacy of the natural, as opposed to the Linnean, system of plant classification. Subsequently Smith's letters to his friends and associates grew increasingly astringent in their criticism both of Salisbury's personal and professional life. For Ancient Pistol's maxim *Se fortune me tormente sperato me contento* see Henry IV (2), II, 4.
[3] *A trompeur, trompeur et demi*: Every deceiver has his match. [N. du Fail, *Contes et Discours d'Eutrapel*, 1548.]

think so too. She turns out every thing, indeed surpasses every thing I could have hoped. We are all well in health, but overwhelmed almost with the horrid blow.

Pray remember us kindly, that is to say Mrs Johnes & myself to Mr & Mrs Kindersley. Had our strange Sister followed his advice it would have been better for her.

I am my dear Doctor,

Yours always,

T. Johnes

To James Edward Smith, in Norwich   Linn. Soc. (Smith), 16, f.160

Wednesday [August 20 1806]

My dear Sir,

As I have an idle half hour I cannot better employ it than in thanking you for your letter of the 13th, received yesterday. I fear your friend Col. Preston will come here when I am from home, for I shall set out tomorrow for Cardigan Assizes, to pay visits etc. I go with Col. Wallis our Sheriff & my guardian angel Hugh Smith, both of whom I expect this evening. Mrs Johnes cannot accompany us for she has had a sharp return of the spasms, and unless she is better when I return she will not be able to see any strangers. Poor Beddoes has been very ill, most dangerously so, but is now a convalescent. He is you know our sheet anchor, and as he knows our Constitutions so well, is successful. He has been ordered wine!!!

I have made great improvements both within and without doors, by taking away a bad circular stairs, and all its dirty appendages, and making of the place a very handsome anti-library in which I have introduced part of my painted Glass. I have had sufficient besides for a fine painted Window in my Church & for those at the end of my gallery upstairs. I have made some new walks & thrown a beautiful chain bridge over the River, which if *properly* tried, would I dare say prove as efficacious as Dr Graham's celestial bed.[1] I have let out my farm I had in hand to 5 substantial tenants, and at three times the rent it was when I took it in hand, and have begun on improving a large tract of wild ground to the amount of 2000 acres, which I shall hope to let out very advantageously indeed in four or five years when I shall continue my improvements farther afield. So you see however desperate I may think public affairs, I do not act accordingly. Somebody will be benefited, and I am employed and amused.

I am interrupted by the arrival of three maiden cousins by my Mother's side, whom I have not seen these thirty years. They are on their way home from bathing in Aberystwith.

Excuse my saying more.

Always yours,

T. Johnes

To George Cumberland, in Bristol   Add. MS. 36500, f.370

Hafod, Sept. 15, 1806

My dear Sir,

As you put no date to your last obliging Letter, the Lord knows how long I have delayed thanking you for it. But I have been attending Cardigan assizes, paying visits etc and when at home I write a sheet, correct a sheet & revise a sheet daily, so that you must allow I have causes sufficient to excuse my silence.

I think with you in what you say of Knight's book. Taste may be felt, but not taught—and I differ from him in some of his other remarks.[2]

[1] James Graham (1745-1794), the celebrated quack doctor listed among his numerous inventions the 'Grand Celestial Bed', a 'magnetico-electrico' contrivance whose movement and agitation was designed to assist barren couples to conceive. Graham's lyrical advertisements of its sensual effects duped many, but not Horace Walpole who tersely summed up the preposterous creation as 'the most impudent puppet show of imposition'. [G. Williams, *The Age of Agony; The Art of Healing c. 1700-1800*, London, 1975.]

[2] R. Payne Knight, *An Analytical Inquiry into the Principles of Taste*, London, 1805. In this work, which was widely read and went through four editions, Knight attempted

I have almost finished printing Joinville and have ordered a copy to be put aside for you. I think you will like it. I do, and believe it may please as well as Froissart. I am now at work on Monstrelet, and shall close my career with Comines. So you see I have cut out work enough for myself within doors, & without I am not idle. I have let out the farm I had in hand satisfactorily, and am working into shape a beautiful, but ill-licked Cub of two thousand acres, that will amply repay in beauty & profit within a few years.

I shall thank you to send me a rough drawing, as rough as you please, of an Arch like to the one General Conway erected at Park Place. There is an engraving of it in Robertson's *Bath Road from London*. I wish it to be 20 feet high, and 14 feet wide, and to be built of very large rough stones, such as I have ready for it. It is to cross the high road on the *point* of the Turnpike leading from Hafod to the Devil's Bridge, and will be flanked with plantations of Larch.[1] I want it as a working sketch to show the masons. I know you will excuse the trouble I am now giving you.

As to politicks I believe we are as bad as may be and unless we correct ourselves must be undone. As for a Foreign enemy invading us, it is a farce if we be but true to ourselves. But we are proceeding in Luxuries with Giant Strides; and I could quote instances from these poor Countries that would astonish you.

Our weather is miserable since the Feast day of that pissing St. Swithin.[2] I fear for our hill harvests, & for our poor labourers that are constantly wet.

My ladies send you their best Compliments.

I am, my dear Sir,

Always yours,

T. Johnes

Mariamne is making great progress in drawing.

to formulate a universal standard of taste. Like others of his works, the *Analytical Inquiry* was a piece of considerable erudition, yet, as his recent biographer observes, 'The cumulative effect of his verbal meanderings is frequently more than mildly soporific'. [F. Messmann, *Richard Payne Knight, The Twilight of Virtuosity*, Mouton, 1974]

[1] Cumberland's drawings had arrived at Hafod by October 5th, and Johnes erected the arch during the course of the following spring. It still remains in position [Add. MS. 36500, f.389].

[2] July 15th.

To George Cumberland, in Bristol   Add. MS. 36500, f.405

Hafod, Oct. 15, [1806]

My dear Sir,

We were greatly glad to hear of your safe arrival at your fireside. The old adage of 'who has a companion has a master' was proved true in your case when here. When you next come, come alone. You will see more and be your own master.

I agree with you as to the great mismanagement of Estates. How should it be otherwise when they are turned over to attornies and Agents. Infinite improvements may be made, but they must not be looked for in the present race of proprietors. These are however daily changing. I am completely against the paring system unless in very bad lands indeed, for the proprietors must be ruined by it. What may do for Lord Fife's country, would not do here. It is indolence only which is our enemy.[1]

I offered Addington to let these 7800 acres to a Colony of Grisons at 1/6 an acre for three lives, and 20 years after if he would advance the 100 families 10,000£ for their expenses & travelling etc. His eyes did not see the wealth these 500 persons would bring to such a Country, and deserves to be cursed for it. But it was lucky for me; it would have ruined my Child & broken my heart, for I must have clung to them and if they had not succeeded, and the chances were against them, I must have been involved. This individual loss would have made the Country. Candide was a grand Philosopher.[2]

I am just going to build my new Paraclete [sic]; it shall have white walls, and a silver spring is beside it. My sale is on Thursday and a most magnificent catalogue it makes of near 200 articles. Those who love a dairy, should give any price for what I dispose of—and yet perhaps so ignorant are we yet in these parts, they may not sell for one third of their real value.[3]

[1] As Johnes implied in *Landlord's Advice,* the practice of paring and burning the turf overlaying mineral soils would rapidly exhaust the organic matter level and hence the potential fertility of such soils. On deep peats, however, the procedure was quite acceptable as he demonstrated on his own uplands.

[2] In his garbled version of Leibnitz's teaching Voltaire's Pangloss argued that individual misfortunes were frequently essential for the general good. Johnes's natural generosity would have obliged him to finance his Swiss colony in the event of their (inevitable?) failure.

[3] The disposal of the home farm dairy, established three years previously. [See Add. MS. 36501, f.65]

Last post brought me a letter from our good friend Anderson. You never mentioned a word here of *Home!!*

Viganoni left us this day sennight on account of Gould(?) the Opera on the 3rd next month.[1] We have now lost our delightful concerts, and the weather weeps his loss, for we have not had one dry day since he went away.

We are all quite well & the Ladies send you their kind compliments. Mariamne thanks you for the music.

I am, my dear Sir,

Yours always,

T. Johnes

To the Rev. John Jenkins, Cilbronnau   N.L.W. MS. 1891 D, f.32

Hafod, Oct. 27, 1806

Dear Sir,

The King having dissolved the Parliament, I beg leave to offer myself again as Candidate to represent this County. I have so often had experience of your friendship that I shall flatter myself with the honour of your support at the ensuing Election.[2]

My attachment to the County is too well known for me to trouble you with professions for I can assure you that I shall never feel greater pleasure than when contributing to its prosperity.

I am, my dear Sir,

Your most obedient humble Servant,

T. Johnes

[1] Francis Gould, manager of the King's Theatre, Haymarket from 1803-1807 [S. Sadie (ed.), *The New Grove Dictionary of Music and Musicians*, London, 1980].

[2] Johnes was returned unopposed as member for the County.

To George Cumberland, in Bristol   Add. MS. 36500, f.417

Hafod, Nov. 17, 1806

My dear Sir,

I should have thanked you before for your last letter but I waited until I should be re-elected. This took place last Tuesday with greater unanimity than ever, and I returned here two days ago.

The Library I bought was from the Pesaro family, not Pisani. It is now on its road hither, and the bookcases come from Carmarthen tomorrow to be in time to receive it. Aldus was not more celebrated for the beauty of his types, than for his correctness; his editions are equal to Manuscripts and I believe I have the most complete set existing. They amount to upwards of 600 volumes. Your *Sogno of Polisilo*, 1545, was the second edition. The first & rarest is of 1499 and is a prodigious fine specimen of his printing in the Roman character. I do not think I have in this Library the books you quote nor a complete collection of the Collana, but the Catalogue is now in London, and I cannot refer to it.

There is a fine press established now at Pisa, whence has been published a grand edition of Dante etc., but the letter is too sharp and the broad & fine parts too strongly contrasted to make the reading pleasant. But never quote Stockdale as an example for our fine printing. He is *I am told* a very bad character by his brothers in the trade, for I never (had) any connection with him myself. [1] But surely Bursley, Bulmer, McCreevey, Burnantine etc. may vie with any on the Continent. [2]

This long continuance of war makes paper & other materials so dear, that to publish books at any moderate rate, worse materials than would otherwise be the case must be used.

I am very sorry you have experienced so ill a return to your friendship. I have met with such ingratitude from those whom I have made, that I am now thankful to any one not to injure me. And those very men whom I have made, would have ruined me & mine had I not

[1] John Stockdale (1749-1814), publisher. His 'bad character' may have been occasioned by the jealousy he excited among regular book traders by establishing a series of book auctions in various parts of the country.
[2] Contemporary typographers [See, K. Day, ed., *Book Typography, 1815-1965, in Europe and America*, London, 1966].

had the good fortune to meet with so active & steady a friend in Mr Hugh Smith, who has absolutely saved us from destruction.

I hate to think on politicks, but they will force themselves upon me. Unless this Tyrant is cut off before his Return, which I somehow think he will, I see no peace for us.[1] Unanimity at home must be our sheet anchor, but I would dismiss all the emigrants, for I am satisfied though fed by us, they would turn to the invader.[2] Should any accident befall him I shall expect to see his mushroom kinglets fall as speedily as they rose, and I hope our Ministers will have the good sense no more to interfere in the arrangement of their government when reduced to its ancient limits.

Adieu, my dear Sir,

I am, yours always,

T. Johnes

To George Cumberland, in Bristol   Add. MS. 36500, f.436

Hafod, Dec. 14, 1806

My dear Sir,

I thank you cordially for your congratulations on my re-election. The expenses were comparatively small to what your town amounted to, and every one was well pleased. They scarce came to more than hundreds for your thousands.

I am much obliged to you for your very flattering compliment as to saving the Country. I really do not despair, if we keep but true to each other. For notwithstanding all the conquests of Napoleon they hang on his sole life, and any one that will risque his own may put an end to it. Remember the conduct of Alexander's lieutenants and so it will

---

[1] Napoleon had shattered the Prussian army at Jena in October and occupied Berlin a few weeks later.

[2] i.e. emigrés from France.

be with him. [1] I have no reasonable grounds for thinking it, but I have a strong presentiment that he will never return to Paris. His conquests alone must destroy him, and I should not be surprized at rebellion at home by the many who must detest him. I hear frequently from Paris, and am surprized at the language of their letters. In my answers I never notice it, but confine myself to the business of my correspondence. [2]

My only intelligence is *The Courier*, whom I have taken in from the beginning as I well knew Parry the original editor, and I can see from Nap's bulletins etc. that he is very far from being at ease. But I suppose this is always consequent on Ambition.

I hope your weather is better than ours, for we have had but one dry day since the 13th Nov. & such floods the oldest person does not remember. I am confined to the house & growling like a bear with a sore head.

I heard a few days since a curious anecdote which I have introduced as a note that I am printing in my *Life* of St. Louis & which I shall hope to send you before February. A Lieutenant in the 20th Regt. that behaved so well at Maida, writes word that the French advanced to the Charge like Lions, but that when within 5 yards, one of our men set up a *huzza* & was followed by the whole line. The French panic struck turned tail, & in about 2 minutes were all bayonetted, except one officer, to the amount of 700. [3]

Always yours,

T. Johnes

[1] Alexander the Great (356-323 B.C.). During the course of his bloodsoaked adventures in Asia, several of Alexander's officers, alarmed at his growing megalomania and despotism, conspired against his life, for which they paid with their own.

[2] Letters to France were liable to be intercepted by the authorities and scrutinised for seditious or treasonable content.

[3] A small force under Sir John Stuart defeated a French army on the plain of Maida in Calabria on July 4th 1806. Johnes's interest in the *huzza* relates to his concern to establish the origins of the medieval *crie d'armes*.

To Robert Liston, in Edinburgh   Liston MS. 5611, f.3

Hafod, Jan. 10, 1807

Indeed, my dear Liston, I have thought it very long since I had the pleasure of hearing from either of you; and your last has, contrary to the usual receipt of your letters, given me much concern.

At our times of life, everything has a strong churchyard aspect, and I no longer look for any very pleasurable sensations. I endeavour to occupy my mind as much as possible, which I believe to be the sole resource in our days, and grateful am I that I can do so. I remember Dalyel perfectly, he married our good Doctor's daughter, and when I saw his death had begun a letter to you, but picqued at not hearing from you on the loss of my dear Sister, I burnt it.

Mr Hanbury Williams came here from the funeral, and after some months went to Cheltenham, Clifton & into Norfolk. He came here on Wednesday, much better in health & spirits. The first is however but very indifferent, and you will say how can it be otherwise, when he consults every Physician he meets with. Beddoes has done him great good and I think were Mrs Liston to consult him she would reap benefit, for of all the physicians I have known, 'and I have had my share', he is the only one I have an opinion of. I know not how long he will remain with us, for he is very unsettled. I understand that he has made his will, & from the hints he has dropped, for of course I never make any inquiries, he has made my daughter his heir. In this he says he has followed what his late angel intended but I know no particulars, and catch this solely from hints occasionally dropped.[1]

In the course of your journey I wish you could make this place. Our air is particularly good, and I flatter myself you would both derive benefit from it. We do not intend going to London until the month of March, probably the latter end, but even that depends on circumstances, so that you will assuredly find us at home.

I have been very busy within & without doors, and have from the profits of my pen, gained a very rich & considerable library from Venice. My room is ready for it, and I shall expect it here in the course of ten days or a fortnight.

Public affairs I say nothing of, but so long as we keep from quarrels at home we may defy our enemies, and I am not afraid.

[1] i.e. Mariamne Johnes would inherit the Hanbury Williams properties.

I must however now conclude. My ladies are not very well — they unite with me in kind love to Mrs Liston.

I am, my dear Liston,

Always yours,

T. Johnes

Jane Johnes in the role of Thetis dipping the infant Achilles in the Styx,
by Thomas Banks

(by permission of the National Library of Wales)

To Robert Anderson, in Edinburgh   Adv. MS. 24.2.12, f.319

Devils Bridge, March 23 [1807]

My dear Sir,

You will have heard of the horrid accident that has befallen me. It is a severe blow indeed, but I thank God it was not worse; that my family escaped unhurt, and that we are all vastly well. I cannot dwell upon it. Three short hours destroyed the labours & collections of nearly 30 years. I am insured, but shall the offices pay the whole, it will not cover half my losses; some indeed are irreparable, for my library is gone.

We shall set out for London this day sennight, and I shall carry with me Mr Laing's letter, and do all I can through the aid of others to satisfy him, for alas my books are gone.[1] Among the rest I am sorry to tell you that every paper, drawing, & collation for the supplementary volume of *Froissart* are destroyed!!!

Joinville has been in London some time & I suppose you must shortly receive your copy. The *Travels* are nearly printed and Monstrelet about half written.

I am so confounded, that I can resolve on nothing as to my future intentions until more calm; for now one thought drives out another. I cannot write more.

Adieu, my dear Sir,

I am always yours,

T. Johnes

[1] William Laing (1764-1832), the Edinburgh collector, bookseller and bibliographical authority.

To Robert Anderson, in Edinburgh   Adv. MS. 24.2.12, f.321

Devils Bridge, March 29 [1807]

My dear Sir,

I had the pleasure of your very kind letter yesterday. I am very glad I wrote you my thanks for the one enclosing Mr Laing's. I am stunned, but not knocked down—for so long as death keeps off, there is a remedy for all things else. My mind is become very calm, and most grateful for the preservation of my Wife, Child & family, and I have infinite consolation in the kind part my friends take in the misfortune.

We leave this place tomorrow for London where we shall probably remain two months at my friend Hugh Smith's, Bloomsbury Square, & any thing I can do for you in the Metropolis, I shall most willingly perform.

Among the irreparable losses are the papers, & drawings which I had arranged for printing, of the supplementary volume of *Froissart*. These I regret most exceedingly.

I suppose you will have your *Joinville* in a few days, and wish it may please. The *Travels* are just printed and then Monstrelet will be begun on, but whether *immediately* finished I know not, for I have as yet formed but one resolution, which is never to involve myself in debt again. My true friend Mr H. Smith has cleared off every debt, and in September I shall have a very large annual income, with a very considerable sum of ready money that I shall settle on my daughter to carry with her whenever she pleases to marry, & wait for the rest until I am gone. My future plans therefore will depend in a great measure on the liberality of the Insurance Offices. If they pay the whole, which I fear they will not, I shall realise the fable of the Phoenix. It was lucky the Pesaro library was not arrived or it would have suffered the same fate to the other.

I must conclude. Mrs Johnes & my daughter desire you & your family will accept of their best Compliments.

I am, my dear Sir,

Yours very truly,

T. Johnes

To George Cumberland, in Bristol   Add. MS. 36501, f.65

Devils Bridge, March 29, [1807]

My good friend, all may yet turn out well; for if the offices behave liberally, Hafod will be rebuilt and though perhaps not so large, it will be more compact & handsomer. But as I have formed a rigid resolution not to involve myself again, my future measures must be guided by the conduct of the Offices.

The outward walls are standing, & I hope will serve. It seems by their entire appearance as if it were intended to be continued in the same design. On coming to it, there is no look of desolation for the conservatory, wonderful to say, is in perfect preservation. All Nash's buildings are gone, & you will say, perhaps, no loss; but Baldwin's stand firm. I shall employ him again for he is an able &, I believe, an honest man.

My late farm I divided last year, and let out to four several tenants, on leases of 7, 14, 21 years and since then farms are so risen that in six years time I shall double their rents. I have the lawn and field above the farmyard and all the lands between the road to the North & the river in my own hand. The farmyard is pulled down to make new houses & offices for the tenants in various parts & it cost me about 1200£ to make their buildings.

I am now planting & improving the wild farm between this place & Hafod & when you next see it, I do not think you will know it again.

Joinville is printed, and will I suppose soon be sent you. I hope you may like it. It was fortunate my new Library was not arrived or it would have been gone. I am too much attached to my mountains to quit them for the 'flaunting town'. It may be well to visit it for a few weeks, but *Flumina amem sylvasque inglorius.*[1] We set out tomorrow for Hugh Smith's house in Bloomsbury Square, where I shall hope to hear from you. We shall return certainly through Bath & probably Clifton, for my brother-in-law Mr Hanbury Williams has behaved so truly kind in adopting our Girl that we cannot pay him too many attentions; and our visit at Bath will be to him. I shall probably go thence to see Fonthill for I understand Beckford is to pull down the old house and there may be many things that may suit me, for rebuild I suppose I shall. But I resolve as yet on nothing. Were I avaricious I

[1] Virgil, *Georgics*, II, 486. [Love rivers and woods, unglamorous though I may be]

have had tempting offers to cut down my woods; upwards of 100,000£ so scarce is that article *now* in this Country, paid in 4 years on the supposition I should not rebuild.

My ladies send you their best Compliments.

I am, my dear Sir,

Ever yours,

T. Johnes

To George Cumberland, in Bristol   Add. MS. 36501, f.72

No. 6., Bloomsbury Square,

Monday [April 1807]

My dear Sir,

You will be glad to hear that we are arrived at my guardian angel Hugh Smith's house perfectly well.

Since my last to you I have been offered such an enormous sum for my wood at Hafod, on the supposition I should not rebuild again, that I am puzzled how to act. Would you suppose that 100,000£ has been offered, to pay for, & cut down in 4 years. I am sure I would not, had it not been offered. Now I think this sum by far too large to lie idle, and too dear to pay 5000£ per annum for a residence, but again I shudder at disfiguring a Country, and a place that I have brought to light, and which I love. For I fear that should I cut down two thirds the place will be very like our modern dressed belles.

Supposing I cut down the whole & instantly replant with beech & oak 4 feet high, it will have a horrid look for longer than I can expect to live. I must therefore look out for some other residence, building perhaps a small habitation at Hafod for a month or six weeks residence. I can in this place buy a handsome town house, for my Girl is like all young persons desirous of seeing & being seen. My good Friend here has cleared me of all debt with a handsome sum of money that I mean to settle on my daughter, for her to carry with her & more perhaps when she marries, & then she must wait [sic] the remainder. If I cut down the whole my income will be very splendid, and among my many Castles in the Air (for as yet I have determined on nothing, nor shall I until I see my way perfectly clear) I have recollected what you told me once about Prinknash, which I understand is to be sold. The rental I hear is 1500£. Now my dear Sir I shall thank you very much for as accurate a description of the place, House & Country as you can recollect. The distance is rather further from London than I wish, but it is not far out of my road to Cardiganshire whither I shall always go once a year. For should I part with the wood I shall not sell the lands, as they are every year advancing in value.

I say nothing to you about politicks, but that I fear we are going from bad to worse, and that the Enemy could not have a better friend, than we possess at home.

I am, my dear Sir,

Always yours,

T. Johnes

To Robert Liston, in Edinburgh   Liston MS. 5611, f.82

Castle Hill, Aug. 19, 1807[1]

My dear Liston,

I had the pleasure of yours Saturday and can with truth say I am perfectly well. I thank you much for your kind expressions about me, as I know they come from the heart. And I entirely agree with you as to our present governors; when we are in the greatest danger the helm

---

[1] Presumably Johnes had leased Castle Hill, Llanilar from the Williams family. John Williams of Castle Hill had died in May 1806 (and lies in the churchyard of Llanilar) and his wife had retired to the family's Shrewsbury home where she died in 1825.

is seized on by ignorance & worse passions.[1] I trust we shall not be overwhelmed, & that some daring hand, not from St. Giles's will seize the reins and by steering us safely get quite clear of *all* continental connections. We can make our way better by far without them as allies.[2] Keep them as purchasers, well & good, but we are become too proud & luxurious not to require some clipping, but I hope we shall not be shorn.

Make your mind easy about the expenses of my rebuilding for I shall not in *all* exceed the allowance from the Offices, and with prudence that will pay for everything I shall want. Mrs Johnes made with me an excursion of nine days to see Beddoes at Clifton, to inquire about what was become of my architect Baldwin at Bath, and to examine the furniture at Fonthill.

Beddoes gave us great encouragement as to our healths, for Mrs Johnes has been very indifferent. Baldwin brought the contractors to us at Clifton on our return, where all was signed, & they begin next Monday. Every expense is included, carriage and all so I know the exact sum, for the walls are perfectly good & sound, and it is not *estimates* but *contracts* for works specified to be done of such & such materials, & by such a time. It is to be covered in by Christmas, & finished in the course of next year, under heavy penalties, and I have also sufficient securities for the due performance of the whole to mine & my architect's approbation. I have been thus minute that you may not have any fears.

At Fonthill we saw many very grand things, but great *disparates*. For instance in all the bedrooms were magnificent glasses and the beds & bedding very indifferent, not worth thinking of. We marked a variety of fine things which if bought at our prices will be very fortunate; if not *Je m'en contenterai*. To the honour of the Country the wretched owner is more detested than you can conceive; under his very nose he is spoken of with contempt by his very servants. His

---

[1] Grenville's Whig ministry had fallen early in 1807 to be succeeded by a mixed government of Tory complexion under the nominal leadership of the Duke of Portland. In the Commons, Canning, Castlereagh and Spencer Perceval played increasingly important roles in Portland's government.

[2] Napoleon was now at the height of his career. He controlled the Netherlands, Italy and the Rhine states and had crushed Prussia and Austria at Jena and Austerlitz. With the defeat of the Russian army in June 1807 and the conclusion of the Franco-Russian Alliance at Tilsit the following month, only Britain remained between the Emperor of the French and total mastery of Europe.

Abbey is just finished (though not shown), wherein I hear he exists in Eastern magnificence.[1]

Brown lives in Frith Street, or at least his successor, for the person you know is dead. His retorts are flat & round & very good. I think they are sold for 5s or 6s apiece, but I would advise you to wait until we meet for I propose heating our Conservatory from the kitchen etc., and have written for [sic] an excellent Russian stove maker to consult him on warming my house, as I propose introducing those stoves everywhere. Damp used to annoy us, and Beddoes tells me that ever since Whitbread erected them at Southill colds have been unknown in his family while residing there. You shall know all about it so soon as I am perfect in the business.[2]

As to my saying the house will be more magnificent than before, it is true. But it will also be more comfortable. This however regards the internal distribution in which I claim the sole merit. The walls are perfect, and you will not see any difference in either of the fronts. The offices will be distributed otherwise than before, & curtailed, for I intend to spend my own money.[3]

What was the music room will be Mrs Johnes dressing room & our bedchamber. The small pavilions my dressing Rooms, bath etc. Mariamne's apartments will remain as they were.

The Colonade will be glazed in winter, & have wires before it in the summer to form a sort of Conservatory for hardy plants. The Hall will be nearly as before, and so will the eating Room, but in this last there will be a stove instead of a Chimney piece, and a double door in the center of the lefthand side on the entrance leading into a library 36 feet divided by four antique Columns Nero & biancho from a circular room of 24 feet, having a dome from the center of which a double door will open into the large library. That will be nearly as before, with the

[1] Beckford's servants, it was said, trembled in fear at his fits of temper, were not permitted to look at him and were obliged to hide or turn away when he passed them by. However, by the standards of the day he was a humane and generous employer who rewarded servants encountering his fiery moods with the gift of a guinea. Indeed, it was widely reckoned that servants attempted to provoke their employer into fits of rage in order to gain the golden recompense. [B. Fothergill, *Beckford of Fonthill*, London, 1979.]

[2] Southill in Bedfordshire was the home of Samuel Whitbread, the politician (1758-1815). The heating equipment and stovework for Hafod was eventually provided by one Anthony Romilly of Sloane Square who was still seeking payment for his services in February 1810. [Edinburgh University Library Ca II, 646/130]

[3] i.e. he proposed to curtail the number of servants employed at Hafod.

exception of no Gallery, but lighted from a lanthorn, and the dome supported by sixteen double Columns of a beautiful green marble, statuary, cups & vases.

A double door will lead from this circular room to the passage, and as these libraries will be all vaulted, I shall have iron or bronze doors to the eating room & passage that will save me from fire.

Opposite to the door from the circular room will be a handsome marble staircase under which is to be an entrance to an excellent billiard room that was the Servants' Hall. And thence you go into the music room, which was the tapestry drawing room. In this I shall hang my pictures etc.

Now you see my improvements tell me how you like them, for any alterations can be made as all is referred to Mr Baldwin at so much per square.

We are very glad to hear that Mrs Liston has got rid of her troublesome complaint—as for colds they are natives.

We all unite in kind compliments to you both.

I am,

Always yours,

T. Johnes

You would oblige me much if you would get Wilkie to paint me a picture. I leave the subject & price to himself.

To James Edward Smith, in Norwich   Linn. Soc. (Smith), 16, f.162

Castle Hill, Dec. 9, 1807

Did you not set me so bad an example, my Dear Doctor, I should feel greatly ashamed at looking at *Nov. 4th* the date of your letter.

I am very happy you have been pleased with *La Brocquière,* and thank you much for your notes, which with your permission I shall make use of in the next edition. I wish you had made more remarks, for I know my hasty productions require them, as well as much indulgence.

Of late I have been much harassed by Lord Lansdowne's flying off his purchase of the Priory, on the faith of which I had entered into many engagements which have irritated my mind greatly.[1] Indeed I begin to fear in spite of my exertions I shall never throw those blisters off. In consequence of his dirty conduct I have been forced to resell this property for much under the former price, and what is worse I fear I cannot force him to make good the deficiency. I am also tempted to cry out in my heat, 'That all men are *Lawyers*'.

Having now growled, I am somewhat easier and shall say that I *will* clear myself and be contented, for after all there will be fully enough for dear Mary to live as she has been brought up when we are gone, if these French devils 'do not push us from our stools'. A propos of Mariamne, she is become a prodigious fine miniature paintress. This is fact, though the Father says it and his hands are so cold he can scarcely write. She now figures herself that if the arts survive she can get her livelyhood by her pencil.

As to myself I am working hard on Monstrelet. The first Vol. is printed and the 2nd will be finished about March. You will say I work hard, when I can keep three Printers constantly employed.

I have got around me in grand confusion my Venetian library that escaped the flames by performing Quarantine. It far surpasses my expectation —*c'est tout dire*. A propos of books, I have lost the 1st Vol. of the *Flora Graecae* by the fire. As I subscribe do you think the executors of Dr Sibthorpe would give me a first volume? Otherwise my set will be incomplete, and this Vol. is the dearest of all. I have also lost all my Linnean Transactions, and I wish to restore my Library as handsome as before. If your Friendship could thus far reinstate my losses, your petitioner will ever pray as in duty bound. This is the usual close of petitions, and shall be of my letter.

My ladies are all well but starved with the severity of the weather. I could say a great deal more of Houghton having been offered and that it was once thought we should have become your countrymen etc. etc., but cold & paper tell me to finish.

Our kind Compliments to Mrs Smith.

Yours ever,

T. Johnes

[1] i.e. the Priory Estate, Cardigan.

To Robert Anderson, in Edinburgh   Adv. MS. 24.2.12, f.291

Castle Hill, Dec. 20, 1807

My dear Sir,

I am very much obliged to you for all the trouble I am giving you about the names in Monstrelet, although he is I think much more correct than his predecessor the jolly Cantor of Chimay.[1] And likewise for all the very kind & flattering things you are pleased to think & say of me. I shall try to deserve them.

I believe Laing has reason to complain, & I thank you for hinting it to me. As he has not written himself, I shall beg of you to tell him that if he will draw on me for the amount of my whole debt to him, that it may fall due on the first week of April, I will accept the draft & make it payable in London, which would perhaps suit him perfectly well. Otherwise it shall be arranged at a shorter date.

You compliment me on my philosophy; alas, no one has so little, but *cui bono* to complain. *Levius fit patientia quidquid corrigere est nefas.*[2] I have had many & serious disappointments, but having been always able to look fully into my own heart, I let the blame & consequent feelings fall on those who have deserved them. I truly forgive.

'Forgiveness to the injured does belong
For they ne'er pardon, who have done the wrong'.[3]

This severe weather checks my building, but it will (be) done in time, and next Summer twelvemonth I shall hope to have the pleasure of seeing you there. Nothing would give me greater pleasure. That poor place has made me many enemies, and you know not how much has been done to prevent my re-building. It is strange that such pains should have been taken by those who pretend to hold it cheap.

I have my books now in grand confusion all around me, and the Venetian Library far surpasses my expectations. In printed books I shall be richer than ever.

The Insurance Offices behaved very handsome. That Sum will be sufficient, and that Sum shall not be exceeded. I am fortunate in having my original architect (Baldwin of Bath) who is the only honest one I ever met with. But the late Miss Pulteney nearly ruined him.

---

[1] i.e. Jean Froissart (b. Valenciennes, ca. 1337) who became a priest at the collegiate church of Chimay.

[2] Horace, *Odes*, I, XXIV, I [But what may not be altered is made lighter by patience]

[3] John Dryden, *The Conquest of Granada*, Pt. 2, 1, (ii).

The house will be more comfortable than ever, & much more magnificent. I purchased some of the finest articles at the sale at Fonthill, which arrived safe a few days ago, after having been wind-bound at Milford these two months. We go there tomorrow to unpack. I have four of the finest glasses, I believe, in Europe, a grand heroic figure of Bacchus, Grecian sculpture [sic]. I could tell you a great deal more but it is late, & my paper is nearly at an end. If you would wish to see the plan I will have it copied & sent to you.

I shall cut down a large fall of wood, for when I plant so much yearly I think I have a right to fall what is in a decaying state, and instantly replant it. At no time can timber or bark sell for such sums as now when the whole continent is shut against (us).[1] Our present ministers have reduced us to the state of Cain, with every man's hand against us.[2]

Always, my dear Sir,

Yours very truly,

T. Johnes

To Robert Anderson, in Edinburgh   Adv. MS. 24.2.12, f.293

Castle Hill, Jan. 10, 1808

My dear Sir,

I am going to request a great favour and which I hope you will not think impertinent. I am in want of a servant, a *working servant*, not a butler or fine gentleman—for those are two creatures I abhor. My household consists of two footmen, for I wish to spend my own money myself, & not squander it on idlers. One of them will attend my dressing which requires only to have my Cloathes, Shoes etc. well

[1] France's inability to invade England ushered in a period of economic warfare. The Berlin Decrees of November 1806 had closed all European ports under French contol to British ships and when the British responded by attempting to force neutral vessels to pay customs duties, Napoleon issued the Milan Decrees (November 1807) whereby all neutral shipping passing though British ports was liable to confiscation.

[2] Genesis, IV, 1-15.

cleaned, and to shave my head once a week. He will have also the chief charge of the plate of which the quantity is very great, and the malt Liquor. The Wine I take care of myself. I wish him to be very *cleanly* & *sober*, and *honest* and not averse to work. Any one possessing these qualities will have a most excellent place, for excepting three or four months in the summer, we do not see much company, nor indeed do I desire it, as I have alway [sic] enough to keep my body and mind fully occupied. Wages are no object, and I keep them both out of Livery. The person I want, by attending on me will have the advantage of my Cloathes, except Linen & flannel & woollen stockings which are given to the poor.

Now my dear Sir could you recommend me such a treasure I shall be exceedingly obliged to you, for I think your people much less dissipated & more sober than ours. I am not in any immediate want, but if you could find me such a one, I will instantly take him. Ours is a very strict & regular family, and I wish the person not to be under thirty, as he will have the principal charge in the house. I hope you will not think me impertinent in this request, and let me have the pleasure of hearing from you soon on the subject.

I am, my dear Sir,

Yours very sincerely,

T. Johnes

To Edward Williams　　　　　　　　　N.L.W. MS. 21281E, f.218

Castle Hill, Jan. 18th, 1808

Dear Sir,

I had not the pleasure of yours of 28th Dec. before last Saturday, and to avoid the delay of the postmaster at Cowbridge as much as I can, I shall inclose this letter to him which I suppose he may have next Saturday.

I thank you much for your account of the Marbles etc. It is the alabaster I should wish to have, if of a fine colour, and in single blocks, provided the expenses per column do not amount to more than I have allowed. I was to have had some prodigious fine ones from Italy but these blockadings have now totally prevented me. You will oblige me much by sending me as early & correct information on this subject as you conveniently can. [1]

Your idea of a tower is a very good one, but as the outside walls are all excellent I must conform nearly to the old plan, making some improvements within side. For instance our own bedrooms will be on the ground floor, and I shall have my libraries arched above & below, with iron or copper doors—no garrets, for in them the fire began— But how, God knows! So that with constant precautions (for a burnt child dreads the fire) I hope no such accident will ever happen again.

All the books in the gallery and anti-library have been destroyed, but the most part of the four bookcases in the large library have been saved. Very luckily a fine library that I purchased at Venice was in London when the fire happened and thus escaped. My MSS are gone and I shall not again attempt to collect more. But in regard to printed books I shall be richer than ever, for independant of what has been saved & this Venetian library, I have purchased a fine collection of Topography and of our early printers' works. I have now nine of Caxton's printing, and all in very good condition. [2]

The winds & weather have been against me so that I do not expect to be comfortably in the new house until September twelvemonth when or at any other time I shall be very happy to shew it to you.

Mrs Johnes sends you her compliments.

I am, dear Sir,

Yours very truly,

T. Johnes

---

[1] As a stonemason Williams would be well-placed to advise Johnes on the availability of marble for both the library columns and staircase of the new Hafod.
[2] From the libraries of Rogers Ruding and Stanesby Alchorne.

To Robert Anderson, in Edinburgh   Adv. MS. 24.2.12, f.287

Castle Hill, Jan. 29, 1808

My dear Sir,

I had the pleasure yesterday to receive yours of the 21st and beg you will accept my best thanks for it, and for the trouble I have given you.

I fear Joseph Coombs is too fine a gentleman for my family. But was he not his wages are so much greater than I ever gave in the more extravagant time of my youth, that I must not now set so bad an example. I could wish for one who has been under a strict and cleanly loving master, for I dread the name of a butler, from sad experience of the worthlessness of the race. We are very regular, cleanly, & strict, and keeping but two men servants they must, especially in the summertime, have a great deal to do.

I have written a post or two since to Laing to draw on me at 6 weeks which I would accept & make payable in London. I do not wish those books that are half bound and lettered to be bound nor am I a great expert in bindings, and I shall beg of your friendship to order him to have those wanting it bound plain & neat. I have no objection to Vellum bindings, having very many in the Pesaro library.

Mr. Constable sent me his Catalogue from which I have ordered a few, but I do not think on the whole it was superior to Laing's, at least in what books I wanted. [1]

I bought nothing at Mr. Reed's for the person to whom I wrote on the subject thought all the articles I wished far too dear.

I know very little of Mr. Cromek having I think seen him but once, when I called to see Stodhard's picture of the pilgrims, and when he called at my hotel to see some of my daughter's miniatures. [2] She will shine in them as much as she does in music & singing. I trust on your first expedition southward that we shall have the pleasure of seeing you, although I do not wish it until (the) new Hafod is fairly completed.

Since you have not seen my friend Malkin's account of his very extraordinary Child I shall write for its being sent you & beg your

---

[1] Archibald Constable (1774-1827), publisher, book collector and friend of Scott. Constable published the *Edinburgh Review*, of which the first number appeared in October, 1802.

[2] Robert Hartley Cromek (1770-1812), engraver and acquaintance of William Blake.

acceptance of it. You will see an account of Blake and an eulogium of your humble servant. Blake is certainly verging on the extravaganza.[1]

But talking of artists have you ever seen the productions of a most extraordinary Genius from Scotland called Wilkie? His works are equal to any of the finest Flemish paintings. I fear he proves another example that a prophet has no honour in his own Country. Liston is his Patron and I wish very much for a picture from him, but it will probably be in vain.[2]

I beg you will give my best Compliments to Lord Buchan. His musical converzationes [sic] must add very much to the amusement of Edinburgh, and I wish my daughter was near enough to partake of and add to them.

The winter has been more changeable than I ever remember, with prodigious high winds, and I am sorry, though not surprised you complain of colds. I have been very well, but Mrs Johnes is a great invalid, and a Physician (the nearest to us, 49 miles distant) from Carmarthen left us this morning. I suppose the sight of the Doctor did the business for she is much better, although she has not taken anything. Her daughter & myself were much frightened at her looking so ill & sent for our Physician to the great annoyance of a puppy Apothecary who thinks himself the Magnus Apollo. He is not a bad surgeon etc., but hurts himself by his confounded conceit.

Had Mrs Johnes been quite well I should probably have gone to give my vote against the present Gothamites who now govern this land. They have robbed us of our honesty which without enriching

[1] Benjamin Heath Malkin had met Blake in 1803 and their mutual interest in radical politics and art sustained a growing friendship. Malkin's son had died in 1802 at the age of 6 and the father was moved to pen an appreciation of the artistic talents of the dead child. The work, with a frontispiece designed by Blake and engraved by Cromek, appeared in 1806 under the title of *A Father's Memoirs of his Child* to the lukewarm reception of the *Monthly Review* and *Monthly Magazine* and the downright condemnation of the *British Critic*, wherein it was described as, '. . . one of the most idle and superfluous works that we have ever seen'. The book was dedicated to Johnes and contained a biographical notice of Blake in the form of a long introductory letter to the dedicatee. [G.E. Bentley, *Blake Records*, Oxford, 1969.]

[2] Sir David Wilkie (1785-1841). His early works, including, 'The Village Politicians' and 'The Blind Fiddler' earned him instant fame and success, such that he was christened 'The Scotch Teniers' and became the toast of Society. Subsequent to his European travels in 1825 his style, methods and materials changed dramatically and his popularity began to wane. (D. and F. Irwin, *Scottish Painters at Home and Abroad, 1700-1900*, London, 1975.]

them has made us poor indeed!!!¹ But I shall conclude wishing you every health & happiness.

I am, my dear Sir,

Yours always very truly,

T. Johnes

To George Cumberland, Culver Street, Bristol   Add. MS. 36501, f.182

Castle Hill, Feb. 28, 1808

My dear Sir,

I should have thanked you for your two very friendly letters much sooner, but I have been unwell, from fretting at the perversity of Mankind, who I fear have very much increased and are increasing in lying and Roguery. The consequences are easily foreseen.

Alas my good friend I am in opposition to the present Baratusian Governors as well as yourself, and cannot think of asking favours from such men. I give you credit for not asking Long. I would do the same. He has been weighed in the balance & found by us both wanting. His thoughts, if ever he took them forward cannot be very pleasant. Party, I have ever said will ruin our Country, and that ruin is coming on us with hasty strides without the proper preparations to avert it. Had I the power your Son should be promoted, and yourself appointed to the place you mention as I think it would be every way suitable to you. But mine unfortunately are only barren wishes. Times may change, and you may then command the very trifling power I may have.²

¹ Members opposed to the Duke of Portland's ministry ineffectively attempted to defeat the Government over the issue of the bombardment of Copenhagen and the seizure of the Danish fleet in September 1807, seeing the latter as an act of naked aggression against a neutral country.

² It appears that both Johnes and Cumberland had unsuccessfully sought favours from their erstwhile friend Charles Long who, as Paymaster General, wielded considerable influence.

I thank you for sending me the Catalogue of Julio Bonasoni, and my daughter desires me to say every thing for her in regard to your kind intentions toward her.[1] We shall be at Bath the latter end of next month, when it shall be hard if we do not meet.

My intentions [sic] is to plant trees of all sizes, ages and sorts when I intend cutting down, for at my years I must not lose a day if possible.[2] My Reverend Brother some years younger is about, as I hear, taking a wife. Whether young or handsome I know not, but I fancy he may say with Dundas, 'that he never goes to bed nor rises in the morning without finding that he had more to perform than he could accomplish'. You remember the speech in the House.[3]

Cobbett has committed himself odly [sic] enough in his answer to Roscoe, by saying that War is necessary for the display of Men's talents.[4] Why, the only peace Minister we ever had (was) Sir Robt. Walpole, who kept us I believe 18 years without War. It was during his reign that Addison, Pope, etc. etc., our golden Age flourished.

These confounded blockadings deprive me of the drawings I want from Paris to print Monstrelet or rather to publish it, for two volumes are already printed. But there they must I suppose remain. I was to have had some Columns from Rome, but they must now be dispensed with. And I had an offer of a grand collection of prints, but must rest satisfied with the Catalogue, which I will bring with me to Bath to shew you.

The weather has been so uncertain that my Ladies feel it, and the

[1] Presumably the Catalogue included in Cumberland's *Anecdotes* of Bonasoni of 1793.

[2] The same year Johnes felled for sale some 80 acres of timber 'with great regret and heartburning'. However, 'the produce will make me every way most comfortable'. [Add. MS. 36501, f.147]

[3] Johnes reminds Cumberland of one of the Commons speeches of Henry Dundas, Viscount Melville, the hard-drinking Scot who served as First Lord of the Admiralty in Pitt's second ministry. Johnes's brother Samuel, rector of Welwyn, married Anna-Maria, eldest daughter of General Sir Cornelius Cuyler of St. John's Lodge in Hertfordshire in 1808 [*Gentleman's Magazine, LXXVIII, 1808.*]. He subsequently succeeded to the estates of his mother when she died in 1813. [*Gentleman's Magazine, LXXIII, 1813.*]

[4] Cobbett's *Letters to William Roscoe*, published in the *Political Register* of February 13th 1808 were devoted to a refutation of Roscoe's arguments in favour of peace. In response to Roscoe's assertion that war itself was inherently evil he argues that it was necessary, '… as conducive to the elevation of human nature (and), to the general happiness of the mankind'. [G.D.H. Cole, *The Life of William Cobbett*, London, 1927; Asa Briggs, *William Cobbett*, Oxford, 1967]

building is delayed. I think you will like it when done. I will not issue a positive decree against Water warming Pans, but I will (if I can) prevent another fire. An Inundation will not be so ruinous.

My paper forces me to stop.

I am, my dear Sir,

Yours always,

T. Johnes

To Robert Anderson, in Edinburgh   Adv. MS. 24.2.12, f.295

Castle Hill, Feb. 28, 1808

My dear Sir,

I am very happy you approve of my house & of my domestic arrangements in having no Butler. I want cleanly, honest and working servants, and having been such a grand gull for every knave to shoot his bolt at that I am now determined, like Falstaffe [sic] 'to live cleanly and like a gentleman' with some sort of prudential wisdom in my old age. Since there seems such difficulties in finding me this Phoenix, I think I shall keep what I have, and whose bad & good qualities I know, 'than to rush to other evils I wot not of'. This is not correct but I have not time to look at Hamlet.[1]

I am therefore exceedingly obliged for the trouble you have so kindly taken, and if a Phoenix comes in your way, pray have the goodness to inform me. My wages are 25£ a year or 30£. My wife says she wants another Phoenix, but a female one, under the name of Housekeeper, one that having seen better days would wish for an Asylum; all that would be wanted of her would be to overlook the family under her Mistress's directions, for she is in fact her own housekeeper, take care of the Linen & China with a maid under her. She will make breakfast & prepare for tea—but no Fine Lady. It would be a most desirable place for any person about forty. The wages

[1] '... than fly to others that we know not of?' (Hamlet, *III(i), 52*)

would be low, 10£, but then she would be allowed to show the house, which perquisites amount to from 15 to 20£. Such is the curiosity of the world to see a House, when nine in ten neglect to go through the walks which are *worth* seeing.

I have read Roscoe's pamphlet with great pleasure. Cobbett's answer is clumsy and he has fairly committed himself by stating that war is *necessary* to display Men's talents. I suppose the present ministry will profit by it, and produce their faultering rushlights of Talent. Cobbett forgets Sir Robert Walpole's administration, the only peace Minister we ever had, when the lustre of our golden age was in full brilliancy!! But Cobbett (like to some of our conceited Statuaries who think seeing & copying the ancient Sculptors of no avail) holds ancient learning cheap!!!

Have you seen the last Edition of Dibdin's introduction to the Classics?[1] It seems to me very well done? It has made me route [sic] among my Aldus's, and I am more & more pleased with them, for I never saw such fine copies. I believe I sent you a copy of their Catalogue. It was not well printed, for I had it not to correct. I shall make out a list of my deficiences, for having so nearly a complete collection of all the works of that excellent family of printers, I shall try to complete it.

I am thinking of a *basso relievo* in front of my house with 'Nunc revivisco', the motto to the Iunta Cicero 1536. How do you like it?[2]

I am, my dear sir,

Yours very truly,

T. Johnes

---

[1] T.F. Dibdin's *Introduction to the Knowledge of the Editions of the Greek and Latin Classics* had first appeared in 1802, with subsequent editions being published in 1804, 1808 and 1827.

[2] The Giunta family, the principal publishing rivals of Aldus, maintained premises in Venice and Florence. The 4 volume edition of Cicero, bearing the Giunta device on the title page, was edited by Vettori and Navagero and appeared between 1534 and 1537. [See N. Binns, *An Introduction to Historical Bibliography*, Library Association, 1960.]

To William Roscoe, in Liverpool   L.R.O.(Ros), 2223

Castle Hill, March 15, 1808

My dear Sir,

I beg you to accept of my best thanks for the copy of your excellent pamphlet which I received from your booksellers on Saturday last. I had before read it with the greatest pleasure, and agree with you in all you say, for I fear the farther we advance in Warfare the more we shall be bewildered.

I have remained here ever since my Election, from ill health in the first place, of which I am now quite recovered, and various causes; but I propose soon setting out for London to join my voice with our friends in opposition, for I think the present Ministers the worst in every respect this country has been cursed with. However they will keep their places, and that is enough for them should the country go to the Devil. There are some of the late Sir Charles H. Williams satirical odes very applicable to them, and among my losses the only complete copy existing has been destroyed.[1] In one of them I remember these two lines :

'Go on most fit and willing
. . . . . . lay any Tax
No matter if it breaks our backs
It wont cost you one shilling.'

I parted on Saturday with a protegé of yours, Mr Bullock, a very clever fellow, and who is to fit up my house, when ready for it.[2] He will I trust give you such an account of my wilderness that you may be tempted to come & see it. Mrs Johnes desires to add her Compliments with mine to Mrs Roscoe.

I am, my dear Sir,

Your most obedient humble Servant,

T. Johnes

[1] Sir Charles Hanbury Williams (1708-1759), satirical writer and diplomat who died by his own hand on his Monmouthshire estate of Coldbrook. Johnes's sister Elizabeth had married Williams's son and heir. An octavo edition in 3 volumes of Williams's collected works appeared in 1822 and contained notes by Horace Walpole. The work was based upon 'originals in the possession of his Grandson, the . . . Earl of Essex'.

[2] Possibly William Bullock, Liverpool antiquary, goldsmith and jeweller.

To George Cumberland, Culver Street, Bristol   Add. MS. 36501, f.278

Castle Hill, Oct. 12, 1808

My dear Sir,

I know not on whom the fault lies in the failure of correspondence, but I begin to sense it first, being probably the idler body of the two.

I have not stirred from here but once to our Assizes, and a few occasional visits to Hafod, since my return from London the middle of July. Everything is going on vastly well, and I have not a doubt of its being finished for us next summer.

I am still plagued with that fellow Hart Davis who I understand has purchased the Altieri Claudes from Beckford for 10 or 12000£.[1] I wish he had thought proper to have completed his contract with me, when I was in London. It would have saved me a wonderful deal of fretting.[2]

During my stay in town, as the bailiff was making a stone wall near to the Devil's Bridge, a fine vein of lead was discovered. It promises well, and I am offered at Bristol 21£ per ton according to the sample sent. I was never any great speculator in mines, nor am I now, so that should it fail I shall be no way disappointed & if it turns out well God grant I may make a 'goodun' of it.

We had as you know formerly a School for 12 Girls & a few young boys at Hafod, but you do not know what I am ashamed to relate that they all turned out bad, Whores and Liars, and all through the worthlessness of the Master & Mistress, the first of whom enjoys his pension of 20£. Now we do not intend to abandon this school, but on our return to renew it, as I hope under better auspices and as one of Mr Lancashire's School(s) is established at Bristol, perhaps we might get a steady person from thence.[3] If you would inquire I shall thank

[1] Richard Hart Davis (1766-1842) of Clifton, Glos. Having gained a fortune from the wool trade, Hart Davis built up an impressive collection of paintings reckoned by Farington to have cost him in excess of £100,000 [R. Thorne, *The Commons, 1790-1830*, III, London, 1986].

[2] Davis had purchased land from Johnes the previous year. On December 11th he wrote to Cumberland; 'Hart Davis has completed his purchase. Of the two evils, a Chancery suit or closing with him I chose the least desperate, for I could not do otherwise. That man must have a mint for he squanders away at a fine rate.' [Add. MS. 36501, f.308]

[3] The schools established by Joseph Lancaster (1778-1838) were based strictly upon the inculcation of the three R's by a system of drill and learning by rote,

you, but as we shall not want one this twelvemonth, I have full time to look about me.

I say nothing of politics, for what can be expected from the present men? Would you like to have a Salmon or Cask of Salt butter? Let me know that I may beg your acceptance of it.

I am,

Yours always,

T. Johnes

My ladies send you their best Compliments.

To James Edward Smith, in Norwich   Linn. Soc. (Smith), 16, f.166

Castle Hill, Dec. 18, 1808

My dear Doctor,

Had I not been exceedingly engaged you would not have had the advantage of the first inquiry, but as I cancelled this day in the week to inquire after my friends, you have had the start.

I am anxious to finish Monstrelet out of hand and when I tell you that I write six Sheets a week *constantly* you will allow that I am not idle. For I want to take the whole of next year to make visits I have so very long promised to the North, and that I may fully enjoy my idleness at Hafod on my return. I have now no doubt of the house being finished for us to reinhabit in next September.

Your bishop I have long admired from his speech on the Catholic question, and the more as that speech effectually cuts off any further preferment. Would that all were like him.[1] We must not complain of

reinforced by a regime of harsh discipline. Although the childrens' education progressed little beyond these bleak principles, Lancaster's ideas were widely followed.

[1] Henry Bathurst (1744-1837), Bishop of Norwich was a staunch supporter of Catholic relief, being for many years considered the only member of the bench of bishops to hold liberal views. [S.L. Orchard, F. Crosse and M. Bond (eds.), *A Dictionary of English Church History*, London, 1912]

ours, as I believe that I am a great favourite with him. He wishes, I think, to do good, but is a high Churchman.

When I read Laing's first edition, I was more shocked to find that we had been such beasts at home after calling the French all manner of hard names, which was like to the Pot & Kettle of old.[1] I am told that old Rose is about answering Mr Fox's book; until he can obliterate such damning facts as Laing states, it would have been wise not to have thought of such folly. But self-sufficiency & a wish to please the higher powers will make folks expose themselves in all shapes. Had he thought of a new edition of Cocker, why, it would have been in Character. But to attempt answering the book of a person who is now no more, and who never gave even a hint for its publication in the imperfect state it was in, would be worthy of a chapter of another Erasmus.[2]

I am very sorry Mr Kindersley did not let me have the pleasure of seeing, or at least hearing from him when he was travelling through the Country, for though we could not offer beds, we should have been very happy to have seen him at Dinner & one consequence would have been that all Hafod would have been opened to him. No rule is absolute with me, but according to circumstances.

We are all vastly well. Indeed we may thank Beddoes for it. Mrs Johnes caught cold at St. Pauls, when the grandest sight I ever saw of the Charity Children took place, and was indifferent all the summer. He was so good to come here, cured her and has wonderfully relieved Mariamne's headaches. Poor man, he has since been exceeding ill and is I fear even now not out of danger. I know not such a loss as his would be to those who are invalids.

---

[1] Malcolm Laing (1762-1818) published his, *A History of Scotland from the Union of the Crowns on the accession of King James VI to the throne of England, to the Union of the Kingdoms*, in 1802. A second and corrected edition followed two years later and was regarded by Fox as 'a treasure'. [Lord Holland's introduction to Fox's *History of James II, p. XIV*]

[2] Charles James Fox's *History of the early part of the reign of James II* was published by Lord Holland in 1808 two years after the author's death. Fox's portrayal of James as a man bent upon establishing civil despotism rather than attempting to overthrow the Church of England was criticised in the Tory George Rose's *Observations on the Historical Work of the late C. J. Fox*, London, 1809. In his reference to the arithmetician and calligrapher Edward Cocker (1631-1675) whose astonishingly prolific corpus of works included such productions as *The Pen's Triumph . . . adorned with incomparable knots and flourishes* (1657) and *Cocker's Urania or the Scholar's Delight* (1670), Johnes was probably enjoying a joke at Rose's expense.

My ladies unite with me in kind Compliments to Mrs Smith, & Mrs Johnes desires me to remind you of the Seeds you thought you could get her from Lady Hume, of the *Paeonia*.

I am, my dear Doctor,

Yours always,

T. Johnes

To George Cumberland, Culver Street, Bristol   Add. MS. 36501, f.321

Castle Hill, Dec. 25, 1808

My dear Sir,

I am exceedingly obliged to you for your two very friendly letters of the 16th & 18th which came at the same time, and for the trouble you have been so good to take respecting my mine. Matthews unfortunately is mistaken; I do not believe there are 20 tons, and not so cleaned. At present this mine is disputed and until it shall be finally settled I do not work it with any spirit, but when that shall happen I will push it forward and ship the ore for Bristol. I should imagine next Hereford Assizes must settle it. It is too long to detail in a letter, but I will tell you the whole when I have the pleasure of seeing you.

But à propos of mines, I have another to talk to you about in Carmarthenshire that I had in former times a great opinion of, but timid & ignorant myself I would not work it, & could not get a Company to do so. I heard only two days ago that Messrs Fox & Co. (pray tell me who they are & their address) have offered to risk 16,000£ and erect a fire engine if necessary, if Mr Johnes of Dolecothy near whose house it is will give them a lease. The case is this: the minework is called Cogové [sic] & has been worked by the Romans who had a station at Pimsaint for that purpose, and great ruins still remain. I sold this estate to my said *worthy* brother-in-Law, but reserved this minework. Whether for a term of years, or in partnership I have now forgotten, but it is not more than about 14

years ago. And as he has behaved most ungratefully to his Sister &
myself ('For they ne'er pardon who have done the wrong'), he has I
believe refused this splendid offer because Dog in Manger like, he
thinks I may be benefitted by it. I shall send my Lawyer to him one
of these first [sic] days to ask to see the Deeds that I may know what
right I have in this mineworks, & as I expect no favour from him shall
be forced probably to file a bill to oblige him to produce the deeds, and
then if I have any right close with the proposal of Messrs Fox & Co.

I have the grant of Brecon forest, about 8 miles long & 4 broad, full
of all sorts of minerals, & where the Romans have also been, which as
this company seems so enterprizing would probably, were they
acquainted with the circumstances, adventure their speculations to
our mutual advantage, for in escaping the fangs of the harpies I have
lost some feathers, and wish to make up by turning everything to
account. [1]

To say the truth I intended to leave off the *Monthly Magazine* when
Dr Aikin withdrew his services. He was the father & nurse & it has
fallen off very much of late. *The Athenaeum* is daily gaining ground. Sir
Richard's exhibition determined me, for having thrown away by folly
& iniquity such an editor as Aikin, he would be unable to support it
himself. [2]

If a collector may be believed I have done, and shall never in future
purchase anything until I have the hard cash ready.

I am afraid poor Beddoes is very ill, though recovering. His loss will
be great, but I hope that is far distant.

Dr Jones was so good to give me a hogshead of Cyder from his
parish in Devonshire, but unfortunately it was very sour when it was
to be bottled a few weeks ago. Pray can you tell me how to make it *quite*
vinegar, for then it will be as valuable to us as if it had been according
to the Doctor's good intentions.

---

[1] Johnes had obtained from the Crown the mineral lease of Brecon Forest in
October 1800. For a yearly rental of £1 together with royalties on ores raised, the
lease enabled him to enjoy mineral rights for a term of 31 years. [J. Lloyd, *The Great
Forest of Brecknock*, London, 1905]

[2] Sir Richard Phillips (1767-1840), author and publisher founded the *Monthly
Magazine* in 1796. An irascible character of eccentric views and Jacobin tendencies
(he had previously been imprisoned for selling Paine's *Rights of Man*), he quarelled
with his editor John Aikin who was replaced in his post by George Gregory in 1806.
The *Monthly Magazine* ran from 1796-1826 and the *Athenaeum* was at its peak of
circulation from 1828-1921. [W. Ward, *British Periodicals and Newspapers, 1789-1832*,
Kentucky, n.d.]

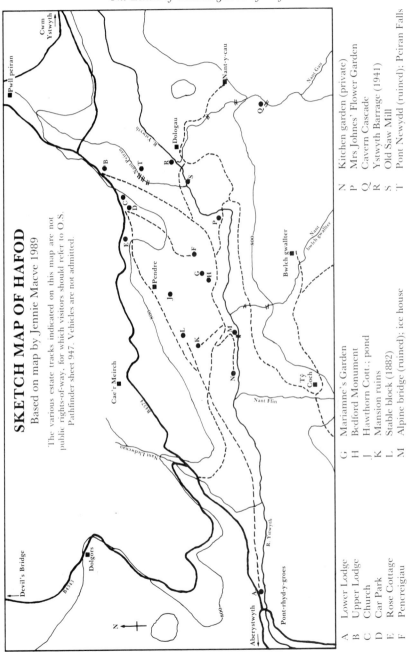

SKETCH MAP OF HAFOD
Based on map by Jennie Macve 1989

The various estate tracks indicated on this map are not public rights-of-way, for which visitors should refer to O.S. Pathfinder sheet 947. Vehicles are not admitted.

A   Lower Lodge
B   Upper Lodge
C   Church
D   Car Park
E   Rose Cottage
F   Pencreigiau

G   Marianne's Garden
H   Bedford Monument
J   Hawthorn Cott.; pond
K   Mansion ruins
L   Stable block (1882)
M   Alpine bridge (ruined); ice house

N   Kitchen garden (private)
P   Mrs Johnes' Flower Garden
Q   Cavern Cascade
R   Ystwyth Barrage (1941)
S   Old Saw Mill
T   Pont Newydd (ruined); Peiran Falls

I must return to the Brecon Forest, for as I do not think things are going on as I could wish, I am anxious to procure a Company, & if you know anything of these Foxes (I believe they are Quakers & Cornish men) they might perhaps take it.[1]

Mrs Johnes & my daughter are both well & send you their best Compliments.

Always yours,

T. Johnes

Mrs Johnes thought you knew some person at the Cape, for the Bulbs you gave her were from thence.

To Robert Anderson, in Edinburgh   Adv. MS. 24.2.12, f.307

84, Wimpole Street, April 14, 1809

My dear Sir,

It is so very long since I have had the pleasure of hearing from you that I fear I am out of your remembrance and thus write abruptly to know how you are. We came here two days ago to remain for two months, and since you will not visit Wales we propose visiting Scotland some time in the month of June. Indeed I have long promise(d) Mr Liston a visit and unless I accomplish it this year, I much fear that I never shall, for if once again I can reinhabit my own house, I shall strike root rapidly & strongly. By this excursion I shall also be prevented from overimpatience to gain possession before it will be quite finished, as we are determined not to go in until the workmen are all gone out.

Pray who is my *kind* friend in the *Edinburgh Review*? I wish to know to whom I am so much obliged, for I suspect that the critique was

---

[1] Welsh landowners rarely worked minerals on their own account, preferring either to lease the workings or to share the risks of the operation in partnership with an established mining concern.

written here.[1] It is so personal & coarse that I cannot attribute it to any of your Townsmen, to whom I must be personally unknown and I imagine it was sent from England, cooked up & perhaps curtailed in Edinburgh. In return have you read or seen a little Poem called 'English Bards & Scots Reviewers' written with much severity & force by a very young man? If you have not I will send it to you.[2] The Leader of the Gang, Master Jeffery must feel the satire, unless thickly covered with Brass. It is to him the booksellers attribute my article.[3]

I wrote before I left Wales to Mr Blackwood (whose catalogue was sent me) to desire he would send me some articles I had named, but I have never heard from him & shall be very much obliged if you would take the trouble to inquire whether he ever had my letter.

I have finished Monstrelet, but we shall wait for the engravings I fear long after the work will be printed. The third Volume will be printed early in May, and I hope the whole finished by the end of August. I know not what the Monthly Arbiters may say, but I like it full as well as *Froissart*, and shall console myself with what a much abler man said, (the Count Alfieri) when he (was) told that a work of his (was) sadly abused : *Basta che parlono*.[4]

Adieu, my dear Sir,

I am always yours,

T. Johnes

[1] i.e. the criticism of Johnes's *Joinville*.

[2] Byron had commenced work on *English Bards and Scots Reviewers* in 1807 and the work was published anonymously in March 1809, two months after the author's twenty-first birthday. In his preface he argues, with respect to the Edinburgh reviewers, that 'it would indeed require an Hercules to crush the Hydra'. Jeffrey and his fellow critics,'Combined usurpers on the throne of Taste', bore the brunt of Byron's savage satire and were treated to a dose of similar medicine in *Hints from Horace* which Byron began to draft in 1811.

[3] Francis, Lord Jeffrey (1773-1850), critic, judge and, later in life, close friend of Dickens. As a regular contributor to the *Edinburgh Review*, he became editor of that journal within a year of the publication of the first number.

[4] 'It is sufficient that they speak'. Vittorio Alfieri (1749-1803), playwright, sonneteer, satirist and lifelong champion of liberty. [E.H. Wilkins, *A History of Italian Literature*, revised edition, 1974]

To Robert Anderson, in Edinburgh   Adv. MS. 24.2.12, f.311

84, Wimpole Street

April 27, 1809

My dear Sir,

I feel very strongly your kind letter of the 21 which I had the pleasure to receive yesterday. And I thank you for sending me the Catalogue of your exhibition. Would you like to have our Catalogues in return? I never saw the Panorama of Agincourt, as when exhibited here I was not so much interested in it as I am now, and besides having been much disappointed in West's pictures of Edward the Third's history, I was not anxious to experience another.[1]

I met on Tuesday Mr Walter Scott at dinner at Longman's, and was likewise sadly disappointed, for William Stuart Rose to whom he has dedicated one of the cantos of *Marmion* sate between him & his friend Mr Erskine to whom another canto was also dedicated, and totally engrossed Scott by earwigging him all the time. Mr Erskine had sate up late the preceeding night and fell asleep. I wished for much conversation with Scott, as I had come there purposely to meet him, but this young sprig of a critic totally prevented it. By the bye I believe that it was this young gentleman who has criticised *Joinville,* out of pique for my having joined opposition on the Catholic question. I was formerly very intimate with that family, and they imagined, foolishly enough, that my line of politics were to follow theirs. *Hinc irae.* I am the more persuaded of this because I understand that he does dabble in Reviews, and from the ignorance of the greater part of his remarks.[2] Mrs Liston tells me that Jeffery spoke so handsomely to her of me, that she had promised him to meet me at their house when I came to them in the summer. I always thought the popgun had been charged here & that Jeffery only drew the trigger. I am certainly anxious to know the author and write thus confidentially to you.

[1] Benjamin West (1738-1820), the historical painter and President of the Royal Academy had been commissioned to decorate St. George's Hall, Windsor with eight scenes from the life of Edward III.

[2] William Stuart Rose (1775-1843). Son of the politician George Rose, William became caught up in the prevailing fashion for medieval romance and published a rhymed version of the first 3 books of *Amadis*, together with translations of a number of Italian works, among which one of the more notable was a version of Ariosto.

I had no idea the sale of the *Review* was so extensive, for the booksellers here only estimated the last quarter at 8500.

Monstrelet will not be published some months, for it is intended to send them out all four together, and we shall wait for the engravers, who have not even yet begun. Indeed I am in expectation of the outlines daily from France, as I heard by letter dated Jan. 9, that they should instantly be set about so soon as the weather became warmer, and forwarded to a correspondent in Holland.

I cannot send you any good news from hence, as I fear Ministers will attempt to brave the storm. A partial change is talked of, Ld. Wellesley *vice* Ld. Castlereagh & Ld. Melville to the Admiralty or Board of Control, but this will not bring any additional weight but much obloquy. Some satisfactory measures must take place, or others will I fear rush in and wrest the government from the present feeble hands, whose only care is to keep their places although the ground is crumbling under their feet.[1]

As I have some spare franks I shall enclose you a very ingenious prolegomenon to a catalogue by my friend Christie whose excellent scholarship & good manners are buried under the auctioneer's hammer![2]

Our friend Martin dined with me yesterday, and I am sorry to say I think he looks but very indifferently.

I am, my dear Sir,

Yours always,

T. Johnes

[1] Reverses on the Peninsula, economic difficulties and Castlereagh's mismanagement of Indian patronage caused great embarrassment to the Duke of Portland's ministry which nevertheless staggered on until October 1809 to be succeeded by the government of Spencer Perceval.

[2] James Christie the younger (1773-1831), antiquary, critic of the fine arts and auctioneer. Christie's catalogues came to be recognised as important contributions to the history of fine art and taste.

To James Edward Smith, in Norwich   Linn. Soc. (Smith), 16, f.168

84 Wimpole Street,

April 30, 1809

My dear Doctor,

Your letter of the 24th was returned me from Wales yesterday, and I lose no time in acknowledging & thanking you for it, that your inclosures may be received before you leave Norwich.

A surgeon at Aberystwith has used cuperose with great effect in epileptic fits on a young man whom he cured, and if Lady Hume would like to try this medicine I will write to him on the subject. [1]

We have certainly had a great loss in our friend Beddoes. He came to see us in the autumn & as usual cured Mrs Johnes who was then seriously ill. His widow has sent me a handsome memorial of him, but which I needed not to remember & regret him. [2]

We came here a fortnight ago. My wife & daughter are very well & I am now recovering from a severe cold. I have dated where we are and shall be always very happy in the pleasure of seeing you & Mrs Smith.

In three other covers I have returned your MS and have only altered *Itswith* to *Ystwith* [sic], the date of the building of the house, and curtailed the extent of the Domain, of which you had been too liberal. You know my partiality for the place, and therefore cannot think any painting too highly coloured. We shall find time to talk over the additions you propose to make and if you would like to give a plan of the present house, you may have the free use of a plate that Baldwin had engraved me. You shall see it, and then decide. Or any information that I possess, I need not say, is at your service. [3] I certainly shall be very proud of any dedication from you and regret

---

[1] 'Copperas' (L. *cuprosa*) was a generalised term used to describe the sulphates of copper, zinc and iron. In English usage it generally referred to iron sulphate (green vitriol), used widely in the dyeing and tanning processes. Any association with the treatment of epilepsy I have been unable to establish.

[2] Thomas Beddoes died on Christmas Eve, 1808. 'From Beddoes', wrote Southey, 'I hoped for more good to the human race than any other individual', while Coleridge claimed 'that more had been taken out of my life by this than by any former event'.

[3] Smith's *Tour to Hafod* finally appeared in 1810.

much that various causes have thrown us so much asunder of late years.

You will have seen the vulgar abuse of me in a miserable criticism of *Joinville* in the *Edinburgh* (Review). I have just had reason to suppose it was fabricated here by an ancient supposed friend, and you know as well as I do the bitterness of such animals.

I never experienced such a change in men's minds as I find here since last year. They all seem unhinged and all abroad, expecting something they know not what, and ready, by appearances, to submit to anything. Such have been the effects of the folly of the present Ministry in not putting a stop to the disgraceful scenes that have been exhibited, before they were brought before the House. I see not now where things will stop, for we have no heads nor leaders.[1] I heartily wish myself among my dear mountains, where when once re-established I do not think I shall soon remove again.

My ladies unite with me in every kind Compliment to Mrs Smith.

I am, my dear Sir,

Yours always,

T. Johnes

To Robert Liston, in Edinburgh   Liston MS. 5614, f.116

June 22, 1809

My dear Liston,

I thank you for both your letters and have got the book which I will bring with me. We have been much alarmed lest our Journey would be altogether put off, for our dear Girl has been very seriously ill, & though better is so indifferent I cannot say positively when we set out.

---

[1] Public confidence in the ailing Duke of Portland's ministry was not helped by the bickering and rivalry of two of its most important members, Canning and Castlereagh, both of whom hoped to succeed to the premiership. Canning's persistent intrigue against Castlereagh eventually led to a duel and the resignation of both men.

We did intend it next Monday. You shall however hear from me when the day is determined on, and whether we go to Woburn or not. Dr Bain is now with her. He was called up yesterday at 4 o'clock a.m. and came three other times in the course of the day. I hope all danger is past, but she had symptoms yesterday of strong internal inflammation which a slight bleeding cured. She could not lie down yesterday & today she cannot sit up. The weather is excessively hot and oppressive. *I hope* to leave town on Tuesday or Wednesday, but you shall hear.

You will see this post the Speech, which is uncommonly strange as no notice has been taken of the many strange things that have passed in & out of Parliament since it met.[1] There are a variety of rumours abroad & I hope some may be true. Oh, how fortunate if Nap should have gone to feed the fishes in the Danube. It will cool him beforehand.[2] But should this be the case, we shall have war I fear at home from the eggregious [sic] folly & obstinacy of the present men. I dined a few days ago at Glocester House when the Duke made *aloud* the most honourable mention of you.

Our united kind love attends you both.

Yours ever,

T. Johnes

---

[1] i.e. the King's Speech before Parliament.

[2] In April 1809 Bonaparte marched once again against Austria at the head of 240,000 men. Having successfully pierced the Austrian front he attempted to cross the Danube at Aspern-Essling when a sudden rise in the river broke his bridges and he narrowly avoided defeat at the hands of Archduke Charles of Austria. Regrouping and summoning up reinforcements, he attacked the Austrians on July 5th and 6th, inflicting a decisive defeat at the colossal Battle of Wagram in which 40,000 men fell.

To Robert Anderson, in Edinburgh   Adv. MS. 24.2.12, f.315

Castle Hill, Sep. 2, 1809

My dear Sir,

I was most exceedingly disappointed in not having the pleasure to meet you when I was in Scotland, and very much concerned to hear of the distress you were in by the sudden loss of your young companion. I had hopes that you might return before we returned Southward, and it was with great regret I found that you were not expected.

We were delighted with all we saw & met with on our Travels, and I am not yet recovered my surprize at the wonderful improvements which have taken place since I was at Edinburgh. It is the most imposing Capital I ever saw, & your countrymen pay a great compliment to London when you leave it. Hospitality having been driven by formality from England has fixed herself in the North, and if our friends perform their promises of visiting us, you may be assured we shall with pleasure return their visits in the course of the succeeding year.

I passed some very pleasant days with the good bishop of Llandaff in & about Liverpool, but hurried homeward in the expectation of reinhabiting Hafod as yesterday, my birthday of sixty one. But alas the workmen taking advantage of my absence, have been so negligent, that I have no chance of regaining possession before next April or May.[1] It has been a grievous disappointment but as I am an optimist, I grin & abide it.

I am now an idler, having only a few sheets to correct of the 4th Vol. of Monstrelet which will come out I suppose early in the Winter. I was in company with some of your redoubted Critics, and was much pleased with them. The criticism of *Joinville* did not come from them, but from a quarter (as I believe) I had before fixed on, originating in party motives; and no enemy is more severe than an old friend (calling himself so) when he turns against you. But as *he* also has

[1] Richard Watson, F.R.S., (1737-1816), Bishop of Llandaff. Having gained the see of Llandaff in 1782 he published a variety of theological works including a vigorous defence of Christianity in reply to Tom Paine's *Age of Reason*. His plantations and farming activities at his retreat at Calgarth Park, Westmoreland were widely celebrated. [See *Memoir* in *Gents. Mag. LXXXVI, 1816.*]

written a book, which deserves to be lashed for its insolence & falsehoods, he will have it in his turn.[1] *Exoriare aliquis* etc.[2]

Adieu, my dear Sir. I shall hope soon to have the pleasure of hearing that you are in good health. Pray present my best Compliments to the ladies under your roof.

Always yours,

T. Johnes

To James Edward Smith, in Norwich   Linn. Soc. (Smith), 16, f.170

Castle Hill, October 31, 1809

My dear Doctor,

I have not had the pleasure of hearing from you this age, and we have been great ramblers since we saw you, having gone north about home. My daughter was very unwell from the ill consequence of a neglected cold and as soon as we could leave the faculty, we set out Northwards and passed our time most pleasantly in making some very long promised visits near to Edinburgh & in the South Country of Scotland. We came through Westmoreland to visit the Bishop of Llandaff and thence by Liverpool where we staied a few days. Pray have you ever seen Mr Blundell's collections at Ince?[3] If not you have a great pleasure to come when you next go into that Country. He has some very fine Marbles indeed— a Theseus that would not disgrace the Apollo if placed beside it. He made me a present of the *real* hand of my Bacchus so that now he is complete.

You may however guess our disappointment on coming to Hafod to find that the Workmen had been as idle as ourselves and that instead of regaining possession last September as I was promised, it can not be sooner than May or June. I am heartily tired of this place

[1] A reference to William Rose's translation of Le Grand's version of *Partenopex of Blois* (1807) in which he was accused of plagiarism from Scott's *Marmion*.

[2] *Exoriare aliquis nostris ex ossibus ultor.* (Arise from my ashes avenger to come) [Virgil, *Aeneid, IV, 625*]

[3] Henry Blundell (1724-1810), of Ince-Blundell, Lancashire, art collector.

for I have now nothing to do and no pursuit!!! We ride to Hafod generally once a week, to drive them on and to plan future schemes. Could I but get back there again, I should have enough to do. This new edition of the house will certainly be a very well amended one and I shall remain there to enjoy it as long as I can, for these are times that no great permanency in anything can be looked to.

There has been a report so very industriously propogated, and *I believe* by my own kind family, that when you publish your Tour I wish you would if possible throw in something to contradict it. I heard it first when in London, and the person who told it assured us that it originated in Portman Square.[1] It has come to this Country & several persons have regretted when they saw Hafod, that I should have expended such sums of money on a place *that was entailed in the male line*. The last person who mentioned it was a Mr Ogle from Norfolk, and it was with difficulty that Nancy at the Devil's Bridge convinced him her young Lady was the real heir. I am very indifferent as to what may be said of myself so long as I find no blame in my own breast, but this attempt to make the world believe that my daughter will have nothing is scandalous in the highest degree. Every acre I possess is in my own absolute power, and I have left it (the moment I heard this report) where it ought to go, and she will have more than enough for any person's happiness.

My paper forces me to end.

My ladies unite with me in every kind compliment to Mrs Smith.

I am, my dear Dr,

Yours always,

T. Johnes

---

[1] Johnes's mother's London home.

To William Roscoe, in Liverpool   L.R.O.(Ros) 2225

Castle Hill, Dec. 15, 1809

My dear Sir,

You must not write me such kindly flattering letters as your last, for I shall fancy myself the thing your friendship has formed, and I know full well *quantum valeo*, not to feel that I am very far behind. However I shall endeavour to be deserving of your praise, & act so that you may not be ashamed of it. My house is not larger than before, but I think better arranged, and when you see it first, as I hope you & Mrs Roscoe soon will, it appears very small. Perhaps I should not have done one half as much as I have, but the house and place have served as inducements for Travellers to visit this Country, and of course to spend money, which has done both good and evil, for what has been gained by the expansion of wealth, has been lost in the morality of the people.

As an old builder, will you allow me to suggest two alterations in the plan you have been so good to send me. [1] In the first place, I would have no door from your library to the dining room. It will be more retired, and warmer, for the door leading to the dining room is opposite to the Chimney. In the second, I would have the door to the Storeroom just opposite to where you have placed it, as being more convenient in all respects. I should also be apt to put the housekeeper's room where the butler's pantry now is, make the Servants hall the butler's pantry, and the Servants hall where the housekeeper's room now is. These strike me as the only changes, but perhaps not knowing more of the locality I may be quite wrong, and beg pardon for my impertinence.

I wish the world thought as you & I do respecting peat lands for I have several very large tracts that I wish to let out to more active tenants than can be found in this Country. There is however very great expenses necessary to bring these lands into proper cultivation. I think Mr Smith's (of Ayrshire) method the shortest and easiest accomplished in this country. [2] My farming will now be on a very

---

[1] Roscoe had purchased Allerton Hall in 1799. The rebuilding of the older part of the house was completed in 1812.

[2] In 1798-99 a Mr Smith of Swinridgemuir received a gold medal from the Highland Society for the improvement of peat lands in Ayrshire. [*Trans. Royal Society of Arts, XX, 1802*]

Thomas Johnes: engraving by E. Engleheart
(by permission of the National Library of Wales)

reduced scale, merely sufficient to maintain my house, for I incline more to planting than farming, and believe it will be found more profitable on large extensive tracts of little or no value in their present state.

As for politics it is distressing to look at what is acting in our Country. Such obstinate weakness must end in ruin. Indeed I see no means to avert it, but a total change in measures, so that the people may again confide in their rulers, for at present there is an apathy & prodigality in all manner of persons and nothing done to make the country sensible of its danger. All seem now to trust to the Chapter of accidents.

My Ladies are vastly well & unite with me in every Compliment to yourself & Mrs Roscoe, hoping that she is perfectly freed from all anxiety about your Son.

I am, my dear Sir,

Your very much obliged friend & humble Servant,

T. Johnes

To William Windham   Add. MS. 37916, f.174

Castle Hill, April 20, 1810

My dear Windham,

I feel most sensibly your very kind letter which I had the pleasure to receive yesterday. Our friendship will I trust continue to the grave, for whenever you are in distress, or I am unwell, you kindly take alarm, and write to me. I shall never forget your two letters from the Northern Coast, and when I was very ill some years ago. I attribute my accident to stooping down too much, packing up books, & in a strongly camphorated atmosphere, for I had been plentifully washing them with Camphor & spirits of wine to destroy the worms which this damp house had generated. My fair Companions & my Doctor were too much alarmed, for though, as Foote says, 'I bled like a pig', I did not feel myself weakened. It would have been sooner stopped, but they thrust a pledget up my nose, which turned the current of blood down my throat & through my mouth. The coughing this caused, prevented the stopping of the hemorrage [sic]. Should you ever have such an accident the cure is quite simple, & I hear it will stop most hemorrages. It is this. Double a towel 3 or 4 times, and dip it thoroughly in a liquid composed of the whites of three or four Eggs beaten up with 2 wine glasses full of Port wine & the same of Vinegar. Then apply this cloth to your Navel, and it almost instantly stops any bleeding. Should it fail at first, repeat it again & again. I can answer for its good effect.[1]

I have undergone pretty severe discipline in bleeding, blistering, & Physic and my Doctor, though of the right way of thinking in politics would not suffer me to go to London or to move from home. However I did attempt in spite of him to come to the Walcheren infamous business, but was forced to return.[2]

I think whatever may have been the cause of this, my health will be bettered, for I shall now be more careful than I have hitherto been and I now no way regret it having happened since it has brought me so very kind a letter from you, for whom I always had & must have the sincerest friendship & esteem.

Believe me my dear Windham,

Always to remain yours most truly & sincerely,

T. Johnes

---

[1] Aged 62 and considerably overweight, Johnes probably suffered from high blood pressure which would in part explain his frequent and lengthy nosebleeds.

[2] The primary objective of the Walcheren adventure, inspired by Castlereagh early in 1809, was to seize the Dutch island of Walcheren at the mouth of the Scheldt, occupy Antwerp and thence to join forces with the Austrians. Due in large measure to the vacillations of the commanders, the Earl of Chatham and Sir Richard Strachan, the expeditionary force failed to get underway before the Austrians had been defeated at Wagram on 5th and 6th July. The British army's losses from disease, together with the failure of the Government to order a prompt withdrawal, caused an uproar in the country and helped to destroy Portland's moribund ministry.

To Robert Anderson, in Edinburgh   Adv. MS 24.2.12, f.317

Castle Hill, April 24, 1810

My dear Doctor,

I should have acknowledged & thanked you for your very obliging letter of the 19th March much sooner, had I not unluckily burst a small artery somewhere about the head, which caused many repeated & violent hemourhages. Thank God I am now quite well again, but am following the regimen & diet ordered by my Physicians. I think it was caused by Stooping too much when packing books and in a strongly camphorated atmosphere, for I had plentifully washed some of my ancients in a solution of that and spirits of wine. It was this that detained me from attending my duty in Parliament & expressing my sense of the imbecility of these men who call themselves Ministers.

'They shall betray & lie, but all in vain; Spite of themselves, their posts they shall maintain.'[1]

I was very much concerned at the indifferent account you gave of yourself. Change of air I would strongly recommend and as I trust we shall be fairly settled at Hafod in July, I need not say how happy we shall be in the pleasure of seeing you there. My return to Scotland must depend on circumstances, and it would be too bold in Sexagenarians to pretend to fix any time beyond perhaps a few months.

I thank you for what you say of Monstrelet. It is not yet published, but what is singular, the whole Edition my booksellers write me one word is sold, and at an advance of 25 per Cent on that of *Froissart*. I shall now lay aside my pen, having full in my mind Horace's wholesome precept:

Solve senescentem mature sanus equum ne peccet ad extremum ridendus et ilia ducat.[2]

Should any severity of Criticism fall on this work I do not believe that it will come through your review but the *Quarterly*, as I have good reasons for believing the [sic] Walter Scott had a principal hand in the criticism of *Joinville*. Nothing equals 'a damned good natured

[1] From Sir Charles Hanbury Williams's satirical verses?

[2] Horace, *Epistles*, I, i, 8. [Be wise in time and turn your horse to grass when he gets old unless he end up with a ludicrous breakdown.]

friend.' When we meet I will tell my reasons for thinking thus. It is too long, and hardly worth writing on paper. [1]

I did all I could for John Henderson although he made use of my name to Lord Liverpool without consulting me, which was not so pleasant. I have not heard anything of him a long time. Instead of attending to his duty as an officer, I believe he employed himself in writing essays for the better government of that Country. Lhind's conduct was not correct at the fire, & ever since I have been absent he has been very idle. His printing of the last volumes is not nearly equal to the former ones. If he does not alter his conduct—indeed, they theirs—they must be beggars.

I fear Mr Cooper Walker is very ill, for the last letter I had from him was not written by himself, and it is now some time since I had a letter. [2]

I beg my best Compliments to your Ladies with many thanks for the poems they were so good to send me.

Mrs Johnes & my daughter send you their kind Compliments.

I am, my dear Doctor,

Yours very truly,

T. Johnes

---

[1] Piqued by Jeffrey's sharp criticism of *Marmion* in 1805 and by what he regarded as the 'unpatriotic' tone of some of Jeffrey's other reviews, Scott ceased writing for the *Edinburgh Review* and threw in his lot with the publisher Murray and the *Quarterly Review*. [M. Ball, *Sir Walter Scott as a Critic*, New York, 1907]

[2] Probably Joseph Cooper Walker (1761-1810), the Dublin antiquary, who died in April 1810.

To Robert Liston, in Edinburgh   Liston MS. 5616, f.118

Castle Hill, May 6, 1810

My dear Liston,

I was very happy in the pleasure of seeing your handwriting again, and should have said so sooner, but I also have been laid up with a severe cold, in addition to which by the untidiness of the people at the D's Bridge I fell down and escaped with a bad sprained ancle [sic]. It is well it was not worse. I am however now rapidly recovering my ailments, but we have a sharp easterly wind that will I fear hurt Gardens & farms as well as poor invalids.

We hope that this will find you both convalescents and as nearly well as this Eastern will permit. You need not advise temperance to me, for I am very temperate. I have left off all malt liquors and only drink water dashed with Hock at my meals, and 3 glasses after dinner. But I agree with you I shall not be well until resettled, for I have here no occupation *now* within or without doors.

I thank you for the model of the gate. It is at Hafod but I have not opened it, nor shall I until I have some place to put it in.

I have made a catalogue of the books these dear women saved. It is wonderful how they could have done it.[1] I fear many have been stolen, for *whole* sets are gone that they threw out of the bookcases. But I am grateful for what has been saved, and in those sets, very few indeed are incomplete. When they are all arranged together, my library will be far more valuable & choice than before.

We, that is, my Wife & Self, shall go the the D's Bridge Tuesday, and I hope by the latter end of this Month we may all squeeze ourselves into Hafod, for until that is done we shall never drive the workmen out.

I am interrupted, and as I cannot move, am surely caught.

My ladies unite with me in kindest Compliments to you both.

Always yours,

T. Johnes

---

[1] i.e. volumes saved from the 1807 fire.

To Mrs Robert Liston, in Edinburgh   Liston MS. 5616, f.166

Hafod, June 10, 1810

My dear Madam,

At length I have the pleasure of dating my letter from this place, and we sincerely hope that it may find yourself & Mr Liston quite recovered. I can send you an excellent bill of health from all here. We came hither on the 4th but our bed was not put up until many hours after our arrival. Mary joined us the following day, and we are as comfortable as people can be amid the noise and dirt of workmen. I hope to get rid of all by the beginning of August and if I have been detained by the negligence of builders & upholsterers from inhabiting my house sooner, I am now amply repaid by the pleasure I enjoy. It is certainly one of the best distributed houses I ever saw, for if you choose to act the Prince you have wherewithal, and if you choose to enjoy the attendant comforts of a *very moderate* expenditure, you can do that also. I am quite happy with all the comforts I see around me. The grounds are in higher beauty than ever although we are sadly in want of rain, for our Cascades are full of dust instead of water.

I was too quiet at Castle Hill, but here we are all in the greatest bustle, and all pains forgotten.

I hope you have received *Monstrelet*; it has a handsome appearance, & will I hope please. After the extraordinary sale of the whole edition before the day of publication I shall close my inkpot and resume my farming occupations, but somewhat more systematically than before.

If there were any things to answer in your letter I wish you would repeat them, for that with several other letters were so carefully put by when I quitted Castle Hill I cannot now find it.

Our united kind loves attend you both.

I am, my dear Madam,

Yours very truly,

T. Johnes

Mrs Johnes will write so soon as she has the Flax which is not yet arrived.

To George Cumberland, Culver Street, Bristol   Add. MS. 36502, f.235

Hafod, July 6, 1810

My dear Sir,

It has been your own fault that you have not heard from me oftener, for I have not had any answer to my last letter until I received yours of the 1st of last month. I am now quite well ever since my return hither, and the accident I had was I think beneficial. We came here the first week of June, and are now very comfortless, not having a single room finished, nor any beds put up but those we ourselves occupy. I am exerting myself as much as I can to make the workmen do the like, but doubt my being fairly quit of them until towards the end of September. I have however had my Statues & glasses put into their places without any accident to them or to the labourers who assisted. This last I so much dreaded would not have been the case from their awkwardness & eagerness, that my agitation brought on a slight return of hemmorhage. But it lasted so short a time that I consider it as nothing.

The sale of *Monstrelet* was so rapid, that the whole was engaged long before the day of publication. Many of my orders were curtailed. I have therefore been forced to direct a copy of the second edition, which will probably be the best, to be sent to you as well as to others. It will be out in a very few weeks.

I thank you very much for your intelligence respecting the arts, which seem rather on the decline. The booksellers as Johnson said, are after all the best patrons, for they make at least the names of the artists known.

You should not republish your account of Hafod until you have revised your first edition on the spot as very many & great improvements have been made since then, and I need not say that when my house is completed, we shall be very happy to see you here. I am at present all hurry & confusion, and if you have a spare half hour I shall thank (you) to call on Hancock a stone mason in Guinea Street who is one of my contractors & hurry him & his men hither as fast as possible to repair the Staircase which through their blunders has cracked. Indeed I have reason to complain of all the contractors except the Plasterer; and of my Upholsterer above all!!

We know not I believe the treasures we possess in this country. A few months ago a very curious clay or marle was discovered on my farm. It answers the purposes of Fuller's Earth, but if (it) should turn out Marle it will be of prodigious use. I understand from a friend at Birmingham to whom I sent a sample that small shells are in it, and (he) has advised me to have it liviqated [sic] when it will make an excellent polisher. In other covers I send you some of it, & shall thank you to let me know what it is & to what other purposes besides agriculture it may be turned to. I have plenty of it. [1]

My ladies are well and send you their best Compliments.

I am, my dear Sir,

Yours very truly,

T. Johnes

To George Cumberland, Culver Street, Bristol   Add. MS. 36502, f.322

Hafod, Nov. 11, 1810

My dear Sir,

I thank you for your two obliging letters, for I thought it long since I had heard from you. As to the Clay, I believe you are mistaken in its properties; it cleans cloth from grease as well as Fuller's earth, and I hear from Birmingham that it would answer there particularly well if I could clear it from *small shells*, observable only by a microscope. It also effervesces (but slightly) in acids. It is now under trials in London & Wiltshire in both of which places they have a high opinion of it. I am satisfied it will answer all my purposes for a manure. I beg of you to accept my best thanks for all the trouble you have been so good to take with it. I am sure we do not any way know what we possess in the under strata of this Country, and I propose to make, when more at leisure, some trials by boring etc.

---

[1] Fuller's Earth was principally used for the thickening of woven woollen fabrics, the bulk of the material used in west Wales being imported from the south-east of England whence it arrived at the seaports of Cardiganshire and Merioneth. [J.G. Jenkins, *The Welsh Woollen Industry*, Cardiff, 1969] Marl is a calcareous clay traditionally used on light, sandy soils to reduce acidity, or on heavier land to improve soil texture.

I differ from you as to foreign politics, for I judge we are doing well in Spain & Portugal, or perhaps rather that the French are going on badly, and my grounds for this conjecture are the foolish decrees of Napoleon against commerce.[1] They have arisen from intemperance & irritability which must have had some serious cause, and nothing more likely than his failures in these Countries. Our prospects at home are more melancholy, and I dread what may be the consequences. But I will not dwell upon them.

Mr Stodhard is now here busily employed to finish his work to return to Town, which I suppose he will do in the course of next week.[2] Your request shall be complied with, and in another cover I will send you a proof of a portrait that was engraven this year.[3] By the bye you forgot to send me in your first letter the inclosure mentioned in it. Stodhard agrees with me that you ought by all means to revisit this place before you publish your second edition, and if too late to add anything to the text, it ought to make an appendix, for the scenery is much improved since you first described it, and there are morsels in the house not unworthy of notice.[4] If you could manage to come hither before he leaves us, you might then return together, as I believe his intention *was* to have called on you at Bristol, unless your letter to him may have made him alter his route.

I hope you have had *Monstrelet*, as I ordered a copy for you long ago & I wish to have your opinion of it. The plates are far superior to those in *Froissart*, but it was unlucky the drawings from France did not come in time to be engraven for this work.

My ladies are well and send you their best Compliments.

I am, my dear Sir,

Yours always,

T. Johnes

[1] The Berlin and Milan Decrees of November 1806 and 1807.

[2] Stothard was completing his decoration of the Hafod library with eight scenes from Froissart and Monstrelet. At the first annual meeting of the Cambrian Archaeological Association, held in the Aberystwyth Assembly Rooms in 1847, a number of Stothard's Froissart and Monstrelet oils were exhibited. These remained at Hafod, 'until very recently they were purchased by Mr Hackney of Aberystwyth, who kindly granted the loan of them for this occasion, and wishes to dispose of them'. [*Archaeologia Cambrensis, II, 1847*.]

[3] Of Johnes by Stothard.

[4] A second edition of Cumberland's *Attempt to Describe Hafod* never materialised.

To Robert Liston, in Edinburgh Liston MS. 5618, f.16

Hafod, Feb. 3, 1811

My dear Liston,

I thank you most kindly for your friendly letter of the 2nd Jany and for all the good advice you give me. I did not know that you were a fellow sufferer in this complaint.[1] I have not had any returns since my daughter's first letter to Mrs Liston, and should they come, as I suppose they will, I think I know *now* how to manage them. I believe I before mentioned the usage of whites of eggs, vinegar & port wine to stop a hemorrhage (if not let me know & I will send you the proportions) applied to the Navel. This I look on as infallible if the patient will lie down in quiet. I shall in cases of return, in addition apply a *large* blister to the upper part of my back, which the late Dr Darwin said never failed to stop bleedings at the nose, & as blisters never hurt me I shall not be sparing of them.[2] Indeed I have had for some time a small blister behind my ear.[3] I have taken every 8 or 10 days from 2 to 3 grains of Calomel at night, & in the morning an ounce of *purified* Epsom salts, which I prefer to your Brazils. I am exceedingly temperate, eat sparingly & of light things, and drink only Water, of which we have the most delicious, and 3 glasses of hock wine after dinner. I feel myself perfectly well, & have neither wants, nor wishes, but rather too much inclined to indifference and laziness since this last attack. So much & enough of Self.

I am looking to Roxburghshire for Tenants but almost despair of

[1] Liston had written to Johnes on January 11th counselling abstinence, regular exercise and a regimen of Brazil Salts and 'James's Analeptick Pills'.[Liston MS. 5624, f.3]

[2] Erasmus Darwin (1731-1802), radical freethinker, physician and advocate of temperance.

[3] The idea that the *materies morbi*, the essential matter of disease, could be drawn out of the body by external application was a very ancient one. A blister was any device which withdrew blood or fluid, leeches being regularly used for this purpose until the late nineteenth century.[G. Williams, *The Age of Agony*, London, 1975] Calomel (mercurous chloride) was widely used as a purgative. Like so many 'patent' medicines it was of more psychological than physical benefit and when taken in large quantities could be positively harmful.[J.J. Walsh, *Cures; The Story of Cures that Fail*, New York, 1923]

having any from thence. Some Kentish man came & took two of my farms, but they now want to be off. How it will end I know not.

I have been much amused in reading the late King of Sweden's (Gustavus III) letters; his plays were very kingly, and Madame du Deffand's correspondence with Horace Walpole of which I am now in the 2nd vol.[1] He treats her very scurvily, but she must have tried him. Some persons now living will not approve of what is said of them. She mentions use of an expression that I do not understand—pray do you? Speaking of the Duc de Choiseul she says (I quote from memory) '*Il etoit ce fieux la à Paris ou il tint Cloche & diner avec le Cure de Ste Eustache*'. What is *tenir Cloche*? I have looked into all my dictionaries in vain. Have you read *Monstrelet*? Pray give me your opinion frankly of it, for although all authors are more or less Archbishops of Granada, yet I think I am (if one may judge of oneself) free from having any claim to such honour.

I would say something of politicks, but that I consider the game as done. After the late most infamous attacks on the constitution by King Perceval we are done up, and nothing but the severest punishment can make atonement & bring us back to ourselves and prevent every little rascal who can chatter from thinking himself qualified for Prime Minister.[2]

We have a new star in our firmament, Lucien Bonaparte, whom I dare say I shall see here in the course of next summer, as it is become fashionable to see this place and he is not more than 50 miles off. I dare say I am wrong, but I cannot help thinking his coming hither a masterpiece of refined policy, considering the vast numbers of prisoners and officers we have in the island. But should it be otherwise, our wise ministers, by suffering him as a resident, totally prevent any possibility of an exchange of prisoners or any chance of peace, as this man must be a stumbling block in the way of both; and their reception has also displeased him.[3] Until Lymore shall be ready

---

[1] Some 1700 letters passed between Walpole and the blind Madame du Deffand (1696-1780) whose Paris salon was a venue for the intellectual aristocracy of the age.[W.S. Lewis, *Walpole's Correspondence, III*]

[2] Johnes here refers to Perceval's resolute (and ultimately successful) handling of the Regency crisis of 1810-1811.

[3] At odds with his brother Napoleon, Lucien Bonaparte (1775-1840) attempted to flee to the United States in December 1807. He was captured at sea by a British naval vessel and taken to Malta and thence to England where he resided (under limited surveillance) with his family until 1814.

he now resides at Dinham!! where I was born, and which I sold to Ld. Powis, but it had been rebuilt in great part since you were there.[1]

Do you propose being in London this year? My doctors will not let me move as yet, and I suppose it may be about Easter before I shall be there. For my own part I wish to remain here always, but it is otherwise decreed.

We have had a shocking winter and are now uncomfortable enough. We have had all severe colds, but unite well or ill in every kind compliment to you both.

Yours always,

T. Johnes

To James Edward Smith, in Norwich Linn. Soc. (Smith), 16, f.180

London, June 10 (1811)

My dear Doctor,

Never make any apologies for sending your letters to me. I have franked yours this day to Mrs Smith.

I wish I could send you good news of our dear Girl, but she is exceedingly ill & yesterday we called in Bayley & Pearson. They agree that it is a strong nervous affliction & I fear will require a long time to recover from. Alas, so far are my visits hither like to Spring; they more ressemble the dreariest winter. They say there is no danger, but when I look at her helpless state, *si je n'ai pas peur, je tremble*. I cannot write more.

Our best Compliments to your Cousins.

Yours always,

T. Johnes

[1] Dinham House, Ludlow, was purchased in 1717 as a town residence by the ironmaster Richard Knight, great-grandfather of Thomas Johnes. When Johnes's mother Elizabeth Knight married Thomas Johnes of Llanfair Clydogau in 1747, her parents insisted that the couple lived with them at the family home of Croft Castle, purchased by her father in 1746. The elder Johnes was prepared to do so, but probably insisted as a condition upon the complete remodelling of Dinham which took place between 1747 and 1749. Thomas Johnes of Hafod lived at Dinham as a child and occasionally in later life, eventually selling the property to Edward Clive, Earl of Powys in 1794. It is now a craft centre.[D. Lloyd, *Dinham House and its grounds*, Ludlow, 1982]

To William Roscoe, in Liverpool   L.R.O. (Ros), 2226

Stoke House, July 28,[1811]

My dear Sir,

That you could write to console us in our affliction when you were
suffering so severely yourself was so kind, we can never forget it. [1]
We had heard of your son's illness from our good friend Shepherd and
very sincerely condoled with you all. I hope that he will soon be
restored to you, for he has youth on his side, & that you may enjoy
many many happy years in his Company. Our blow has been hard,
but it has been tempered with infinite mercy and I trust that we are
duly resigned, for if ever there was a righteous death it was hers. And
the spirit had left her with such a smiling countenance that it was some
hours before the event was ever suspected, although Miss Harley was
sitting by her bedside watching her, as she thought she was sleeping.

We shall return homeward soon, and endeavour to do as much
good as we can that we may all meet again hereafter. I wish any
inducement could prevail on you & Mrs Roscoe to favour us with
your company; 'a fellow feeling would make us wond'rous kind'. [2]

Mrs Johnes unites with me in kindest compliments to Mrs Roscoe,
yourself & family.

I am, my dear Sir,

Truly yours,

T. Johnes

---

[1] Mariamne Johnes died on July 4th, 1811.
[2] 'A fellow-feeling makes one wondrous kind'; [David Garrick (1717-1779),
Occasional Prologue on Quitting the Theatre.]

To James Edward Smith, in Norwich   Linn. Soc. (Smith), 16, f.181

Stoke House, Aug. 5th (1811)

My dear Doctor,

We thank you much for your very kind letter, but were very sorry to learn by it that you had been so ill, and hope this may find you quite well at Norwich. Our blow has been heavy indeed, but we look to the same merciful power that gave it for support, & trust that we shall bear it with the proper resignation. The calm of this place & the attentions of our kind friends have done us great good. We leave this place tomorrow for home in the hope that we may be enabled to endure it, for it is there where we can do the most good, which must now be our sole object. I did intend to write more, but I cannot.

Yours always,

T. Johnes

To George Cumberland, Culver Street, Bristol   Add. MS. 36503, f.56

Hafod, Aug. 15, 1811

My dear Sir,

I thank you kindly for your friendly letter, which I found on my arrival here a few days since. Our blow has been indeed severe, but I trust the same Almighty power that ordained it will support us under it. We must now do all the good we can to enable us to hope for a happy meeting when we shall follow her. I was afraid we should not have had strength to endure this place, now robbed of its brightest Charm, but I think we can stand it.

When we last met, I was in the utmost anxiety for Mrs Johnes, then extremely ill, but little did I look for the sad event that would follow, & could at that time think of nothing but her. I cannot write more.

Believe me,

Always yours,

T. Johnes

To James Edward Smith, in Norwich   Linn. Soc. (Smith), 16, f.182

Hafod, Aug. 17, 1811

My dear Doctor,

I did intend thanking you yesterday for all your kindness which we sensibly feel and had begun a letter to your brother-in-law, but was forced to send it off half finished. We are very much obliged by all your attentions and wish you could have sent us better accounts of your own health. We came here this day se'enight, and hope we may be able to endure it although deprived of its brightest Charm. It is here, we can do the most good, and that must now be our only endeavour, to shew some gratitude for mercies already received, & they have been manifold, & to indulge a hope that we may all meet again hereafter. By placing our dependance on the sole source of happiness & comfort, we have been wonderfully strengthened, not only to bear our loss with resignation but with thankfulness. My wife is still very low though calm. She cannot see any Company, but if you could favour me with a visit, I think it would do us both good.

I never saw this place in such beauty, and I trust that we shall enjoy it as we ought within a short time, for we daily regain Strength. Tomorrow will I fear unhinge us again for we must go to Church & I expect Mr Chauntrey [sic] here Thursday to consult about a monument.[1]

Our thoughts now will be attached to all that loved her and to everything that may remind us of her excellencies. I do not think I shall ever again bear music!!

Adieu, my good friend,

I am always yours,

T. Johnes

Our kind Compliments to Mrs Smith.

[1] Sir Francis Chantrey (1781-1841) one of the most distinguished English sculptors of the nineteenth century, had been introduced to Johnes by Stothard early in 1811. Stothard and Chantrey were close friends and the former may have made suggestions regarding the design of the Mariamne Johnes monument.

Hafod, Aug. 31, 1811

My dear friends,

I have long intended writing to you, but put it off from day to day, until I could say that we were determined to remain here & that we trust to be enabled not only to bear it with resignation, but with thankfulness and enjoyment. I believe I should not now have mustered courage to sit down to write, were it not upon business, and I shall refer all the account of ourselves to Mr Chauntrey who will call on you about 9 o'clock on Wednesday morning, with a short letter from me. You perhaps do not know Mr Chauntrey? but his fame as a Sculptor will very soon blaze abroad. It was he who made my bust, and who has undertaken a monument to our dearest Girl, that if the Sculpture answers the design, must fix his name. At least I have never seen any thing that more affected my feelings, and I think it will come home to every breast. [1] Marble is now so scarce & dear, not less than 6£ per foot, that I am going to request you would endeavour to send me a shipload of *Statuary* Marble, whether from Carrara, Paros, or anywhere else does not signify. And if such a quantity may not be had, or freight found for it, you could perhaps prevail on some of (the) Captains of King's Ships to bring a few large blocks, which would answer my purpose if procured immediately, & save me many hundred pounds. But Mr Chauntrey will explain to you all this more fully than I can. I am however very impatient to have this memorial finished with all due dispatch, for at my time of life no time must be lost.

I cannot write more, nor read over this. Our kindest Compliments attend you. Mr & Miss Harley are now with us & send you their Compliments.

Ever yours,

T. Johnes

[1] The celebrated monument, showing the dying girl on a couch with her mother seated at her feet and her father standing beside her, marked an important stage in the breakdown of the eighteenth century allegorical tradition, being a simple, dignified and semi-realistic treatment of a death scene on a scale never previously attempted. At the time of Johnes's death in 1816 and his wife's in 1833 the work had not been paid for and it was ultimately placed in the Church at Hafod by the 4th Duke of Newcastle. It was destroyed by fire in 1932. [M. Whitney, *Sculpture in Britain, 1530-1830*, London, 1964]

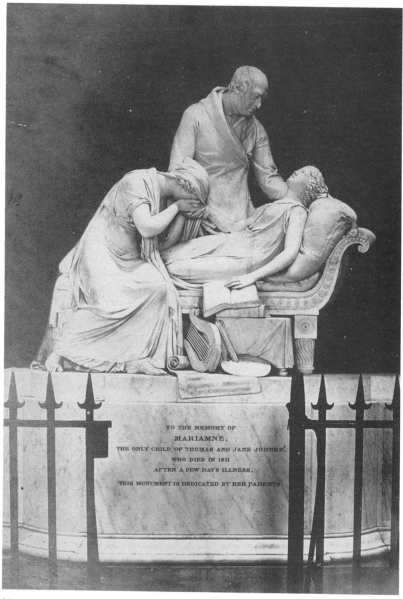

TO THE MEMORY OF
MARIAMNE,
THE ONLY CHILD OF THOMAS AND JANE JOHNES,
WHO DIED IN 1811
AFTER A FEW DAYS ILLNESS,
THIS MONUMENT IS DEDICATED BY HER PARENTS

Chantrey's Monument to Mariamne Johnes of which the remains lay in the church of Eglwys Newydd following its destruction by fire in 1932.

(by permission of the National Library of Wales)

To George Cumberland, Culver Street, Bristol Add. MS. 36503, f.74

Hafod, Oct. 17, 1811

My dear Sir,

I thank you for yours from Salisbury Street, and am glad you are pleased with what you saw at Chauntrey's. I have great ideas of his abilities, & think that what he is about will do him infinite credit, and establish his Character for a first rate Sculptor. Your thought of our Schist forming the background is worth considering, for it may be had I believe of any size slabs & will bear a sort of polish. I do not like your Nightingale so well. It is a Concetto—and I propose the Lyre to lay on that beautiful song of Handel's and which she sang so delightfully, 'What though I trace each herb & flower etc'. I would have put, 'I know that my Redeemer liveth' but that is already placed on the tomb of Handel. [1]

You will judge from my composure in this talking that I am better in mind and I trust we shall bear our irreparable loss with the resignation & hope of Christians.

I have no doubt but that your account of this place will answer. Much has be(en) done in every respect since you were last here, & any assistance I can give you may always command.

Pray what Marbles has Fagan to dispose of? [2] I should wish to know, and their price, although perhaps I may not purchase, for I am no way settled. And not having any relative that cares for me, nor I for them, 'The world is all before me where to choose and Providence my guide'. [3]

I am glad you & Long remembered me so kindly when you were at

---

[1] Cumberland had suggested that Chantrey's group might be set against a background of local rock and that a singing nightingale might with effect be placed on the lyre resting beside the dead girl's couch. Johnes fortunately rejected the proposal as, no doubt, would Chantrey have done.

[2] Robert Fagan (d. 1816), diplomat and collector who, during his stay in Rome between 1794 and 1798 purchased numerous masterpieces from the Altieri Palace. It was from Fagan that William Beckford acquired the Altieri Claudes, including *The Landing of Aeneas* and *The Sacrifice of Apollo*.

[3] Milton, *Paradise Lost,* XII, 645.

Bromley, for though we may differ in politics, I love him much.[1] I did intend writing further, but Mr Baldwin is just arrived to settle the rascally accounts of my Contractors.

Adieu,

Always yours,

T. Johnes

To George Cumberland, Culver Street, Bristol   Add. MS. 36503, f.80

Hafod, Nov. 10, 1811

My dear Sir,

I hasten to thank you for the very beautiful verses you were so good to send me last post. I admire them much, more especially the three last stanzas. They came from the heart, and speak to the heart. My printing office has been long since broken up, or I would have sent you the copies you desire. When I have them printed you shall be sure to have same.[2] I still however continue in my former opinion about the nightingale, as it would require an explanation; and everything in such subjects as do not a(t) first sight declare their purpose I think misplaced. I hope & indeed, doubt not, but that Chantrey will fix his name by his work.

I am no way surprized at what you say of your late cousin Richard. His life fixed my opinion of his character, which has since been confirmed by his Will. This I suppose you have seen, as it is printed in the *Panorama* or one of the monthly publications.

Lord Elgin has I think been hardly used, for by his exertions we possess the finest sculptures in Europe, and have now nothing to complain of as to want of models to imitate & work from. But it must

---

[1] Cumberland's visit to Long in 1811 was commemorated by his *Bromley-Hill, The Seat of the Right Hon. Charles Long, M.P.*, London, 1811.

[2] Cumberland's *Elegy* on Mariamne Johnes. It was apparently never printed.

be taken up by the nation if we expect to excell.[1] I thank you very much for what you say about Fagan, but I am not even personally known to him, and we have all around some very fine young statues, that are so much in want of drapery that I must now attend to the clothing & feeding of them, as my most worthy employment.[2]

Our weather for these last 8 weeks has been uncommonly wet, which has ruined our harvests; and I am sorry to say that much corn is now out rotting on the ground. Our potatoes & herring fishery have failed, so that our prospect is very miserable and I dread the consequences, for a scarcity will come like Pandora's box, but without hope at the bottom.

Ministers when the(y) suffered Lucien to come here should have treated him properly, or kept him away. The Dutch King is the only good one of the family.[3] I have no great idea of his Epic poem, but it will sell well, which is all a bookseller looks to.[4]

We shall go somewhere in the spring, but cannot determine whither. Should we come to Clifton, which is probable enough, one inducement will (be) to meet you.

Mrs Johnes sends you her kind Compliments.

Yours always,

T. Johnes

---

[1] Thomas Bruce, 1st Earl of Elgin (1766-1841) had formed the notion of removing the celebrated marbles from Athens during his tour as British envoy in Constantinople. After considerable procrastination (and against the advice of Richard Payne Knight) the government purchased the marbles from Elgin in 1816 for £36,000 and caused them to be deposited in the British Museum.

[2] A reference to the children on the Hafod estate?

[3] Louis Bonaparte (1778-1846), proclaimed King of Holland by Napoleon in 1806.

[4] Lucien Bonaparte's *Charlemagne, ou l'Eglise delivrée* was published in two volumes in 1814.

Hafod, Feb. 9, 1812

My dear Shepherd,

I thank you for your two letters from Bath & home, and I forwarded your enclosure to Mulpomene the day after I received it. I was aware of the difficulties of the Transit from Liverpool here in this season, for in summer we have carriages rattling on all sides of us and there is a Coach from Shrewsbury to Gloucester, which crosses a Coach from Hereford hither twice a week. At least so I hear it will be when the Cuckoo sings.

I am become a great enthusiast for the Fiorin grass, and trust that what you used to see as bogs will in short time be converted into Hay grounds producing 3 Tons per acre, for I am moderate and only state *half* the produce. Pray ask Mr Roscoe if he has ever tried it; if not let him not lose time but begin instantly. Dr Richardson is sending two labourers to a Dr Thackeray at Chester to instruct the Cestrians in this culture, and should our friend wish for information he cannot have a better opportunity of gaining it than from these men. I really see no end to its advantages, and firmly believe all Dr Richardson says of it, for very many facts stated by him I have witnessed here. I want to know what that dogmatist Arthur Young will *now* say when he so impudently asserted that *all* beasts rejected it for *any* other food, when the contrary is just the truth.[1]

I am planting this year 200,000 trees of all sorts, and making such improvements you will hardly know parts of the place again. I shall continue to plant & improve just the same as if we were not the miserable branchless trunks we are.

I cannot say much for indoor work. I have begun a catalogue according to the contents of each bookcase, preparatory to a complete one, but alas I have not advanced more than 3 shelves. The truth is that every day we are out of doors as long as we can, & then I am too

---

[1] The celebrated pundit was not alone in his scepticism. Professor David Low of Edinburgh University, one of the foremost authorities on agriculture in the early nineteenth century, argued that Fiorin might have had some use as a grass species in irrigated meadows, '. . . otherwise it does not possess properties to entitle it to be ranked amongst the superior grasses'. [D. Low, *Elements of Practical Agriculture*, London, 1838.]

tired to do anything but read a newspaper, although their contents are most disheartening. I see no cheering prospect on any side & should we go to loggerheads with America we shall be like the two Cats across a string tearing ourselves mutually to pieces for the advantage of others, who must laugh at our weakness. I never expected much from the present Governor. His mind is so much occupied by frivolity & personal vanity there is no room for any grand or permanent good. [1] The old maxims will be pursued, 'do my job & I will do yours', until the ground, now crumbling shall sink & swallow them up.

Mrs Johnes sends you her kind Compliments.

I am always yours,

T. Johnes

To William Roscoe, in Liverpool   L.R.O.(Ros), 2228

Hafod, March 2, 1812

My dear Sir,

I feel much obliged for your very flattering letter of the 19th and I am happy that what I wrote to our good friend Shepherd about Fiorin achieved so much à propos. I have no doubt but that in the course of next Spring I shall be able to send you any quantity of it, for it grows here most abundantly, & I dare say that you will find plenty among your bogs.

You, I believe, have lime every where around you, but here alas we are forced to send to Pembrokeshire for it. However, for this grass Dr Richardson seems to prefer ashes mixed with earth and my bailiff has hit upon an ingenious & simple contrivance to procure ashes enough.

[1] Commercial rivalry, continued British rule in Canada, and American support for the French cause had soured Anglo-American relations since the end of the American Revolution. Tension thawed somewhat after the Peace of Amiens only to return after the 'Chesapeake' incident in 1807 and to escalate rapidly over the coming years. After much procrastination and soul-searching the Americans declared war against Britain on June 17, 1812. [R. Horsman, *The War of 1812*, London, 1969.]

He has built a Kiln exactly similar to a Lime Kiln of sods of earth and makes layers of Peat, faggots & Clay which he burns. The produce is very great, & has perfectly succeeded. Our peat by itself yields so small a quantity of ashes it would not be worth the burning, but with the above additions we have plenty. Should the Kiln itself burn, so much the better, for we should have more ashes, and it can be rebuilt in a day's time. We propose therefore building such in all the fields we work. I am now digging upwards of 20 acres of deep peat bog which I shall manure with ashes & turnip it as a preparation for Fiorin in November next. I can only lay down about 4 acres this Spring which I shall do so soon as weather permits.

I wish I could speak as confidently and as well of my indoor pursuits. My Catalogue alas, has not proceeded more than my unfortunate three shelves. To arrange them with any regard to System would require more room than I can allow for I am now full and I shall content myself with numbering them, and referring to the Catalogue for the different bookcases. This is to be sure very slovenly, but I am ashamed to say that indolence is taking fast hold of me. Were I to follow any system it would be that of De Bure, but then I might be tempted to add more to make up deficiencies & my ardour is much cooled as a purchaser.[1] I was always afraid of entering on drawings & prints, which has been the reason why I refused several fine offers. Indeed I mistrusted my own judgement in these articles, which I know are most seducing.

As to politics, what can save us after such a total dereliction of all principle & honorable feeling as we have just witnessed. A quarrel with his Parliament will soon follow, for I suspect this juggle of voting in the Catholics will be a two-edged sword, and should it be in their favour, which I doubt, it will have been so very ungraciously done that it will be considered the contrary to a favour.[2] I agree with you

[1] G.F. de Bure, bibliographer and author.

[2] '. . . his Parliament'—i.e. the King's parliament. The question of Catholic relief had smouldered as a political issue since the Revolutionary Settlement uniting Church and State and excluding Catholics and Dissenters from civil power. Anti-Catholics were paranoid in their fear and distrust of the Papacy and viewed every Catholic as a potential traitor to the English crown, especially during the wars with France when the possibility of an invasion of Catholic Ireland, (and the consequent threat to mainland Britain) was uppermost in many people's minds. Irish Catholic pressure groups succeeded in achieving some relief by way of the Franchise Act of 1793 whereby they gained the same voting rights as Protestants, and the struggle for full emancipation came in the wake of the Act of Union in 1800. Despite the efforts

that a war must take place with America, & after a time we shall cry out, but when too late, like Peachum and Lockit in *The Beggar's Opera* 'we are both in the wrong'.

Should India be thrown open as it ought to be this may give a little spirit to our Trade, but I fear it will soon be annihilated. In short, look which way you will all is misery. I fear as much evil as good will follow a reform in Parliament for no three people seem to agree on the mode.

I congratulate you on having finished your house. I have had sad rogues in my building & hope you have escaped better. As for sheep I was forced to sell mine for I could not keep them out of my plantations, & my neighbours took the advantage. Several years ago I had the Merinos, but I was not then forward enough for them, and besides I could never keep them free from footrot. How do you manage this?

Mrs Johnes unites with me in every Compliment to yourself & Mrs Roscoe, with our best thanks for your kind invitation, but we hope to have the pleasure of seeing you both here this Summer as I can assure you it will give us much pleasure, and we will return it the following year.

I am, my dear Sir,

Your very sincere humble servant,

T. Johnes

of Pittites and Whigs in the various ministries holding sway in the first decade of the nineteenth century, George III was adamantly opposed to further reform, especially to measures which would allow Catholics to hold commissions in the armed forces and to sit in the House of Commons. Like many of his subjects the King believed that if the Irish Catholics were admitted to Parliament they would form a large and tightly-knit pressure group with its own particular ambitions, which might even include the eventual severance of political ties with England. In the event the Catholic Relief Bill reached the Statute Book in 1829. [G.I.T. Machin, *The Catholic Question in English Politics, 1820-1830*, Oxford, 1964]

To James Edward Smith, in Norwich   Linn. Soc. (Smith), 16, f.187

Hafod, July 5, 1812

My dear Doctor,

I heartily congratulate you on your recovery. No one knows the value of health until after being deprived of it some time. I can send you as good a bill of my own health, but I wish I knew what it was, for a weakness about the left hip remained for some time, and made walking disagreeable. My Wife has been very unwell & low, but now this sad week is passed, I hope that we shall recover our tone again.[1]

I duly forwarded your inclosure to Mrs Spragge the day I had it, for we have now a daily post, which is convenient and pleasant.

On looking over the Wiltshire agricultural report, I find that your brother botanist *Sole* of Bath declares the *Agrostis stolonifera* to be black Couch & the worst grass that grows.[2] He should have taken more time before he made such a declaration for I trust that he will stand *Solus* in this business. I wrote to you about it, but you prudently have never answered me. I am more & more convinced that it will prove the most beneficial discovery that has been made, and all travellers now stop to look at what plantations I have made of it on the roadside. It more ressembles fine healthy wheat about 3 months old than grass, and the Cattle, who first made me acquainted with its virtues by their greediness in seeking for & devouring it, now eye it with longing Eyes. I shall sow in October & November and I hope by the end of next year to have nearly a hundred acres of it. I really see no end to the advantages that may be derived from its cultivation.

From what I hear of weather elsewhere, I believe we have been better off than our neighbours. We have had one very rainy day such as I never saw at this period, but everything looks well & promises a year of great plenty. I hope so, for I dread scarcity, as that would probably produce more evils than all Pandora's box.

Politics are disgusting, and where there is no moral character, for after all we must come to that, the usual routine of intrigue will not do. You see the Catholics will be thrown aside, notwithstanding all the

[1] i.e the anniversary of Mariamne's death.
[2] The botanist William Sole had produced his account of the principal British grasses for the *Bath and West of England Agricultural Society* in 1799.

fine promises, for in the Cabinet there is a majority of three against them, which must carry it.

Mrs Johnes unites with me in best Compliments to Mrs Smith & yourself.

I am, my dear Doctor,

Yours always,

T. Johnes

To George Cumberland, Culver Street, Bristol   Adv. MS. 36504, f.273

Hafod, Oct. 25, 1812

My dear Cumberland,

I have waited to send you the inclosed until I could do it free of expense. Mrs Bryon was a great favorite with her we have lost, and if you could be of any service to her in her professional line we shall think ourselves very much obliged.

I am very sorry your Citizens have rejected Romilly as he would have done them more honor than all the blood & tallow of the Davis's for a hundred generations.[1] We have his young hopeful now at Cardigan stirring up the breeze that has been going on for this last fortnight.[2] But I trust that he will lose it. Inclosed is a state of the Poll. My re-election was highly flattering to my feelings.

I have not time to say more than that,

I am,

Yours always,

T. Johnes

[1] Sir Samuel Romilly (1757-1818) the Whig law reformer, was adopted as candidate for Bristol at the General Election of 1812 but stood down after seven days of polling thereby allowing the Tory Richard Hart Davis to win the seat which he held until 1831.

[2] i.e. Herbert Evans of Highmead (See Add. MS. 36504, f.3)

To George Cumberland, Culver Street, Bristol   Add. MS. 36504, f.3

Hafod, Jan. 3, 1813

My dear Cumberland,

You are become a most lazy correspondent, and had it not been for your sprained knee which I suppose gave you a twinge of compunction, I should not have heard from (you) at all.

I agree with you that we are so far advanced toward ruin that I cannot see any way of perfect deliverance. A peace, which I think might *now* be honourably made, had we heads for it, would perhaps right us a little, and another system of economy etc. adopted together with a total reformation in our manners. But without all these taking place at the same time, we shall but botch up the business.

Our election for the Boroughs in which your townsman Hart Davis has so greatly interfered has ended with a petition & duel; in the last no harm was done, but I think the first must be voted frivolous & vexatious. That fellow does not seem to know what to do with his money, for he has now 3 petitions on hand, and if he succeed in all, great expense must attend them.[1]

I am busying myself in gaining every information respecting a rail way to bring us coal & lime more abundantly & far cheaper than we have it now. Should I succeed I shall do more good to these poor Countries than ever Howel Dha [sic] did. I really think I shall succeed & if I can shew that subscribers will have from 6 to 8 per Cent for their money, I trust this speculating age will soon find enough of the means to carry it on.

The idle blackguards, in spite of all endeavours to check them, are throwing down the battlements of our bridges. That at the Devils Bridge is become dangerous & I propose to take the stone battlements

[1] In the election for the Cardigan Boroughs in November 1812, Hart Davis attempted to gain electoral capital from his purchase of the Manor of Lampeter by securing the return of his protegé Herbert Evans of Highmead who stood against the sitting member, the Hon. John Vaughan. After Vaughan's election Evans's supporters petitioned Parliament complaining of electoral irregularities and lack of impartiality on the part of the returning officer—a common enough procedure in eighteenth and nineteenth century elections. Upon examination of the complaint by a Commons Select Committee, Vaughan was declared duly elected although in the opinion of the Committee the petition was not, 'frivolous or vexatious'. [J. Hughes, *A History of the Parliamentary Representation of the County of Cardigan*, Aberystwyth, 1849]

wholly down & lay beams of cast iron across, covering them with 2 feet of good gravel & on these beams to fasten uprights and rails, with a kind of Gothic under-railing to prevent persons slipping through. They cannot cut these, but may they not break them as cast iron is brittle? Let me know your opinion on this for I shall have the measurements Tuesday sennight which I will send to you for your advice & opinion. Winwood & Co are good casters and reasonable, so that I hope it may be done handsomer & cheaper than if in wood.

We have had sharp frost, but no Snow; a fine thaw followed & it is now Spring weather. But I dread a scarcity of Corn as it rises every market.

Mrs Johnes sends you her best Compliments.

I am,

Yours always,

T. Johnes

To William Roscoe, in Liverpool   L.R.O.(Ros), 2230

Hafod Sept. 2, 1813

My dear Sir,

I thank you for your obliging letter & for your paper on Moss culture. But I do not understand how you manage to plow such land a second time. We can do it well enough while the sward remains, but afterwards we should lose our Cattle in the bog. I am preparing 70 acres by previously draining for culture November twelvemonth but I shall dig it and mix lime while I break the Sods, & then sow it with Fiorin, which I think the best use we can make of our bogs. I do not expect such crops as I read of but am quite contented with two Tons per acre on land that three years ago could not be walked over with safety, and this at a trifling expense comparatively with its present value with what it was before.

You flatter us much with the hope that we shall have the pleasure of seeing you here at no distant period & we hope that Mrs Roscoe will accompany you. We are now in high beauty and I shall not be from home excepting our assize week, from the 9th to the 18th of this month.

I have been somewhat disappointed that no rich man has come forward in *earnest* for the reversion of this place. Only two have been here that seemed really to wish for it, but one had not (the) wherewithal & the other's Lady would not consent to be buried in such a solitude!! One blessed effect of the present mode of the [sic] educating females.

It would be a most advantageous purchase, for I entered yesterday on my 66th year, and the woods in 20 years would pay the whole of the purchase money. I shall thank you if you know of any rich man of taste to advise him of it. Mr. Carrington, a land surveyor from Barton on (?) was to look at it, but would not say from whom only that it would exactly suit his employer in all respects. It was reported at Hereford assizes that a Mr Ireton had bought it, but I know not who this Mr. Ireton is, not having ever heard from or seen him.

We have delightful weather for our Harvests which promise abundantly. And I hope Peace may be restored, but I fear & doubt that; our wise heads from highest to lowest are not capable of playing the cards that have been so unexpectedly thrown into their hands. [1]

Mrs Johnes joins me in kind regards to Mrs Roscoe & yourself.

I am, my dear Sir,

Yours very truly,

T. Johnes

---

[1] Russian offers to mediate between Britain and America in March 1813 had been eagerly accepted by the latter. Britain, however, was less than enthusiastic and the government dragged its feet in the hope that its forces would shortly be in a position to occupy large tracts of American territory. Castlereagh finally agreed to enter into *direct* negotiations with the Americans and the two sides eventually commenced discussion of terms in Ghent in August 1814. The Peace of Ghent was ultimately settled on December 24th, 1814 on the basis of the restoration of the *status quo ante bellum*.

To James Edward Smith, in Norwich   Linn. Soc. (Smith), 16, f.189

Hafod, Oct. 3, 1813

My dear Doctor,

A few days after the receipt of your letter of the 22 September there arrived a basket of plants that we supposed must have come from you & are what you allude to in your letter. Mrs Johnes desires me to offer her very best thanks for them. We have the *Corchorus* which is very beautiful & thrives well out of doors.

The excursion we made to Weymouth has been of service to us both, and we shall I believe make one annually (in) the spring months, the only disagreeable ones here, toward that or the Devonshire Coasts. Alas your eastern shores are too cold at that season, and I never wish to be absent (from) here longer than March, April & May. I have often chided myself for never having accepted yours or Mr Coke's invitations to Norfolk, nor can I give any good reasons for it.[1] I stay in London until tired, & then always hurry straight home as fast as I can. My journies henceforward will probably be less frequent to the Metropolis. Nothing can be done in Parliament & unfortunately the late disgraceful business of the Princess of Wales has shown *all* parties in base colours.[2] This tearing off the veil has been equally dishonourable to all and I fear when the two great Leaders were taken away miserable, stinking corses were

[1] Thomas William Coke of Holkham (1754-1842), Earl of Leicester, Whig magnate and agricultural improver. Johnes had known Coke since their Eton days together.

[2] The lamentable affair of the separation of the Prince Regent from his wife Caroline of Brunswick (whom he had married under duress in 1795) had dragged on for many years. In spite of the Prince's own pecadilloes he had arranged, in 1806, for a Commission of Privy Councillors to enquire into his wife's extra-marital interests and the resulting censure of her behaviour caused him to decree that she should not see her daughter, Princess Charlotte, more than once fortnightly. After the General Election of 1812, when the Prince threw over his long-standing support for the Whig opposition, several Radicals, hoping to injure the Prince Regent and embarrass Ministers, persuaded the Princess to publish an unanswered letter to her husband in the *Morning Chronicle*. Consequently another Commission was appointed and, with further censure of her behaviour, it supported the Regent's decree regarding the Princess and her daughter. This unsavoury charade provoked widespread public disapproval of the Regent and popular commiseration with his wife. [J. Gore (ed.), *The Creevey Papers*, London, 1963.]

left behind.[1] What I dread is a general crash that really seems fast approaching, & then Lord who would have thought [sic] it?

I have been anxious to dispose of the reversion of this place, for I have been used so very ill by all my relations on every side that I could wish some rich man of taste would purchase. It would be a grand speculation & I should be an excellent tenant in tail. There are yearly so many improvements made you would not know the place again. What I ask is not much, for I would include timber, house, furniture, & if tempted books. It would be a valuable purchase, for I have been much hurt at the conduct of my relations & one of whom I considered as my firm friend & had a very great regard for, but though no relative, he has fled off. I know not why. These are events that are not uncommon when we are 66 years of age. But I shall drop the subject.

Mrs Johnes unites with me in best Compliments to Mrs Smith & yourself.

I am,

Yours always,

T. Johnes

[1] Pitt and Fox.

Hafod: Cascade above the 'Mossy Seat', by John 'Warwick' Smith

(by permission of the National Library of Wales)

To James Edward Smith, in Norwich   Linn. Soc. (Smith), 16, f.191

Hafod, Nov. 28, 1813

My dear Doctor,

I am very anxious for your success at Cambridge & regret my inability to assist you, for having been brought up at Edinburgh & at no English university I am even ignorant in whom the right of voting lies. It is very handsome in the Duke of Glocester to remain neuter. He is the only branch of Royalty I feel myself attached to, & am very strongly to him. I can never forget his very attentive kindness to us when we lost our all.[1]

I have lately lost my Mother. Indeed, from the machinations & Lies of others she has been long lost to us. But would you believe that I was first informed of the event accidentally by an acquaintance! No one of the family, not even a servant, wrote to me & I was told of it some days after by an Upholsterer, I believe of the name of Bywater, in Grosvenor Street. God mend them!

There may be some voters in Wales & if you could find any out I would try to get them to serve you. There is a Dr Nagh at Haverfordwest whom Lord Kensington can influence & Coke I should think Lord Kensington. He was at the Duke's installation & boasts of the fine reception he met with. Every vote is worth trying for, or at least stopping from going against you.[2]

I cannot think our Ministers will dare to continue a war in support of the Bourbons, otherwise I fear we shall have war at home. What a fall has Napoloen had—Phaeton's was a farce to it. And what a wonderful man, had he chosen it, might he have been! His brother Lucien has chosen a wiser plan & he must have forseen the effects of an unbounded ambition. I hear great praises of his poem *Charlemagne*. An acquaintance is translating it into English & seems in raptures. She is a poetess also (and) I am partly promised a beautiful ballad or sonnet she wrote on leaving Italy. I understand he is adored in his

---

[1] Smith's protracted efforts to succeed Thomas Martyn as Professor of Botany at Cambridge eventually failed and notwithstanding widespread support from at home and abroad, he was turned down at the election to the Chair on the grounds that as a Unitarian he could not conscientiously subscribe to the Thirty-nine Articles. He was deeply upset by the 'cabal of bigots' who debarred his appointment.

[2] A reference to potential supporters of Smith's candidature for the Botany chair.

family & they have fully sufficient within themselves to amuse each other as well as any company that may visit them.

We have had a wet autumn, but it now seems set in for frost.

When you see Coke give my best Compliments to him. Mrs Johnes desires to be kindly remembered to you.

I am, my dear Doctor,

Yours very truly,

T. Johnes

To John Fitchett, Solicitor, Warrington.   L.R.O.(Ros), 2232

Hafod, Dec. 14, 1813

Sir,

Mr Roscoe has inclosed to me your letter to him of the 7th instant.[1]

An event has lately happened that has made the disposal of the reversion of this place, unless on my own terms, a matter of indifference to me. In the first place I must have no interference with any part of the Estate until after my decease. Those who know me will not suppose me capable of doing any thing to its injury, but on the contrary for its advantage and ornament. I am too fond of the place even to think of hurting it by cutting down its great ornament, Trees.[2]

The Estate will be at May next full 3000£ and when the leases shall fall in must be greatly increased. The leases I grant are for 7, 14, 21 years determinable at either period giving one year's notice. What the

[1] Roscoe himself had contemplated buying the reversion of Hafod, but eventually decided against doing so, and in the early stages of the negotiations had acted as intermediary between Johnes and Fitchett. [L.R.O. (Ros), 1514]

[2] Fitchett had previously implied that in insisting that the purchaser not interfere with Hafod during his lifetime, Johnes was looking to the chance of felling trees for his own profit. [L.R.O. (Ros), 1517]

amount may be at my decease it is impossible for anyone to say, but I should think 50 per Cent advanced as the present rents are low.[1]

I ask 80,000£ to remain on mortgage with interest for the Estate, Woods, House & furniture, but as I before said I will have no interference respecting it, as I am sure it would end disagreeably to both parties & drive me hence.

If your friend wishes to advance 10 or 18,000£ on it by way of *post obit* it would be an accommodation & I shall thank you to send me an early answer, as others are desirous of advancing this sum.

I am, Sir,

Your most obedient humble Servant.

T. Johnes

To George Cumberland, Culver Street, Bristol   Add. MS. 36504, f.258

Hafod, April 3, 1814

My dear Cumberland,

It is a great while since we have corresponded & I know not on which the fault lies. I should have acknowledged yours of the 16th March sooner had I not been laid up by a neglected Cold.

You are mistaken as to our Winter for I believe we fared much better than many other parts of the island. Our snow was light, excepting drifts, for a high wind blew it off the ground before it had time to harden, and filled up some of our Lanes. The Post was never stopped between this (place) & Aberystwith although we were 2 or 3 days without hearing from London via Radnorshire. And as the frost put an end to all farming work, I found out a fine job for my poor labourers in the making of a new & most beautiful approach from near Pentre. From 40 to 50 poor fellows never lost but two days at this work. It has been laborious, but it more than answers my expectations.

[1] Johnes had originally claimed that the rental of Hafod would be £4500 at his decease.

It is curious enough that your Parson Evans's widow should have applied to me (without ever mentioning anything of her husband) for assistance, & I have got her through a friend a small gift from another Charity, but she must not look for it again I am told. Nor from your statement, should she have asked it.

I fear I cannot meet you in London, for I am ordered warm sea bathing and we shall probably return to Weymouth toward the end of this month to come back again in June. The winters here are never unpleasant, but three months of Spring I shall always wish to spend in a warmer climate, & it will probably end in buying or renting a Cottage on the Southern coast, Dorset or Devon.

I am not that great admirer of Rogers's poetry you seem to be. He polishes & polishes until the Steel wears away as an acquaintance of his justly said. No, give me such a Poet as Ld. Byron, who was born one and makes you feel. The other has no heart, and I can give you proofs enough of it without ascending the rugged hill of Parnassus to look for them.[1]

As for the times, the state of suspense we are kept in is most wearing. It will end I fear badly, for if the war continues, how can we go on without calling on the people for sacrifices they neither can, nor will, make. I am told we are expending from one to 2 millions daily. Feasts & shows will not cover this deformity. It will I dread soon shew itself and then 'who would have thought it? we were going on so vastly well', will be the cry.[2]

Napoleon is no common man and I should suppose his father-in-Law must support him from an absolute fall.[3] And this Carl Jean,

---

[1] Johnes's judgement is very much in accord with the author of Rogers's entry in DNB who describes his talent as '... one of mediocrity elevated to something like distinction by fastidious care and severe toil'. Johnes seems to imply that his personal relations with Rogers, whom he would have met at James Edwards's Pall Mall house, were less than friendly.

[2] Although expenditure on the war amounted to 16% of gross national income, this was exceeded by the total increase in national wealth between 1793 and 1815. Fighting a major war and getting richer at the same time was a unique achievement, yet inflation at the rate of 3.3% per annum, together with a run of bad harvests, meant that the mass of the working people in Britain enjoyed few of the benefits of increasing national prosperity. Johnes was acutely aware of the potential dangers to social stability which might result from the erosion of real incomes among the wage-earning classes.

[3] Napoleon abdicated on April 6th, 1814 and was despatched to Elba with a pension of 2 million francs.

what is he doing at Liège when he ought to be near Paris? Had he any pretentions to the Throne he looked for to be vacant?[1]

Adieu,

Always yours,

T. Johnes

Mrs Johnes sends you her best Compliments.

To George Cumberland, Culver Street, Bristol   Add. MS. 36504, f.283

Hafod, May 15, 1814

My dear Cumberland,

I am sorry to differ with you about Weymouth, for I like it much, the short time we stay (sic) there. We shall set out next week & return here about the 28 June, but I shall go with regret for we are now in very great beauty. I agree with you in all your praises of Clifton; it is a charming spot, but it would bring to us back bitter recollections.[2]

I never heard of so many fools going to Paris. They will have enough of it; 5 guineas per Bed & 5 or 6 in a room, beside the 30 per Cent discount in the exchange. The Parisians know better than any people the *art de plumer la poule sans la faire crier*. I have not a wish for such an expedition for all my friends & acquaintances except Talleyrand are gone—and as for their Shows I have seen them all before.[3]

[1] Charles, Comte d'Artois and subsequently Charles X of France, brother of Louis XVIII. He was at this time, 'delayed in Flanders, and could not arrive (in Paris) until Tuesday in Easter Week'. [A. Palmer, *Metternich,* London, 1972]

[2] i.e. of Mariamne's visits to Beddoes.

[3] The rich and fashionable flocked to Paris in the early weeks of May to witness Wellington's entry into the French capital, to see the parade of Allied troops before Louis XVIII and, perhaps, to attend one of Mme. de Stael's splendid parties in her reconstituted salon. [E. Longford, *Wellington, The Years of the Sword*, London, 1969]

Never was such an overthrow, but I fear we are going to disgrace ourselves in favour of this Crown Prince, who in my Eyes acted a more than doubtful part by remaining so long in Liège. Pardon the pun, he was *corked* up there waiting the event of the campaign near Paris.

Having according to a wretchedly bad custom left all things to the last, I am now interrupted on business that should have been done weeks ago.

Adieu. Mrs Johnes sends you her best Compliments.

Yours ever,

T. Johnes

If you ever intend a new Edition of your *Hafod*, now is your time for I have done wonders to it.

To James Edward Smith, in Norwich   Linn. Soc. (Smith), 16, f.193

Hafod, Jan. 29, 1815

My Dear Doctor,

I do indeed take shame to myself for never having accepted Coke's kind invitations to Holkham—a man whom I so greatly respect. Nor can I any way account for it, although since the receipt of your last kind letter I have been trying to find out why it was so and I am now just as wise as ever. The accounts of his & Mr Fountaine's splendid Collections made my mouth water, and for a moment I was envious, but that soon wore off. I will not promise for this summer, but I do verily that I shall attempt to come & see you in the course of the following supposing all things to be nearly in *status quo*.

I have the pleasure to tell you that I am recovering as fast as you can wish me. I have not seen such a physician as Darwin since poor Beddoes, and he is more prudent. [1]

[1] Robert Waring Darwin (1766-1848), son of Erasmus Darwin and father of Charles. Elected to the Royal Society in 1788 he built up a large and thriving medical practice in Shrewsbury.

We shall I hope set out for our new purchase in Devon sometime next month, but I must be cautious after so severe an illness. It is a most beautiful situation and if you look into Donn's Map of Devonshire you will see nearly opposite to Exmouth a house called Wick, which seems to be the spot though now called Langstone Cliff Cottage.

We have had frost & snow, but a fine thaw is now taking place. I was the only person here who did not feel the Cold. So much for renovated health.

You have I find at Norwich a person of the name of Stiles who cures Herrings superior to the Dutch. You will oblige me if you will desire of him to send me a Keg to taste by the Coach to London & to be forwarded thence by the Shrewsbury mail directed for me at Hafod care of Mr Watton, Chronicle Office, Shrewsbury. I not only want to taste them, but to attempt if I can to induce my good, but indolent countrymen to cure the Herrings on this Coast in the same way.

Mrs Johnes joins me in every Compliment to Lady Smith & yourself.

I am,

Yours always,

T. Johnes

To George Cumberland, Culver Street, Bristol   Add. MS. 36505, f.24

Hafod, Feb. 20, 1815

My dear Cumberland,

As circumstances have turned out I am glad you did not write sooner for I have been most dangerously ill since the middle of last September, and am but now recovering, so that I could not have answered you.

I bought last year a most beautiful Cottage not far from Dawlish, called Langstone Cliff Cottage, whither we are going about this day week for the more perfect restoration of my health. I purchased it with the intent of passing the spring months there, but I shall now perhaps spend the Winter ones too there, always coming hither for those of Summer & Autumn.

I agree with you in liking the peace because it is peace, and I wish most heartily our Governors were of the same mind. But that is not I believe the case.

Your sketch is precisely that of Mr Bentham's.[1] When a new Gaol was building in this County I proposed a similar one & sent to the Magistrates engravings that were given me by Revely. But it was not adopted!![2] Its utility is apparent & something more effectually must be done to prevent such children as we daily read of turning thieves.

I admire your two Societies; & wish you would send me plans of their regulations. I want to establish a bank at Aberystwith for such servants etc. as may have saved any sum however small to receive interest for the same & their capital on demand. I have my doubts of success. The poor are ready enough to borrow, but very few save.[3]

Your City, by the deeds you mention will wash itself from Savage's cutting Rhymes & I wish others would follow the example.[4] I am busy

---

[1] Jeremy Bentham (1748-1832) developed the idea of the 'Panopticon', a circular prison building with cells in the circumference and a central lodge for the gaoler. Associated with the structure would be a system of management which, as he wrote in one of his pamphlets on prison reform, would result in 'morals reformed, health preserved, industry invigorated, instruction diffused (and) public burdens lightened'.

[2] A reference to Nash's Cardigan Gaol, completed in 1793. Willey Revely (d. 1799), the Yorkshire born architect, had studied under Sir William Chambers in 1781-82.

[3] Under Rose's Act of 1793 official encouragement had been given to mutual self-help through Friendly Societies and Savings Banks. By 1815 more than 30 Friendly Societies, primarily of native origin, flourished in Cardiganshire. The Savings Bank Act of 1817 provided for interest to be paid on cash deposited in the Bank of England. Johnes may have been involved in the planning of the Aberystwyth Savings Bank, founded in 1818. [See A.M.E. Davies, Wages, Prices and Social Improvements in Cardiganshire, 1750-1850, *Ceredigion X(I), 1984*.]

[4] Richard Savage's years of poverty in Bristol, where he died in 1743, inspired some acid lines. The posthumously published *London and Bristol Compar'd; a Satire* was penned as Savage languished in a Bristol gaol after imprisonment for debt. Bristol's merchants and citizens are seen as 'deaf to Wisdom's Call', who 'scorn all Learning's as all Virtue's Rules', 'despising all Men and despis'd by all' and much other similar invective. The deeds mentioned by Johnes presumably refer to municipal acts of charity—of which Savage was a recipient from various quarters for much of his life. [C. Tracy, *The Artificial Bastard, a Biography of Richard Savage*, Toronto, 1953; C. Tracy (ed.), *The Poetical Works of Richard Savage*, Cambridge, 1962]

at present in my endeavours to save our fishermen from being lost and when any accident shall happen to assist the wretched mothers, wives & orphans from a County fund. You will hear probably of the result in the Carmarthen paper the latter end of next month, for it will be determined upon at the Assizes. Whatever may be the event, my resolution is formed to establish it myself although not joined by a single individual. A long illness makes one pause & think!!!

I have had a letter from Chauntrey who has been at Paris and in raptures with the grand works of art he saw. He speaks of them as such an artist ought; with gratitude & wonder. He has I believe just finished his work for me, and if you have not seen it it is well worth calling on him, for I have not seen any thing more simple or more pathetick.

Mrs Johnes has gone through my illness most wonderfully, thanks to God. She sends you her best Compliments.

I am,

Always yours,

T. Johnes

Can you give me the direction at Bristol to Mr Dobbins who has a patent for some improved Castors?

To George Cumberland, Culver Street, Bristol   Add. MS. 36505, f.83

Langstone, May 9th, 1815

My dear Cumberland,

You see what bad example does. I have delayed from day to day thanking you for your letters until I have left it so long that I am quite ashamed of myself. I almost always clear my desk once a week at least & then burn the Contents. But you of late have been so very lazy a correspondent I have caught the infection & we are all, more or less, animals of imitation.

I like your idea of the Panopticon much, and diet & close confinement are surely worth trying, for we have been long used to strangling & deportation not to have fully proved its inefficacy in reformation.

I conclude you have seen, or are about to see, the Exhibitions. Report in the papers speaks most favorably of them. Our friend Chauntrey I find has exhibited at Spring Gardens.[1] I am sorry he has quarelled with the Academy, although I think he has been ill used. But still that is a national concern & ought to be supported. Cabals & intrigue have ever existed in all academies, & I believe an artist's & a poet's skin are alike irritable.[2]

I am more & more delighted with this place. It is the finest cradle for old age imaginable and everything is so much under one's hand, it is quite comfortable. I am busily employed in walling my kitchen garden which will be an excellent one. All the rest is a kind of flower garden, which we shall yearly improve.[3]

I say nothing of politics, for I detest them; and the scrape we are about getting into will I fear seal our doom. We are now at the top of the Pinnacle, & consequently must go down, for nothing in this world stands still. Luxury, corruption and vice, 'Kill more sure than del Toboso's eyes'.[4]

Mrs Johnes sends you her best compliments,

I am,

Always yours,

T. Johnes

Evans's widow has quitted Froxfield, and wants relief from other Charities.

[1] His bust of Johnes had been exhibited at the Royal Academy in 1812. [A. Graves, *The Royal Academy of Arts Exhibitions, 1769-1804*, London, 1905.]

[2] Whatever the nature of Chantrey's quarrel with the academicians he was elected to their number in 1818 and left the bulk of his fortune of £150,000 to the Academy in order to found the Chantrey Bequest. [R. Gunnis, *Dictionary of British Sculptors, 1660-1851*, London, n.d.]

[3] Langstone Cliff Cottage in Dawlish is now the Langstone Cliff Hotel. The Gothic windows and two bays of the original single storey 'cottage ornée' have been incorporated into the modern building in which hangs an unattributed late eighteenth century painting of the earlier house. Parts of Johnes's walling of the garden still remain.

[4] i.e. Don Quixote's lady Dulcinea del Toboso.

To James Edward Smith, in Norwich   Linn. Soc. (Smith), 16, f.195

Langstone, June 19, 1815

My Dear Doctor,

Your obliging favour of the 11th was forwarded here from Hafod two days ago and I hasten to thank you for it before we set out tomorrow on our return home. This fair air & fine food has quite made me well again, and I shall ever feel grateful for it. It is really the nicest cradle for old age I ever saw and we shall return the first week of October & probably pass the winter here. We are happy you send us such bills of health & wish you a long continuance of it, for without *that*, all the rest is nothing.

Pray be so good to order some of this Empyreumatic Ligneous acid to be sent to me by a Shrewsbury waggon directed for me to the care of Mr Watton, bookseller, Shrewsbury and the bill with it that I may order payment, for I am very anxious to try it on flesh & fish, although I am no great admirer of smoke-dried food. It may turn out of great advantage. Have you ever seen Slater's Steam Kitchen? It is one of the cleverest & most useful inventions. The roast meat is equally grateful to Eye & palate. It is cheap and of great utility. I have had one put up here & am delighted with it.

I need not say how proud I shall be to have the pleasure of seeing Mr Coke & you at Hafod. But remember I shall set out on my return hither the first week in October and I should be very sorry indeed to miss seeing him, for I consider him a *rarissima avis* in this profligate & corrupt age.

Your opinion of what may probably be the *end* of the French Revolution, for I fear we are not so near it as our Ministers seem to think, is very just. There is a coolness already among the Bourbons I suppose, or rather the part the Orléans branch took in the early time of it (which) has never been fully forgiven. Family quarrels never are, as I well know by experience. Some of mine, in attempting to detain the plate etc. have been so near to (?) point, they must take care or their Steersman (Carr the Solicitor) will wreck them upon it. I wish it not, but if people will run their heads through malice on a brick wall, they must break their pates.[1]

---

[1] Presumably a reference to an attempt by Johnes's brother and others of his remaining relations to have the Hafod silver declared heirlooms thereby preventing their sale.

The person who wrote the verses you inquire after is a particular friend of mine of the name of Merivale. He is of Lincoln's Inn & married to a daughter of my neighbour Dr Drury, late master of Harrow. Merivale has written many other things of great merit such as *Orlando in Roncesvalles*, & very many of the Epigrams in the Anthologia.[1] We thank you much for what you say on the subject. I hope it may be put up before your arrival at Hafod, but I confess I dread the effect of it. I could not stand it, & how my poor Wife will!!![2]

But no more of this.

Adieu, my dear friend,

Always yours,

T. Johnes

To James Edward Smith, in Norwich   Linn. Soc. (Smith), 16, f.197

Langstone Cliff Cottage, Exeter

Feb. 1, 1816

My Dear Doctor,

I thank you very kindly for your letter of the 13th which was forwarded to me from Hafod. We have been here since November and I am just recovered from a most severe cough & inflammation on the Lungs. I am satisfied it was the same complaint I had last year, which that Scoundrel W. Williams wilfully mistook and mistreated. But having at Dawlish as able as honest a practitioner, I escaped with only three weeks confinement & I think I am in better health than for many months past.

[1] John Herman Merivale (1779-1844), scholar, poet and friend of Byron who praised both his *Orlando* and his translations from the Greek in Bland's *Collections from the Greek Anthology* of 1813. Merivale had penned several memorial verses which, he had suggested, might be inscribed on Chantrey's monument to Mariamne Johnes.

[2] The monument was not placed in the church at Eglwys Newydd before Johnes's own death. In any event, Chantrey's fee of £3150 was not paid until 1835.

Alas poor Roscoe!! I am most exceedingly hurt at his failure & from my heart I wish I could assist him. His was the last house I should have thought of failing for I considered him of great prudence. What will become of him & his numerous family?[1] I was not any way prepared for this event & am therefore more shocked at it. I was enjoying myself in thought of your plans, but now they vanish. I do not mean to go to London, for late hours, & hot houses will not do for me. *Non sum qualis eram.*[2]

I fear the Country is in a miserable state & I know not what can be done to assist it, and pay national Creditors. We have no rents, but farms thrown on hand and Coke's tenant has set a notable example of calling out his Landlord. I wish the scoundrel could have been more severely punished.[3]

Limpstone is across the Exe from us. I should be most happy to have the pleasure to see Mr Lane, but you can answer for my being the worst of all visitors except my Wife.[4] She unites with me in kind Compliments to yours & to yourself.

I am, my dear Doctor,

Very truly yours,

T. Johnes

---

[1] Roscoe's bank stopped payment on June 25 1816, and he was declared bankrupt in 1820.

[2] Horace, *Odes, IV, i, 3. (I am not what I was)*.

[3] The acute economic depression following the cessation of the French wars led to difficulties for farmers throughout the kingdom. Generous rent abatements were granted on some estates, yet many abandoned their tenancies leaving landowners with the problem of unoccupied holdings.

[4] I am unable to establish the identity of Mr Lane, although a contemporary drawing by a Mrs A.C. Lane hangs in the Linnean Society Library.

Thomas Johnes of Hafod died at
Dawlish on April 23rd 1816 at 4.00 pm.

Epilogue

When the ageing Duke of Newcastle left Hafod in 1846, to the 'unfeigned regret' of the burghers of Aberystwyth, he carried with him many of the more valuable contents of the house, among which were the bulk of the books and the fireplaces and French glasses purchased by Thomas Johnes at Fonthill. During his occupancy the duke had effected various improvements to the estate (including the complete rebuilding of the Devil's Bridge Inn) but apart from extensively reorganising and refitting the interior, had done little to alter the appearance of the house itself. His successor, however, the Lancashire gentleman Sir Henry de Hoghton (who, it is claimed, parted with £94,000 for the estate) was massively to transform the building. Hoghton, it seems, was haunted by the ill-luck that had stalked Hafod's creator. His first wife ran away; his second died after three years of marriage and yet, with blithe indifference to Dr Johnson's sound advice, he married for a third time in 1854. But Hoghton was not the sort of man to allow these matrimonial misfortunes to blight his plans and shortly after he bought Hafod in 1846 he commissioned the architect Anthony Salvin to extend the house. Engaged at the time in building Penoyre near Brecon for John Lloyd Watkins, Salvin submitted plans for a huge and rambling Italianate wing complete with 'Venetian' windows and a slightly absurd campanile. Notwithstanding the aesthetic hotch-potch which the marriage of this curious concept to the original classical/gothic house would produce, Hoghton approved the plans and construction went ahead. But for one reason or another the interior of the new wing remained incomplete when the manufacturer William Chambers of Llanelli bought Hafod from Hoghton in 1855. Neither Chambers nor subsequent owners made any effort to finish the work and Salvin's shell of local stone and ashlar dressings was doomed. From the moment the contractors left the site the forces of decay stepped into the breach.

William Chambers himself died bankrupt, but not before selling the Hafod estate in 1864 to one John Waddingham, an obscure figure of whom little seems to be known beyond the fact that he refurbished the outbuildings adjacent to the house. His son Thomas succeeded in 1892 and lived on at Hafod for many years, occupying his time in the pursuit of those recondite studies whose nature has never been clearly

defined. Thomas Waddingham died in 1938, six years after fire had
destroyed Chantrey's celebrated monument to Mariamne Johnes in
the church of Eglwys Newydd. The contents of the house were now
sold and Hafod remained empty while the surrounding demesne was
left to the tender mercies of the Forestry Commission. As Johnes and
his family lay uneasily in their vault at Eglwys Newydd the mansion
gradually succumbed to dereliction and what was left of the walks,
gardens and viewpoints became increasingly overgrown by
regimented columns of vigorous conifers. Only the inevitable ghosts
remain witness to the former glories of the Hafod mansion, now an
unsightly pile of rubble. The American poet Jonathan Williams has
starkly portrayed the nemesis of Thomas Johnes's creation and to him
I leave the last word.

> 'in 1958, the Forestry Commission dynamited Hafod as
> ''a menace to Public Safety''
> in 1966, there is a caravan site where Hafod, where
> Eden stood. . . .
> from Kubla Khan
> to Caravan
> a stately
> measured
> doom,
> decreed. . .
> hoo hoo
> hee hee
> say the locals'.[1]

[1] Jonathan Williams, *Thomas Johnes, Master of Hafod Ychdryd (The Summer Palace By the Winding River), Cardiganshire/Eden*, in *Selected Poems, 1957-1967*, New York, 1969.

Hafod: rear view, circa 1880

(by permission of the National Library of Wales)

Select Bibliography

The following is by no means an exhaustive bibliography and is limited to those items which refer specifically and extensively to Thomas Johnes and his works. Most 'general' histories of Wales include references to Johnes and Hafod as do volumes concerned with the Picturesque Movement, and the histories of 'picturesque' travel and printing. Readers will derive considerable benefit from the *Reference Catalogue* currently being prepared by that admirable body of enthusiasts, *The Friends of Hafod*. Together with references to printed material, newspaper items and letters, the *Catalogue* includes photographs, paintings, engravings, maps, artefacts and ephemera associated with Hafod. The two sections so far completed are available to members and to archive libraries. The relevant files in the National Monuments Record (Wales) office in Aberystwyth contain a fully documented record of the house before it was finally destroyed in the 1950s. Other references are given in the text footnotes.

Barber, J. T., *A Tour through South Wales and Monmouthshire,* London, 1803.

Borrow, G., *Wild Wales,* London, 1862.

Cambrian News , The End of Hafod Mansion, August 22, 1958.

Colyer, R. J. The Hafod Estate under Thomas Johnes and Henry Pelham, Fourth Duke of Newcastle, *Welsh History Review, 8(3), 1977.*

Country Life, Last Look at Hafod, February 6, 1968.

Cumberland, G., *An Attempt to describe Hafod*, London, 1796.

Davies, W. *General View of the Agriculture of South Wales*, London, 1814.

Dearden, J. A., Thomas Johnes and the Hafod Press, 1803-1810, *The Book Collector, 22, 1973.*

Dibdin, T. F. *The Bibliographical Decameron*, London, 1817.

Ibid., *Bibliomania*, London, 1809.

Inglis-Jones, E., Hafod and Thomas Johnes, *Wales, June 22, 1946.*

Ibid., *Peacocks in Paradise,* Faber, 1950 [Reprinted, *Golden Grove Editions,* 1988].

Jenkins, D., *Thomas Johnes o'r Hafod, 1784-1816,* Cardiff, 1948.

Kerkham, C., The Hafod Landscape, *Spadework, Journal of the Cardiganshire Horticultural Society, 3(7), 1987.*

Ibid., Hafod, Paradise Lost, *Journal of Garden History, 11, 1991.*

Kerkham, C. and Briggs, C.S., *A Review of the archaeological potential of the Hafod Landscape, Cardiganshire,* in Brown, A.E.(ed.), *Garden Archaeology,* C.B.A. Report, 78, 1991.

Ibid., A Review of the archaeological potential of the Hafod landscape, *Ceredigion, XI (2), 1990*. [Ms. Caroline Kerkham is currently working towards the completion of her University of Wales thesis 'A Study of the Picturesque in the work of Thomas Johnes of Hafod, Cardiganshire'].

Linnard, W., Thomas Johnes of Hafod, Pioneer of Upland Afforestation in Wales, *Ceredigion, VI, 1970*.

Lipscomb, G., *Journey into South Wales*, London, 1802.

Lloyd, D., *Dinham House*, Ludlow Craft Centre, 1988.

Lloyd, T., and Turnor, L., *General View of the Agriculture of Cardiganshire*, London, 1794.

Lloyd-Johnes, H., The Cardigan Boroughs Election, 1774, *National Library of Wales Journal, 7(1), 1972*.

Malkin, B. H. *The Scenery, Antiquities and Biography of South Wales*, London, 1804.

Meyrick, S. R. *The History and Antiquities of the County of Cardigan*, London, 1810.

Morgan, D. J., Johnes of Hafod Uchtryd, Cardiganshire as an Agriculturist, *Journal of the University College of Wales, Department of Agriculture, IX, 1920*.

Morgan, T. O. *Aberystwyth and its Environs*, Aberystwyth, 1848.

Namier, L. and Brooke, J., *The House of Commons, 1754-1790*, London, 1964.

Nance, E. M. *The Pottery and Porcelain of Swansea and Nantgarw*, London, 1942.

Nicholas, J., *Annals and Antiquities of the Counties and County Families of South Wales*, London, 1872.

Nichols, J., *Illustrations of the Literature of the Eighteenth Century*, London, 1817-1858.

Ibid., *Literary Anecdotes of the Eighteenth Century*, III, London, 1812-1815.

Nicholson, G., *The Cambrian Traveller's Guide*, Stourport, 1808.

Piper, J., Decrepit Glory: a Tour of Hafod, *Architectural Review, 87, 1940*.

Rees, E. An Introductory Survey of Eighteenth Century Welsh Libraries, *Journal of the Welsh Bibliographical Society, X(4), 1971*.

Smith, J. E., *A Tour of Hafod, Cardiganshire*, London, 1810.

Summerson, J., *John Nash, Architect to King George IV*, London, 1935.

Thomas, J., The Architectural Development of Hafod, *Ceredigion VII (2), 1973 and VII (3 and 4), 1974-5*..

Thompson, M. W., *The Journey of Sir Richard Colt Hoare through Wales and England, 1793-1810*, Gloucester, 1983.

Thorne, R. G., Two Letters from Thomas Johnes of Hafod to William Adam of Blair Adam, *National Library of Wales Journal, 21, 1979-80*.

Ibid., Herbert Lloyd of Carmarthen, *Transactions of the Cymmrodorion Society, 1977*.

Ibid., *History of Parliament, The Commons, 1790-1820*, London, 1986.

Turner, E. H., *Walks and Wanderings in County Cardigan*, Bingley, ca.1905.

Vaughan, H. M., The Hafod Press and Colonel Thomas Johnes, author and publisher, *Transactions of the Cymmrodorion Society, 1911-12.*

Ibid, Some Letters of Thomas Johnes of Hafod, *Y Cymmrodor, XXXV, 1925.*

Walker, M. *Sir James Edward Smith,* Linnean Society, 1988.

Walters, G., A Catalogue of the late Pesaro Library at Venice now forming part of the Hafod Library, MDCCCVI, *Trivium, 22, 1987.*

Warner, R., *A Second Walk through Wales*, London, 1800.

Williams, M. I. Did Handel visit Cardiganshire?, *Ceredigion 3(4), 1959.*

Williams, W. R., Colonel Johnes of Hafod, *Red Dragon, X, 1886.*

Index of persons and places

In compiling this index I have attempted to include all those individuals of significance to the text and footnotes whose names appear therein. I have only included the more important locations and omitted those to which Johnes only makes occasional passing reference.

Knight, Richard Payne, 5, 12-14, 36, 53, 81, 101, 105, 127, 131, 137-8, 207, 273
Knight, Richard, of Downton Castle, 1
Knight, Richard, of Croft Castle, 1
Knighton, Radnorshire, 147-8

Lancaster, Joseph, 236-7
Lane, Mr, 297
Lane, Mrs, A. L., 297
Langley, Batty, 13, 15
Laing, Malcolm, 238
Laing, William, 216-7, 225, 229
Langstone, Cliff Cottage, Dawlish, 56, 58, 291-7
Lansdowne, William Petty, 1st Marquess of, 21, 98
Lavater, Johann Kaspar, 117
Leominster, 122
le Noir, Michel, 41
Lhind, William, 204, 257
Lhuyd, Edward, 3, 36-7, 73
Linnard, William, 25
Linnean Society, 96-7
Lipscomb, R., 14
Lisburne, Wilmot, 1st Earl of, 120, 125
Liston, Robert, 1, 2, 10, 22, 24, 37, 43, 58-60, 77-85, 91, 93, 95, 97, 117, 161-2, 179-83, 187, 189, 197, 214, 220, 230, 242, 247, 258-9, 263, 269
Liston, Mrs R., 259
Liverpool, 24, 133, 155, 183, 249
Liverpool Botanic Gardens, 68
Llanaeron, Cardiganshire, 16
Llandaff, Richard Watson, bishop of, 249-50
Llandovery, 124
Llanelli, 124
Llanidloes, 169
Llanwrtyd Wells, 146
Lloyd, Herbert, of Carmarthen, 54-5, 124, 128, 176, 189
Lloyd, Thomas, of Coedmor, 141
Lloyd, Mr, of Norfolk, 149
Llysnewydd, Cardiganshire, 16
Lodge, Edmund, 195
Long, Charles, 64, 114, 118, 127, 153, 204, 231, 271-2
Longmans, publishers, 44, 47, 203, 244
Loughor, River, 124
Loutherbourg, Phillipe Jacques de, 177
Lovedon, Edward, 120-1
Low, Professor David, 274
Ludlow, Salop, 1, 2, 122, 198

Lyndhurst, Hampshire, 64

Mack, General, 200
Malkin, Benjamin Heath, 14, 16-17, 24, 177, 205, 229-30
Mansfield, Louisa, Countess of, 191
Marchant, Henrietta, 60
Marchmont, Hugh Hume, 3rd Earl of, 78
Martyn, Professor Thomas, 30, 33, 118, 285
Matlock, Derbyshire, 130
Maurice, William, of Cefn-y-Braich, 36
Meerman, Johann, 37, 184
Merivale, John Herman, 296
Meyrick, Samuel Rush, 18, 74
Miller, Sanderson, 13
Milford Haven, 123
Monthly Magazine, The, 240
Morris, Mr, of Swansea, 34
Morris, family of Carmarthen, 124
Mountstewart, Lord, 60, 86
Mynach, River, 5, 109

Nagh, Dr, of Haverfordwest, 285
Nash, John, 15-16, 20, 22, 95, 218, 292
Nelson, Horatio, 200
Newcastle, Henry Pelham, 4th Duke of, 17, 58, 74, 114, 301
Newtown, Montgomeryshire, 32, 148, 169
Norfolk, Charles Howard, 11th Duke of, 7, 137-8
North, Lord, 10

Octagon Unitarian Chapel, Norwich, 70
Ogle, Mr, 251
Ogofâu, Pumsaint, Carmarthenshire, 92-3, 100, 127, 239
Ormskirk, Lancashire, 133
Owen, Reverend John, of Tynllwyn, 28

Panton, Paul, Jnr., 35, 39
Park Lettice, Monmouthshire, 56, 85
Parry, Thomas, of Llidiadau, 55
Payne, Thomas, 38
Paynter, John, 2
Pearson, Dr, 27
Pennant, Thomas, 36, 136
Perceval, Spencer, 221, 264
Pesaro Library, 37, 217, 228-9
Phillips, Sir Richard, 240
Philosophical Magazine, The, 70-1
Pitcairn, Dr David, 107, 131, 187
Pitcairn, William, 68